THE PEOPLE OF THE
LEEWARD ISLANDS
1620 - 1860

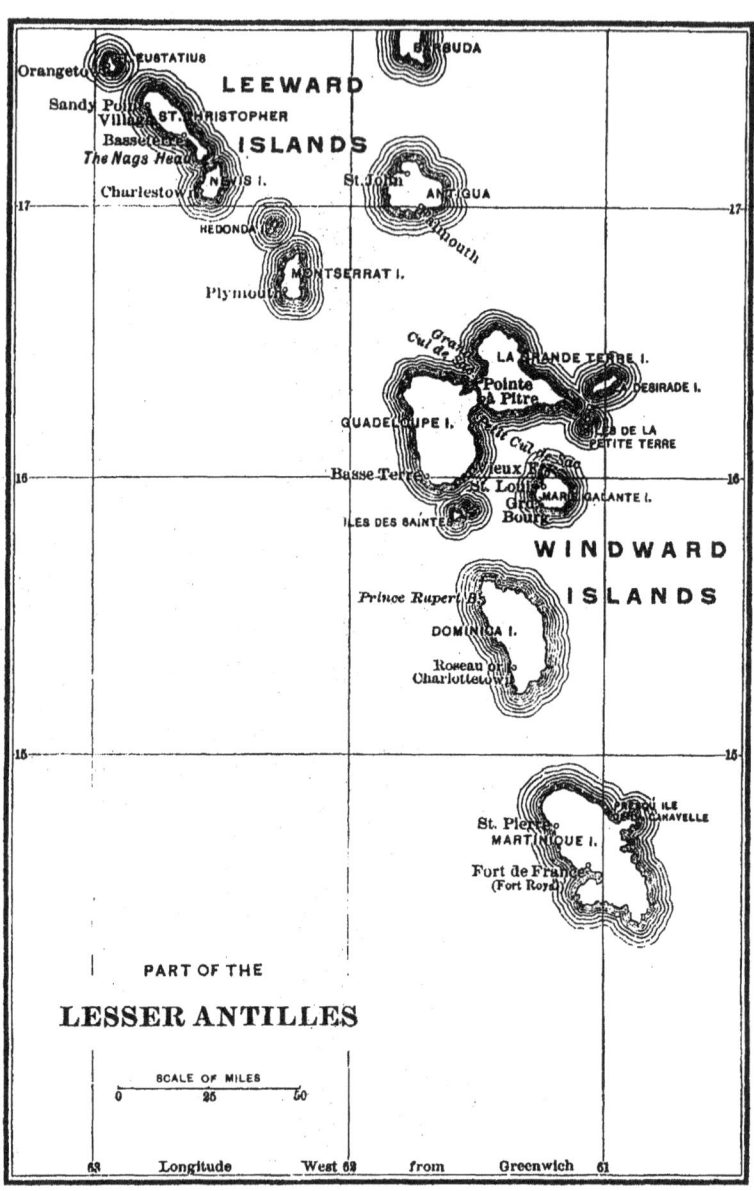

THE PEOPLE OF THE
LEEWARD ISLANDS

1620 - 1860

By
David Dobson

CLEARFIELD

Copyright © 2018
by David Dobson
All Rights Reserved

Printed for Clearfield Company by
Genealogical Publishing Company
Baltimore, Maryland
2018

ISBN 9780806358659

INTRODUCTION

The Leeward Islands form part of the Lesser Antilles which stretch from Puerto Rico to the fringes of Venezuela. Since the seventeenth century these islands attracted immigrants from Europe, initially from Spain but soon also from the British Isles, France, the Netherlands, and Scandinavia. The Leeward Islands comprise of Antigua, Barbuda, St Kitts, Nevis, Montserrat, the Virgin Islands, St Bartholomew, St Martin, Guadeloupe, St Thomas, St Croix, and Anguilla.

In 1494 the Treaty of Tordesillas granted territories beyond 370 leagues west of the Cape Verde Islands to Spain while those lands in Africa, America and Asia east of the line were allocated to Portugal. This gave Spain the monopoly of trade and settlement in much of the Americas, except Brazil which remained Portuguese.

During the sixteenth century the Spanish controlled the West Indies however the English, the Dutch and the French ignored the restrictions of the above Treaty and voyaged to the Caribbean where they engaged in piracy and raiding Spanish settlements. By the early seventeenth century they were beginning to establish permanent settlements there, such as Barbados in 1626

Throughout the seventeenth century the English expanded their Caribbean empire, from Barbados to some of the Lesser Antilles, and by 1655 Jamaica. By 1643 around 37,000 British were settled on Barbados. It is reckoned that by 1705 there were 46,000 African slaves in Barbados alone. The French, based originally in Tortuga, captured Saint Dominique by 1697. Martinique has been a French island since 1635, notwithstanding periods of British occupation. By 1740 there were about 117,000 slaves in Martinique. The French Company of the Isles of America had brought 8,500 settlers from France by 1645. Many Huguenots escaped from persecution in France and settled in the West Indies. After being expelled from Brazil, the Dutch settled in the French colonies, and later in Curacao and St Eustatia. Settlers were also brought directly from the Netherlands by the Dutch West India Company. Many Spanish (Sephardic) Jews fled from Spain to South America to avoid the horrors of the Inquisition; however, when the Inquisition became established there as well, they took refuge in West Indian islands such as Nevis. The Kingdom of Denmark (then comprised of Denmark and Norway) colonised the island of St Thomas around 1670, later adding the nearby islands of St Jan and St Croix. The Danes participated in the Slave Trade from Africa's Gold Coast, whence they transported about 85,000 slaves to their West Indian colonies.

The waning of Spanish power during the seventeenth centuries enabled Britain, France, and the Netherlands to colonise islands in the West Indies, especially the Leeward and Windward Islands. During the eighteenth century Britain and France were generally engaged in a power struggle which meant that from time to time colonies changed hands; for example, Martinique was occupied by the British between 1762 and 1763, and from 1794 to 1815. The end of the Seven Years War between Britain and France in 1763 resulted in French colonies, such as St Vincent and Dominica, being transferred to British rule.

While most of the people in the Leewards today are of African origin there is little data in colonial records to positively identify individuals by race; consequently the people listed in this work are almost certainly of European origin. And most of them derive from Great Britain and Ireland. The majority of the latter possess English roots, with a significant minority coming from Scotland and Ireland. During the seventeenth and eighteenth centuries, the British government disposed of rebels and felons by transporting them for sale to the American Plantations, Cromwell sent Irish rebels, James II sent Monmouth's rebels, the Hanoverians kings sent Jacobites from England and Scotland, as well as thousands of petty criminals. These movements account for much of the Leewards' Caucasian stock. Economic opportunities, especially in the tobacco, sugar, and slave trades attracted many, notably after 1763 to the "Ceded Islands," those islands which were granted to Great Britain as part of the settlement after the Seven Years War. Many of their descendants, both black and white, have in recent years chosen to emigrate to North America and Europe—all of which contributes to the Leeward Islands' complex and fascinating demographic and genealogical makeup.

This book is based on research into manuscript and published sources, mainly located in Great Britain, but also in the West Indies.

David Dobson,

Dundee, Scotland, 2018.

THE PEOPLE OF THE LEEWARD ISLANDS, 1620 - 1860

ABENDANA, RAPHAEL, in Nevis in 1708, [TNA.CO152-157]; resettled there in 1712. [JCTP.1709-1715.386]

ABBOTT, GEORGE, in St Kitts, probate 1660, PCC. [TNA]

ABRAHAM, Mrs ELIZABETH, in Antigua, a deposition in 1718. [JCTP.1718.361]

ABRAHAM, PHILLIP, in Antigua, a deposition in 1718. [JCTP.1718.361]

ABUDIENT, ABRAHAM, aboard the ketch Phoenix, master Robert Flexny, bound from Barbados to Antigua on 25 November 1679. [TNA]

ADAIR, JAMES M., born 1728 in Inverness, settled in Antigua in 1760, an author, judge and physician, died 24 April 1801 in Ayr. [SGS.Library]

ADAMS, JO., aged 16, aboard the Paul of London, master Jo. Acklin, bound from Gravesend to St Kitts on 3 April 1635. [TNA.E157.20]

ADAM, Reverend Dr ROBERT, in St Croix, reference in a deed, 13 April 1821. [NRS.RD5.204.550]

ADCOCK, GEORGE HENRY, born 1803, died in St Kitts on 13 November 1850. [GM.ns.35.222]

ADRIAANSON, PIETER, Governor of St Eustatia, 1665. [SPAWI.1665.1042]

ADYE, Dr, from St Kitts, died in Exeter, England, on 2 April 1804. [GM.74.388]

AIKINE, JAMES, a merchant in St Kitts, who was admitted as a burgess of Glasgow on 24 September 1722. [GBR]

AIRD, JOHN, graduated MA and MD from Glasgow University, later a physician in Antigua. [RGG.7]

AITCHISON, GEORGE, born 1797 in Dryesdale, Dumfries, son of John Aitchison in Borland, died in Guadaloupe in June 1816. [Dryfesdale gravestone]

AITCHISON, JOHN, born 1752, son of John Aitchison in Newbie, Cummertrees, Dumfries-shire, a merchant in the Virgin Islands, died 7 November 1792 in the West Indies. [Cummertrees gravestone]

AITKEN, CHARLES, a merchant in St Croix, married Cornelia Beekman in New York on 22 August 1771, died in St Croix in May 1784. [ANY.I.128]; late in St Croix, 1795. [NRS.RD5.92.723]

AITKEN, GEORGE, in St Croix, a deed, 9 June 1795. [NRS.RD5.92.723]; a planter in St Croix, 1815. [TNA.Probate 37/297]

AITKEN, JANE, daughter of the late Charles Aitken in St Croix, married James Mudie from London, in North Tarry, Angus, on 11 December 1798. [GM.68.1082][AJ.2660]

AITKEN, ROBERT, probate December 1767, Christiansted. [RAK]

AKERS, ARRELAS, of Paradise, St Kitts, was admitted as a burgess of Edinburgh on 9 January 1765. [EBR]; in St Kitts, probate 1785, PCC. [TNA]

AKERS, GEORGE ALEXANDER, third son of the late Aretas Akers in St Kitts, died in Kentish Town, London, on 9 January 1799. [GM.69.83]; in St Kitts, probate, 1799, PCC. [TNA]

AKERS, Miss, daughter of the late Aretas Akers in St Kitts, married William J. Morton in Marylebone, London, on 23 January 1799. [GM.69.78]

THE PEOPLE OF THE LEEWARD ISLANDS, 1620 - 1860

ALEXANDER, CHARLES, born 1822, a merchant from Edinburgh, died in St John, Antigua, on 11 December 1860. [S.1748]

ALEXANDER, DAVID, an accountant in St Kitts, 1730s. [RSM] [HS.7.6/34]

ALEXANDER, WILLIAM, a merchant in Antigua, a sasine, 1792. [NRS.RS.Renfrew.3234]; later in Paisley, testament, Comm. Glasgow, 1806. [NRS]

ALEXANDER and MITCHELL, merchants in Antigua, 1778. [NRS.CS16.1.173]

ALISON, JOHN, a merchant in St Kitts, 1783. [NRS.CS17.1.2]; partner in firm of Allan, Walker and Company in Christiansted, St Croix, died 1820, a deed, 1825. [NRS.RD5.301.447]

ALLAN, GEORGE, in St Croix, deeds, 1819. [NRS.RD5.168.283; RD2.235/2.215]; partner of the firm Allan, Walker and Company in St Croix. [NRS.RD5.301.447]; nephew of Reverend Alexander Allan an Episcopalian priest in Edinburgh, died in St Croix on 18 June 1820. [BM.7.584][EEC.16615][EA.5904]

ALLAN, JOHN, a schoolteacher from Kirkcaldy, in Nevis by 1783. [NRS.CS17.1.2/233]

ALLEN, ROBERT, a mariner from Wapping, died at Montserrat, probate, 1688, PCC. [TNA]

ALLAN, ROBERT, probate 14 June 1775, Christiansted. [RAK]

ALLAN, WILLIAM, in Antigua in 1753. [NRS.CS96.645]

ALLAN, WILLIAM, only son of John Allan a merchant in Tortula, matriculated at Glasgow University in 1801. [MAGU.197]

THE PEOPLE OF THE LEEWARD ISLANDS, 1620 - 1860

ALLANSON, JAMES, in St Kitts, from Liverpool, England, drowned on his passage from St Eustatia to Boston, New England, in 1818. [GM.88.90]

ALLASON, JOHN, a merchant in St Kitts, son of Thomas Allason a merchant in Glasgow, 1782, 1786. [NRS.CS17.1.1/243; 5/278]

ALLERTON, GEORGE, aged 23, bound aboard the Mathew of London, master Richard Goodladd, for St Kitts on 21 May 1635. [TNA.E157.20]

ALSEBROOK, JOHN, born 1760, a clerk from Nottingham, via London aboard the Elenor bound for Antigua in 1775. [TNA.T47.9/11]

ALSEBROOK, SAMUEL, born 1758, a clerk from Nottingham, via London aboard the Elenor bound for Antigua in 1775. [TNA.T47.9/11]

ALSOP, KATHERINE, from Barbados aboard the sloop Katherine, master Andrew Gall, bound for Antigua on 25 November 1679. [TNA]

AMORY, JOSEPH, eldest son of Joseph Amory a merchant in St Kitts, matriculated at Glasgow University in 1793. [MAGU.172]

AMORY, ROBERT, a planter in Antigua, will, 1713. [PWI]

ANBREY, LEWIS, aged 13, bound aboard the Mathew of London, master Richard Goodladd, for St Kitts on 21 May 1635. [TNA.E157.20]

ANDERSON, ANDREW, from Tortula, married Miss H Hetherington, from Tortula, in Durham in 1799. [EA.3688.287] [AJ.679]; she died in Tortula in 1813. [EA.5213.13]

ANDERSON, ANDREW, a merchant in Grenada, later in Antigua, testament, 1784, Comm. Edinburgh. [NRS]

THE PEOPLE OF THE LEEWARD ISLANDS, 1620 - 1860

ANDERSON, ANN, born 1795, died 8 December 1819. [St Paul's. Antigua]

ANDERSON, DAVID, a wright in Antigua, father of Polly Anderson, services of heirs, 1777. [NRS]

ANDERSON, JAMES, in St Croix in 1790. [Caribbeana.5.265]

ANDERSON, Dr JAMES, in St Kitts, later in Midmiln of Cruden, 20 December 1800. [RGS.132.34.35]

ANDERSON, JAMES, a surgeon in Antigua, father of Thomas Anderson, MD, in Trinidad, services of heirs, 1829. [NRS]

ANDERSON, JOHN, a planter in Antigua in 1715. [NRS.RD2.104.724]

ANDERSON, JOHN, a minister sent to the Leeward Islands in 1717, minister of Trinity parish, St Kitts, in 1719, minister of St George, Basseterre, St Kitts, in 1723, minister of Trinity, Palmeto Point, St Kitts, in 1727, died in St Kitts in 1734, probate 1737, PCC. [TNA] [NRS.CH2.14.22; RD3.251.201; RD3.253.542; RD2.278.744] [EMA.11][FPA.272][SPAWI.1728.494.iii/iv; 1729.906] [TNA.CO241.2]

ANDERSON, Dr JOHN, a cleric in St Kitts, dead by 1778. [NRS.RD4.224.1; RD3.253.542; RD2.278.744]

ANDERSON, JOHN, in St Croix in 1790. [Caribbeana.5.265]

ANDERSON, Dr JOHN, in St Kitts, a sasine, 1792, [NRS.RS8.292]; in 1802. [NRS.RS8.PR34.392]

ANDERSON, JOSEPH, probate 22 June 1767, Christiansted. [RAK]

ANDERSON, ROBERT, born 1758, a clerk from Edinburgh, via London aboard the Warness bound for Antigua in 1774, 'going to his uncle'. [TNA.T47.9/11]; son of Henry Anderson a cordiner burgess of Edinburgh, a merchant in Edinburgh, was admitted as a burgess of Edinburgh in 1812. [EBR]

ANDERSON, ROBERT, died on 9 March 1824, probate St Jan. [RAK.1807-1826, fo.131]

ANDERSON, Dr, 'a Scots gentleman who went abroad 25 years ago' died in St Kitts in 1736. [EEC.1987]

ANDREWS, Lieutenant RICHARD, a gentleman on Montserrat, probate,1655, PCC. [TNA]

ANDREW, RICHARD, probate 13 October 1779, Christiansted. [RAK.325.364]

ANGIER, ..., in St Kitts in 1672. [SPAWI.1672.903]

ANGUS, ANDREW, in St Kitts, services of heirs, 1754. [NRS]

ANGUS, JOSEPH, a merchant from Glasgow, settled in St Kitts by 1761, deed. [NRS.B10.12.2]

ANTONY, WALTER, aged 23, bound aboard the Mathew of London, master Richard Goodladd, for St Kitts on 21 May 1635. [TNA.E157.20]

ANTROBUS, CHARLES, born 1725, died 3 November 1765, Captain of HMS Jason. [St Paul's, Antigua]

ANTWISTLE, BERTIE, born 1733, a gentleman and planter, bound via Portsmouth aboard the William and Elizabeth bound for Antigua in 1774. [TNA.T47.9/11]

ARBUCKLE, R. JAMES, probate 26 November 1777, Christiansted. [RAK.334.188]

ARBUTHNOTT, JAMES, a clergyman, emigrated to the Leeward Islands in 1705. [EMA.11]

THE PEOPLE OF THE LEEWARD ISLANDS, 1620 - 1860

ARE, SARAH, from Barbados aboard the sloop Katherine, master Andrew Gall, bound for Antigua on 25 November 1679. [TNA]

ARMSTRONG, ANN, a time-served indentured servant aboard the Francis, master Peter Jefferys, bound from Barbados to Antigua on 28 April 1679. [TNA]

ARMSTRONG, EDWARD, in St Croix in 1790. [Caribbeana.5.265]

ARMSTRONG, JEAN, in Antigua, 1753. [NRS.CS96.645]

ARMSTRONG, KATHERIN, aged 20, bound aboard the Mathew of London, master Richard Goodladd, for St Kitts on 21 May 1635. [TNA.E157.20]

ARMSTRONG, MARTHA, died 11 November 1844, probate, St Jan. [RAK.1835-1882.42]

ARMSTRONG, MARY REDFERN, daughter of Rev. Dr Bunting in London, wife of H. Armstrong, died in Antigua on 21 October 1835. [GM.ns5.335]

ARMSTRONG, THOMAS, in St Croix in 1790. [Caribbeana.5.265]

ARMSTRONG, THOMAS T., in St Croix in 1790. [Caribbeana.5.265]

ARMSTRONG, WILLIAM, a gentleman in St Kitts, surgeon of the Naval Hospital there, graduated MD in Aberdeen on 18 October 1798. [AUL][KCA.143]

ARMSTRONG, WILLIAM, in St Croix in 1801-1804. [NLS.ms5602/3]

ARMSTRONG, WILLIAM, son of Thomas Armstrong, [1731-1805] and his wife Janet Laidlaw [1738-1769] in Ewes, Dumfries-shire, died in Antigua aged 26. [Ewes gravestone]

ARNAUD, VEUVE ANTOINE, in St Vincent in 1777. [JCTP.84.69]

ARROBAS, HANANIAH, was resettled in Nevis in 1712. [JCTP.1709-1715.386]

ARTHUR, MATHEW, aged 18, from Plimpton, emigrated via Plymouth aboard the Robert Bonaventure bound for St Kitts in February 1633. [TNA.E157.18]

ARTHUR, WILLIAM, in Antigua by 1753. [NRS.CS96.644]

ARTHURTON, JOHN, born 1752, via London aboard the Harlequin bound for Nevis in 1774. [TNA.T47.9/11]

ASHTON, Captain HENRY, Governor of Antigua, letters, 1641. [NRS.GD34.933]

ASHTON, WILLIAM, formerly a merchant on St Croix, died in Islington, London, in 1814. [GM.84.300]; a slave merchant in St Croix in 1802. [RDAG.I/2]

ASKINS, ALEXANDER, probate 10 May 1769, Christiansted. [RAK.21.33]

ASSAILIES, KATHERINE, daughter of Peter Assailies in St Kitts, 1720. [PCCol.1720.1225]

ASSAILIES, MARTHA, daughter of Peter Assaillies, a Huguenot and planter, who to escape religious persecution in French St Kitts, fled to Boston before 1695, however his estates were restored in 1715-1716. [PCCol.1715.375.1225][SPAWI.1714.630; 1715.375; 1716.134/173]

ASSAILLIE, Mrs, in St Kitts, 1717. [JCTP.1717.208]

ATHILL, E., daughter of the late James Athill in Antigua, married John Vassall on 13 May 1799. [GM.69.526]

ATHILL, ANN, born 1737, wife of James Athill of Antigua, died 28 February 1802. [Bath Abbey gravestone]

THE PEOPLE OF THE LEEWARD ISLANDS, 1620 - 1860

ATHILL, JAMES, a Lieutenant of the Royal Navy, married Ellen Redhead, daughter of the late George Redhead formerly a Captain of the 3rd Regiment of Foot Guards in Antigua, in London on 13 March 1850. [GM.ns33.657]

ATHILL, JOSEPH LYONS, an Assemblyman and judge in Antigua, died on 18 September 1790. [GM.60.1052]

ATHILL, MARY, daughter of James Athill in Antigua, married Lewis Evans a surgeon from London, in Edinburgh on 22 July 1823. [S.370.480]

ATHILL, SAMUEL, born 1786, eldest son of Samuel Athill in Antigua, a barrister, died in Antigua on 21 October 1811. [GM.81.657]

ATHILL, Miss, daughter of the late Dr Athill, married Captain Bickerton of HMS Sybil in Antigua in 1782. [GM.58.1181]

ATHILL, Miss, daughter of Samuel Athill in Antigua, married Charles Turner in London on 13 January 1804. [GM.74.86]

ATKINSON, ROBERT, aged 23, aboard the Paul of London, master Jo. Acklin, bound from Gravesend to St Kitts on 3 April 1635. [TNA.E157.20]

ATKINSON, SAMUEL, died in Antigua in December 1757. [Willoughby Bay gravestone, Antigua]

ATTWELL, ELIZABETH, born in Nevis, a widow, married Robert Thomas from Elie, Fife, in Curacao on 7 March 1719. [Extract uit het Trouwboek der Gereformeerde Gemente op het eiland Curacao van der jaar 1714 tot en met 1722]

AUCHENLECK, Mrs ELIZABETH, widow of Samuel Auchenleck late Customs Collector of Antigua, died there on 31 August 1819. [GM.89.284][S.142.19]

AUCHENLECK, JOSEPH, a Jacobite prisoner banished to Antigua in 1716. [SPAWI.1716.310]

AUCHENLECK, SAMUEL, in Antigua, married Elisabeth, daughter of Captain Maurice Gouldstone of the 1th Regiment, in Edinburgh on 3 December 1775. [EMR]

AUDAIN, ABRAHAM, in St Kitts, probate 1781, PCC. [TNA]

AUDIAN, ISAAC PETER, a planter with his infant sons Andrew and Peter, in St Kitts in 1722; 1723; 1746. [JCTP.1723.28; 1733.354/365/375/398; 1746.219] [PCCol.1733-1734]

AUSTIN, JONATHAN, an indentured servant bound from Bristol to St Kitts in 1660. [BRO]

AYRES, ROBERT, in St Thomas, probate 1780, PCC. [TNA]

AYSON, THOMAS, in Nevis, probate, 1665, PCC. [TNA]

BABELL, JOHN, in Nevis, probate, 1726, PCC. [TNA]

BACHELOR, JOHN, aged 26, aboard the John of London, master James Waymoth, bound for St Kitts on 2 October 1635. [TNA.E157.20]

BADCOCKE, WILLIAM, from St Hillary, a husbandman aged 20, who emigrated via Plymouth aboard the Margaret bound for St Kitts in 1634. [TNA.E157.18]

BADLAND, JOHN, aged 22, from Northill, emigrated via Plymouth aboard the Robert Bonaventure bound for St Kitts in February 1633. [TNA.E157.18]

BAGIN, HENRY, aged 22, aboard the Paul of London, master Jo. Acklin, bound from Gravesend to St Kitts on 3 April 1635. [TNA.E157.20]

THE PEOPLE OF THE LEEWARD ISLANDS, 1620 - 1860

BAIJER, Mrs, widow of John Otto Baijer in Antigua, died in Exeter, England, in April 1796. [GM.66.444]

BAILLIE, ALEXANDER, of Dochfur, in Nevis before 1752. [NRS.NRAS.0484.4.6]; probate 1799, PCC. [TNA]

BAILLIE, ALEXANDER, a merchant in St Kitts, a deed, 1768. [NRS.GD71.174.2]

BAILLIE, DAVID, in St Croix, probate 1797, PCC. [TNA]

BAILLIE, G., formerly a merchant on St Eustatia, died in Ealing, England, on 7 September 1793. [GM.63.869]

BAILLIE, JAMES, a merchant in St Kitts, a deed, 1768. [NRS.GD71.174.2]

BAIRD, ANTONY, third son of Daniel Baird a merchant in St Kitts, matriculated at Glasgow University in 1808. [MAGU.235]

BAIRD, CHARLES, in Antigua in 1775. [AUL.ms3175/668.3]

BAIRD, DANIEL, second son of Daniel Baird a merchant in St Kitts, matriculated at Glasgow University in 1808. [MAGU.235]

BAIRD, ROBERT, probate 20 July 1777, Christiansted. [RAK.250.19.302]

BAIRD, WILLIAM, born 1744, died 26 July 1779 in Antigua. [St John's Cathedral gravestone, Antigua]

BAKER, ALEXANDER, a mariner, arrived in Boston aboard the brigantine Martha and Hannah from Montserrat, on 14 April 1712. [PA.129]

BAKER, HENRY WILLIAMS, born 1794, from Suffolk, died 17 December 1823. [St John's, Fig Tree, Nevis, gravestone]

BAKER, JAMES, in St Kitts, probate, 1796, PCC. [TNA]

BAKER, JOHN, in St Kitts, probate 1780, PCC. [TNA]

THE PEOPLE OF THE LEEWARD ISLANDS, 1620 - 1860

BAKER, THOMAS, in St Kitts, probate 1780, PCC. [TNA]

BAKER, WILLIAM, on Saba, petitioned the Dutch West India Company in Amsterdam in 1772. [DNA.Inv.1151]

BALAGUER, JOHN, deputy secretary of St Kitts in 1725. [SPAWI.1725.648ii]

BALDERSTON, GEORGE, a surgeon in Edinburgh later in St Kitts, dead by 1767, husband of Euphan Douglas, a sasine. [NRS.RS27.177.244]

BALFOUR, JAMES, a time-served indentured servant, aboard the sloop True Friendship, master Charles Callaghan, bound for Antigua on 4 October 1679. [TNA]

BALFOUR, M. Y., a Lieutenant of the 96th Regiment, died in St Croix in 1808. [EA.4698]

BALL, GEORGE, aged 51, bound aboard the Mathew of London, master R. Goodladd, for St Kitts on 21 May 1635. [TNA.E157.20]

BALL, WILLIAM, a husbandman from Manaton, Devon, bound from Bristol to Nevis in 1660. [BRO]

BALLANTYNE, JOSEPH, a Jacobite banished to Antigua in 1716. [CTB.31.04]

BALLANTYNE, WILLIAM, a Jacobite banished to Antigua in 1715, [SPAWI.1716.310]

BALNEAVES, WILLIAM, a minister sent to Antigua in 1712. [EMA.12]

BANKS, H., died 19 October 1753. [St Anthony's mi, Montserrat]

BANNERMAN, MARK, a Jacobite banished to St Kitts in 1716. [CTB.31.209]

THE PEOPLE OF THE LEEWARD ISLANDS, 1620 - 1860

BARBER, WILLIAM, aged 22, bound aboard the Mathew of London, master Richard Goodladd, for St Kitts on 21 May 1635. [TNA.E157.20]

BARBOUTTAIN, JOHN, a gentleman in Antigua in 1709, dead by 1728. [SPAWI.1709.487ii][PCCol.1729.177]

BARCLAY, ANDREW, born 1791, a Presbyterian resident of St Croix in 1841. [Census]

BARCLAY, CHARLES, born 30 July 1790, fourth son of Reverend Dr Peter Barclay minister at Kettle, Fife, and his wife Margaret Duddingstone, died at Point au Petre, Guadeloupe, on 13 June 1819. [S.134.19][F.V.160][EEC.16877]

BARCLAY, ELIZABETH CLELLAND, born 12 February 1792, daughter of Reverend Dr Peter Barclay minister at Kettle, Fife, and his wife Margaret Duddingstone, married Thomas Martin a merchant in Antigua in 1810, she died on 4 December 1841. [F.V.160]

BARCLAY, SUSANNE, probate 31 August 1774, Christiansted. [RAK.232.225]

BARCLAY, WILLIAM, in Antigua, probate 29 October 1748, PCC. [TNA]

BARKER, MARY, aged 12, bound aboard the Mathew of London, master Richard Goodladd, for St Kitts on 21 May 1635. [TNA.E157.20]

BARLOE, JO., aged 22, bound aboard the Mathew of London, master Richard Goodladd, for St Kitts on 21 May 1635. [TNA.E157.20]

BARNABY, THOMAS, a planter in St Kitts, murdered there in 1753. [TNA.CO186.3]

THE PEOPLE OF THE LEEWARD ISLANDS, 1620 - 1860

BARNES, EDWARD, aged 16, aboard the Paul of London, master Jo. Acklin, bound from Gravesend to St Kitts on 3 April 1635. [TNA.E157.20]

BARRELL, THEODORE, in St Eustatia, a memorial, 1790. [TNA.AO13.1.137/4]

BARRI, JACOBUS, Vice Commander of St Martins in 1728, [Goslinga, 132]; Governor of St Martin's in 1734. [SPAWI.41.592]

BARROW, EDWARD, born 1759, died in Antigua on 8 November 1762. [St Stephen's]

BARRY, CLEMENT, from Exeter, a husbandman aged 22, who emigrated via Plymouth aboard the Margaret bound for St Kitts in 1634. [TNA.E157.18]

BARRY, DANIEL, probate, 28 July 1777, Christiansted. [RAK.252.24]

BARRY, GARRETT, of Montserrat, died in Cornwall, probate, 1659, PCC. [TNA]

BARRY, JAMES, in St Kitts, probate, 1659, PCC. [TNA]

BARRY, Reverend JAMES, born 1708 in County Kildare, was educated at Dublin University, rector of St George's in Antigua for 9 years, husband of Margaret Sherwood, died on 11 December 1747. [St John's Cathedral, Antigua]

BARRY, JOHN, probate, 31 March 1779, Christiansted. [RAK.322.142]

BARRY, JOHN JAMES, probate 11 December 1759, Christiansted. [RAK]

BARTER, WARNER, in Antigua, letters 1794-1796, will, 8 February 1796. [NRS.GD46.108]

BARTOUILH, DOMINIQUE, in Dominique in 1773. [JCTP.1773.334]

THE PEOPLE OF THE LEEWARD ISLANDS, 1620 - 1860

BARWICKE, ROBERT, in St Kitts, probate, 1628, PCC. [TNA]

BATHGATE, ARCHIBALD, born 1779 in Falkirk, master of the brig Robert of London and Montserrat, died 18 June 1827. [St Anthony's mi, Montserrat]

BATTERIE, PIETER, Commander of St Eustatia in 1680. [SPAWI.1680.1358]

BAWDEN, Sir JOHN, in Nevis, probate, 1689, PCC. [TNA]

BAYER, BASTIAEN, in Antigua, 1709. [SPAWI.1709.443]

BAYER, JOHN OTTO, formerly of the 82nd Regiment, a Councillor of Antigua in 1773, died there on 10 May 1817. [JCTP.80.118][BM.1.451]

BEACH, D., from Edinburgh, father of Rachel [1814-1829], settled in St Croix before 1829. [Restalrig burial register]

BEACH, EDWARD, in St Croix in 1768. [SSF]

BEACH, WILLIAM, in St Kitts, probate 1788, PCC. [TNA]

BEAKS, JOHN, on Saba, petitioned the Dutch West India Company in Amsterdam in 1772. [DNA.Inv.1151]

BEAN, DUNCAN, a Jacobite banished in 1716, landed in Montserrat. [SPAWI.1716.313][CTB.31.205][CTP.CC.43]

BEAN, GEORGE, a Jacobite banished to Antigua in 1747. [P.2.30]

BEAN, KENNEDY, a Jacobite banished to St Kitts in 1747. [SPAWI.1716.312][CTB.31.207]

BEARDSFORD, GEORGE, a wire drawer, bound from Bristol to Nevis in 1660. [BRO]

THE PEOPLE OF THE LEEWARD ISLANDS, 1620 - 1860

BEAULIEU, HENRY, in Antigua in 1709. [SPAWI.1709.487ii]

BEAVOR, JOHN, born 1710, from Kingsale, Ireland, died 31 July 1768, husband of Honor ... from Montserrat. [St George gravestone, Basse Terre, St Kitts]

BECK, JANET, widow of John N. Beck, a planter in Antigua, services of heirs, 1794. [NRS]

BEDDLE, WILLIAM, aged 19, aboard the Paul of London, master Jo. Acklin, bound from Gravesend to St Kitts on 3 April 1635. [TNA.E157.20]

BELCHAMBER, THOMAS, in Nevis, probate, 1693, PCC. [TNA]

BELINDER, JOHN, born 1729, a merchant, via London aboard the Good Intent bound for Antigua in 1774. [TNA.T47.9/11]

BELL, JOHN, a doctor aboard a Dutch slaving ship trading between Africa and St Eustatia in 1743. [NRS.NRAS.363/2]

BELL, THOMAS, aged 14, bound aboard the Mathew of London, master Richard Goodladd, for St Kitts on 21 May 1635. [TNA.E157.20]

BELL, THOMAS, probate 1767, Christiansted. [RAK.2.2]

BELLEW, FRANCIS, formerly of St Kitts, but of Cork, will, 1773. [PWI]

BENNET, GEORGE WILLIAM, married Elizabeth Burns third daughter of Patrick Burns of Villa Estate, in Antigua on 5 February 1861. [S.1841]

BENNET, JOHN, probate 3 April 1762, Christiansted. [RAK]

BENTLEY, WILLIAM, a militiaman in Montserrat in 1654. [Remonstrances ...., London, 1654]

THE PEOPLE OF THE LEEWARD ISLANDS, 1620 - 1860

BERKELEY, HENRY, born in St Kitts in January 1734, son of Maurice Berkeley and his wife a Miss Tobin from Nevis. [St George mi, Basse Terre, St Kitts]

BERNARD, MATHEW, a merchant from London, died in 1775. [St John's Cathedral burial register, Antigua]

BERRY, Captain JAMES, of Liverpool, born 1732, died 1764. [St John's Cathedral]

BETHUNE, DAVID, Anglican minister of St Anthony's, Montserrat, in 1715; rector of St Anne, Sandy Point, St Kitts, 1724, 1727. [FPA.270; 274][SPAWI.1728.494i]

BETTS, THOMAS, in St Thomas, Middle Island, St Kitts on 7 February 1678. [TNA.COI.42]

BEVERIDGE, WILLIAM GARDINER, born 1842, an engineer late of Dunnikier Foundry, died in St Thomas on 24 August 1865. [Dunnikier gravestone, Fife]

BEVON, JAMES, in Nevis, probate, 1722, PCC. [TNA]

BICKES, JACOB, a Dutch Reformed Church minister on St Croix in 1754. [RAK.WIC.429]

BICROFT, EDWARD, aged 22, bound aboard the Mathew of London, master Richard Goodladd, for St Kitts on 21 May 1635. [TNA.E157.20]

BIETON, JAN, in St Thomas in 1686. [St Thomas tax roll]

BILFORD, JAMES, a time-served indentured servant, aboard the pink Seaventure, master George Battersby, bound from Barbados to Antigua on 5 March 1678. [TNA]

BILL, WILLEN, born 1606, a husbandman from Great Torrington in Devon, bound from Dartmouth to St Kitts in 1634. [TNA]

THE PEOPLE OF THE LEEWARD ISLANDS, 1620 - 1860

BIRD, GEORGE, a Jacobite transported to Antigua in 1716. [SPAWI.1716.310][CTB.31.204]

BIRKET, BENJAMIN, in Nevis, probate, 1729, PCC. [TNA]

BIRLECK, P. W., born 1759, a gentleman in London, via London aboard the Pemberton bound for St Kitts in 1774. [TNA.T47.9/11]

BISHOP, THOMAS, aboard the Virgin, master Thomas Alumby, bound from Barbados to the Leeward Island on 4 October 1679. [TNA]

BLACK, JAMES, born 1807, died in Cochran, Antigua, on 14 August 1839. [SG.812]

BLACK, JOHN, from Dunfermline, a Justice of the Peace, died in Antigua on 22 August 1840. [W.83][FH]

BLACK, WILLIAM, son of John Black in Antigua, died in Dunfermline on 6 June 1827. [FH]

BLACKADDER, WILLIAM, in Antigua in 1758. [DA.Ogilvie pp.25]

BLAER, JOHANN, a planter in St Thomas in 1686, [St Thomas Tax Roll]; with his Dutch wife Anna David, and two children Gillis Blaer and Robert Blaer, in 1688. [1688 Census of the Danish West Indies]

BLAIN, JAMES, in St Thomas, services of heirs, 1817. [NRS]

BLAIR, DAVID, born 1793, son of John Blair a calenderer in Glasgow, died in St Croix on 3 February 1816. [Glasgow, Ramshorn gravestone]

BLAIR, JAMES, a Jacobite transported to Antigua in 1716. [SPAWI.1716.310][CTB.31.204]

THE PEOPLE OF THE LEEWARD ISLANDS, 1620 - 1860

BLAIR, JAMES, in St Eustatia, letters, 1780-1795. [PRONI.DOD.717/19-27]; a merchant in St Eustatia in 1784. [ASS.125/390]

BLAIR, JOHN, in Antigua, a deed, 24 March 1797. [NRS.RD2.271.419]

BLAIR, LAMBERT, a merchant in St Eustatia in 1784. [ASS.125/390]

BLAIR, WILLIAM, a minister sent to Montserrat in 1750, in Antigua in 1751. [EMA.15][FPA.284]

BLAKE, BRYAN, a merchant in Antigua, will, 1801. [PWI]

BLAKE, EDWARD, in St Kitts, probate 1770, PCC. [TNA]

BLAKE, HENRY, son of the Mayor of Galway, emigrated to the West Indies in 1668. [BFR]; a planter in Montserrat, and by 1719, was in Plymouth, Montserrat, 1719. [TNA.CO152.13]

BLAKE, JOHN, son of the Mayor of Galway, emigrated to the West Indies in 1668; later a merchant in Barbados, thereafter Speaker of the House of Assembly of the Leeward Islands, died in Montserrat in 1692. [BFR]

BLAKE, JOHN, a time-served indentured servant, from Barbados aboard the sloop Resolution, master John Ingleby, bound for Antigua on 18 February 1678. [TNA]

BLAKE, JOHN, in Plymouth, Montserrat, 1719. [TNA.CO152.13]

BLAKE, PATRICK, a planter in Montserrat in 1712. [TNA.CO152.16]

BLAKE, Sir PATRICK, in St Kitts, probate 1784, PCC. [TNA]

BLAKE, THOMAS, in Plymouth, Montserrat, 1719. [TNA.CO152.13]; a planter in Montserrat in 1712. [TNA.CO152.16]

BLANE, JOHN, a merchant in Antigua in 1751. [NRS.RD2.211.1.380]; from Ayrshire, died in Antigua in 1755. [GJ.756]

BLEAKLEY, JOHN, of the Island of St Croix, will, 1804. [PWI]

BLUNDELL, Lieutenant Colonel, the Commanding Officer in Basseterre, Guadeloupe,1795. [NRS.AC7.67]

BODETT, ..., in St Kitts in 1672. [SPAWI.1672.903]

BODKIN, ANDREW, in St Kitts, 1716. [PCCol.1716.275]

BODKIN, ANDREW, third brother of Edmond Bodkin late of Kilaloony, County Galway, married Margaret Denn of St Croix, Danish West Indies, there in 1770. [FLJ.65]

BODKIN, DAVID, a planter in Montserrat in 1712. [TNA.CO152.16]

BODKIN, LAWRENCE, in St Croix, probate, 1797, PCC. [TNA]

BODKIN, MARY, in St Croix, probate, 1797, PCC. [TNA]

BODKIN, THOMAS, in the parish of Sandy Point, St Kitts on 7 February 1678. [TNA.COI.42]

BODKIN, THOMAS, a land-owner at English Harbour, Antigua, 1744. [JCTP.66.186]

BOGARDUS, SAMUEL, a merchant, Tavern Yard, Cape Herriott, in St Croix in 1802. [RDAG.I/2]

THE PEOPLE OF THE LEEWARD ISLANDS, 1620 - 1860

BONDINOT, MAGDALEN, widow and executrix of John Bondinot in Antigua in 1725. [PCCol.1725.87]

BONNEMERE, ..., a Huguenot in St Kitts, 1672 -1690. [SPAWI.1672.903; 1673.1048; 1674.1273; 1690.1212]

BONNIN, GOUSSE, in Antigua, 1709. [SPAWI.1709.487ii]

BONTINAN, DOROTHY, in St Anne's, Sandy Point, St Kitts, 1724. [PCCol.1727.135]

BONVERON, SIMEON, in Montserrat, 1733, 1737. [SPAWI.1733.446; 1737.55]

BONYEA, CHARLES, on Saba, petitioned the Dutch West India Company in Amsterdam in 1772. [DNA.Inv.1151]

BONYEA, SIMEON, on Saba, petitioned the Dutch West India Company in Amsterdam in 1772. [DNA.Inv.1151]

BORINTHON, THOMAS, from Helston, a husbandman aged 22, emigrated via Plymouth aboard the Margaret bound for St Kitts in 1634. [TNA.E157.18]

BORN, JOHAN, a Dutch Reformed Church minister on St Thomas in 1737, husband of Maria Runnels, daughter of Isaac Runnels. [RAK.WIC.431]

BORVELIO, ROBERT, master of the shalop St Dominique seized at Montserrat in 1736. [SPAWI.1737.611]

BOSWELL, Dr JAMES, a physician, died in Montserrat in December 1767. [SM.30.110]

BOSWELL, JO., aged 17, bound aboard the Mathew of London, master Richard Goodladd, for St Kitts on 21 May 1635. [TNA.E157.20]

THE PEOPLE OF THE LEEWARD ISLANDS, 1620 - 1860

BOTTELL, PAUL, aged 32, bound aboard the Mathew of London, master Richard Goodladd, for St Kitts on 21 May 1635. [TNA.E157.20]

BOUDEWYNE, JOHN, master of the schooner Prosperity seized at Montserrat in 1736. [SPAWI. 1737.61I]

BOUDINOT, JOHN, a merchant and planter in Antigua in 1718. [SPAWI.1718.413]

BOURKE, THEOBALD, on Castle Bourke plantation in 1755; a planter in St Croix in 1770, [RDAG]; in St Croix, probate, 1783, PCC. [TNA][SSF]

BOURNE, JOHN, in Nevis, probate, 1631, PCC. [TNA]

BOURNE, THURLOE, a yeoman, bound from Bristol to Nevis in 1660. [BRO]

BOURRYEAU, JOHN, in St Kitts, dead by 1729. [SPAWI.1729.908]

BOURYAU, JOHN, in St Kitts, 1716, 1733. [JCTP.1716.110] [SPAWI.1733.446]; in St Kitts, probate 1769, PCC. [TNA]

BOURRYAU, SUSANNAH, in St Kitts, probate 1785, PCC. [TNA]

BOWDEN, MICHAEL, aged 27, from Holston, emigrated via Plymouth aboard the Robert Bonaventure bound for St Kitts in February 1633. [TNA.E157.18]

BOWIE, JAMES, in Antigua in 1753. [NRS.CS96.645]

BOWIE, ROBERT, a smith, settled in Tortula before 1792. [Kincardine, Blair Drummond gravestone]

BOWIE, Dr WILLIAM, a physician in Antigua, husband of Margaret Mure, 1779. [NRS.CS16.1.175]

THE PEOPLE OF THE LEEWARD ISLANDS, 1620 - 1860

BOWIE, WILLIAM, late in Antigua, son of John Bowie a merchant in Ayr, was admitted as a burgess and guilds-brother of Ayr on 24 September 1790. [ABR]

BOWNE, Reverend SAMUEL WHITBREAD, married Mary Caroline Cassin, eldest daughter of the late Henry R Cassin, MD, in London on 24 March 1852. [GM.ns37.512]

BOWRING, GRACE W., born 1825, daughter of the late William Bowring of Paradise Estate, Nevis, grand-daughter of Rear Admiral Gourlay of the Royal Navy, died in St Kitts on 1 January 1854. [GM.ns.41.329]

BOWRIN, WILLIAM, from Nevis, married Elizabeth Grace Gourlay, second daughter of Captain Gourlay of the Royal Navy, in Bath Cathedral on 23 March 1819. [S.116.19]

BOXWELL, JANE, a widow, an indentured servant bound from Bristol to Nevis in 1660. [BRO]

BOWYER, JAMES, born 1736, died in Antigua on 8 October 1772. [St John's Cathedral, Antigua]

BOY, GEORGE, a Jacobite transported to Antigua in 1747. [P.2.44]

BOYCE, FRANCIS, born 1609, a button-hole maker from London, bound from Dartmouth to St Kitts in 1634. [TNA]

BOYD, ANDREW, a merchant in Antigua, later in Virginia, 1765. [NRS.CS16.1.122]

BOYD, GEORGE, a clerk in St Croix, witness to a deed, 21 December 1784. [NRS.RD3.244.530]

BOYD, HUGH, in Antigua in 1759. [DA.Ogilvie pp.29]

BOYD, JAMES, fourth son of the late Dr William Boyd of Martinhall, Galloway, Scotland, a merchant in London, died on Guadeloupe on 14 September 1794. [GM.64.1150][SM.56.801]

BOYFIELD, Miss, married Thomas Woodyer, in St Kitts in 1785. [GM.55.1005]

BOYLE, JAMES LAWRENCE, son of John Boyle in St Croix, services of heirs, 1777, [NRS]; a merchant in St Croix, 1783. [NRS.CS17.1.2]; son of John Boyle, a merchant in St Croix in 1779. [NRS.CS16.1.175], in 1800. [NRS.CS17.1.19.350]

BOYLE, JAMES, a surgeon in St Eustatia, 1781. [NRS.CS16.1.183]

BOYLE, Dr JOHN, probate 6 November 1763, Christiansted. [RAK]

BOYLE, STAIR, from Inverkip, a merchant in St Kitts, 1761. [NRS.B10.12.2]

BOYLE, THOMAS, probate 28 November 1781, Christiansted. [RAK]

BRADLEY, Reverend WILLIAM GARDNER, in St Mary Cayon, St Kitts, eldest son of Reverend W. Bradley in Nether Whitacre, Warwickshire, died in 1851. [GM.ns37.105]

BRADNER, ALEXANDER, probate 17 November 1781, Christiansted. [RAK.112.339]

BRADSHAW, THOMAS, born 1739, a gentleman in London, via London aboard the <u>Catherine</u> bound for St Kitts in 1774. [TNA.T47.9/11]

BRAITHWAITE, Reverend FRANCIS GRETTON C., son of Reverend Francis Robert Braithwaite the former Archdeacon of St Kitts, married Frances Brown, fourth daughter of the late Thomas Brown of Barbados, in London on 14 August 1861. [GM.ns2.11.320]

THE PEOPLE OF THE LEEWARD ISLANDS, 1620 - 1860

BRAITHWAITE, MARY BLANCHE, younger daughter of Reverend F. R. Braithwaite in Basseterre, the Archdeacon of St Kitts, married George Pilgrim Toppin, in London on 23 July 1863. [GM.ns2.15.369]

BRAMBLE, ANN, born 1795, died in January 1811. [St Anthony's mi, Montserrat]

BRAND, ANDREW, late from Nevis, died in East Linton, East Lothian, on 31 March 1820. [AJ.3771]

BRANDER, JOHN, a planter in St John's, Grenada, later in Tortula, died 18 May 1806, testament, 16 June 1807, Comm. Edinburgh.

BRATTLEY, HENRY, in the parish of St John Capistar, St Kitts, on 28 January 1678. [TNA.COl.42]

BRAYNAN, JAMES, a Scot, was admitted as a burgher of St Eustatia on 8 December 1780. [TNA.CO318.8.84V]

BRAZIER, EDWARD, born 1736, died 20 September 1819, Mrs Anne Brazier, born 1750, died 8 December 1797, and William Brazier, born 1782, died 10 October 1794. [St John's, Fig Tree, Nevis, gravestone]

BRAZIER, JOSEPH, born 1792, son of Edward Brazier, died 24 July 1834. [St John's, Fig Tree, Nevis, gravestone]

BREAD, ARTHUR, from Barbados aboard the ketch Phoenix, master Robert Flexny, bound for the Leeward Islands on 25 November 1679. [TNA]

BREAD, THOMAS, from Barbados aboard the ketch Phoenix, master Robert Flexny, bound for the Leeward Islands on 25 November 1679. [TNA]

BREBNER-GORDON, JAMES, a Councillor of Antigua and Chief Justice of the Ceded Isles in 1761. [JCTP]

THE PEOPLE OF THE LEEWARD ISLANDS, 1620 - 1860

BRENNAN, JOHN, born 1695 in County Carlow, died in Antigua on24 September 1743. [St John's Cathedral, Antigua]

BREWETT, JOHN, in Nevis, probate, 1699, PCC. [TNA]

BRIDGEWATER, E., formerly a physician on St Kitts, died in London on 5 September 1811. [GM.81.293]

BRIGGS, DANIEL, a Jacobite transported to Antigua in 1716. [CTB.31.204]

BRIGGS, PAUL, a Jacobite transported to Antigua in 1716. [SPAWI.1716.310[CTB.31.204]

BRIGGS, ROBERT, born 1784, settled in Antigua in 1802, father of Mrs Neville in Bristol, died in Green Castle, Antigua, on 3 May 1841. [GM.ns16.334]

BRIGHT, EDMUND, a mariner from Whitechapel, died in Nevis, probate, 1688, PCC. [TNA]

BRIMLAY, MICHAEL, bound from Bristol to Nevis in 1660. [BRO]

BRINT, MORGAN, aged 19, bound aboard the *Mathew of London*, master Richard Goodladd, for St Kitts on 21 May 1635. [TNA.E157.20]

BRISKETT, ANTHONY, born in Wexford, Governor of Montserrat, 16…. [SPAWI]

BRITTARGH, WILLIAM, a Jacobite who was transported from London to Antigua aboard the *Prince George*, master James Nairn, on 14 January 1748, landed on 16 March 1748. [TNA.T53.44]

BROADHURST, JOSEPH, in Antigua, will, 1737. [PWI]

BRODBELT, Mrs FRANCES, born 1686, wife of Colonel Richard Brodbelt, died 27 August 1723, parents of Joseph Hill Brodbelt and Frances Hill Brodbelt. [St John's, Fig Tree, Nevis, gravestone]

THE PEOPLE OF THE LEEWARD ISLANDS, 1620 - 1860

BRODBELT, JOHN, a planter in Nevis, 1734. [TNA.CO186.1]

BRODBELT, LAWRENCE, in Nevis, probate, 1661, PCC. [TNA]

BRODBELT, LAWRENCE, in Nevis, probate, 1727, PCC. [TNA]

BRODIE, ALEXANDER, born 1738, son of Alexander Brodie of Windyhills, Moray, and his wife Anne Dawson, settled in Antigua in 1760, a merchant in Windyhills, St Mary's, Antigua, married Anne Kidder [1730-1801] in 1766, died 1800 in Antigua. [Caribbeana.I.98]

BROME, PHILIP. in Nevis, probate, 1708, PCC. [TNA]

BROOKES, RICHARD, aged 16, bound aboard the Mathew of London, master Richard Goodladd, for St Kitts on 21 May 1635. [TNA.E157.20]

BROOKES, WILLIAM, aged 22, bound aboard the Mathew of London, master Richard Goodladd, for St Kitts on 21 May 1635. [TNA.E157.20]

BROTHERSON, BARBARA, widow of Ludovic Brotherson in St Kitts, services of heirs, 1818. [NRS]

BROTHERSON, LEWIS, in St Kitts, probate 1783, PCC. [TNA]

BROUNCKER, HENRY, in St Kitts, probate 1769, PCC. [TNA]

BROWN, ADAM, probate 5 February 1762, Christiansted. [RAK]

BROWN, ALEXANDER, formerly a merchant in St Kitts, services of heirs, 1765/1767. [NRS]

BROWN, ALEXANDER, minister of the Scots Kirk in St John's, Antigua, 1842-1843. [F.7.666]

BROWN, FRANCIS, born 1755, a gentleman in London, from London aboard the Betsey bound for St Kitts in 1775. [TNA.T47.9/11]

BROWNE, J., late President of Nevis, a memorial, 1805. [BM.Add.34928/348]

BROWNE, JACKSON, in St Kitts, probate 1770, PCC. [TNA]

BROWN, JAMES, probate 13 June 1766, Christiansted. [RAK]

BROWN, JAMES, late of Nevis, then in Acton, Middlesex, probate 1779, PCC. [TNA]

BROWN, JAMES, a merchant in Christiansted, St Croix, married Miss Krause, daughter of Colonel Krause in Danish service, in St Croix on 23 May 1820, [BM.7.583]; a deed witness on 13 April 1821. [NRS.RD5.204.550]

BROWN, JEAN, daughter of the late Campbell Brown in Antigua, married Lieutenant W. Hamersley of the 3rd Garrison Regiment on 20 September 1817. [GM.ns87.362]

BROWNE, JEREMIAH, born 1687, educated at Pembroke College, Oxford, Chief Justice of St Kitts in 1729, probate 1755, PCC. [TNA]

BROWN, JOHN, probate 22 May 1767, Christiansted. [RAK]

BROWN, JOHN, born 1836, son of Thomas Brown and his wife Janet Moffat, died in St Thomas on 21 November 1864. [Alexandria gravestone]

BROWNE, PATRICK, in Plymouth, Montserrat, 1719. [TNA.CO152.13]

BROWN, Dr PATRICK, probate 1 February 1767, Christiansted. [RAK.37]

THE PEOPLE OF THE LEEWARD ISLANDS, 1620 - 1860

BROWN, RACHEL, aboard the barque Adventure, master Christopher Berrow, bound from Barbados to Antigua on 17 February 1678. [TNA]

BROWN, SAMUEL, from Cork, a merchant in Nevis, probate 1721, PCC. [TNA]

BROWN, WILLIAM, a merchant in St Kitts, later a planter in Tobago, a deed, died 1767. [NRS.B10.15.7493]

BROWN, WILLIAM, born 1728, a merchant in London, from Bristol aboard the Aurora bound for Tortola in 1776. [TNA.T47.9/11]

BROWN, WILLIAM, from Lochwinnoch, Renfrewshire, died in Antigua in October 1835. [GM.ns5.678]

BROWN, Mr., born 1738, a gentleman, via London aboard the Le Soy Planter bound for Dominica in 1774. [TNA.T47.9/11]

BROZET, JOHN, in St Kitts, probate 1780, PCC. [TNA]

BROZET, PETER, of Guadeloupe, probate 1701, PCC. [TNA]; husband of Anne de Clainenbrong, born 1656, died 1729.

BRUCE, ANDREW, a merchant in St Kitts, executor of Walter Pringle's testament, 1760.

BRULEY, JAMES, in Tortula, witness to a deed, 18 September 1803. [NRS.RD3.303.743]

BRULEY, JOSEPH, died in St Croix on 15 May 1818. [GM.88.373]

BRUN, MANUEL, in Nevis, 1686. [SPAWI.1686.678]

BRUNING, JO, aged 20, bound aboard the Mathew of London, master Richard Goodladd, for St Kitts on 21 May 1635. [TNA.E157.20]

BRYANT, THOMAS, born 1611, a husbandman from Brampton in Devon, bound from Dartmouth to St Kitts in 1634. [TNA]

BRYAN, THURLOGH, in the parish of Sandy Point, St Kitts on 7 February 1678. [TNA.COI.42]

BRYANT, THURLOGH in Halfwaytree Division, St Kitts on 7 February 1678. [TNA.COI.42]

BRYCE, ROBERT, in St Kitts, 1766. [NRS.CS16.1.125]

BUCHANAN, ARCHIBALD SHANNAN, of Drumhead, Dunbartonshire, died in Antigua on 18 September 1791. [GM.61.1062][SM.53.568][GC.35]

BUCHANAN, GEORGE, in Nevis, probate, 27 May 1679, PCC. [TNA]

BUCHANAN, JAMES, late in St Thomas, was admitted as a burgess of Montrose in 1783. [MBR]

BUCHANAN, J. S., in St Croix, 1790. [Caribbeana.5.265]

BUCKE, GRAYSTON OCTAVIUS, born 22 November 1778, died 9 September 1798. [St Anthony's mi, Montserrat]

BUCKE, WALTER LEWIS, born in Bungay in 1780, settled in Nevis in 1802, died there on 23 February 1857. [GM.ns2.2.624]

BUIST, ANDREW, died 6 September 1823, probate St Jan. [RAK.1807-1826.fo.107-108]

BUNCOMBE, CATHERINE ESTRIDGE, in St Kitts, probate 1772, PCC. [TNA]

BUNTIN, JASPER, probate 11 April 1780, Christiansted. [RAK.5.4]

BUNTIN, RICHARD, probate, 7 April 1781, Fredericksted. [RAK]

THE PEOPLE OF THE LEEWARD ISLANDS, 1620 - 1860

BUOR, PIERRE, a Major in Colonel Alexander's Regiment, a planter in St Kitts in 1726. [SPAWI.1726.236]

BURGESS, HENRY GILBERT, born 1824, eldest son of the late H. W. Burgess in London, of the Ordnance Department in St Kitts, died 21 April 1848. [GM.ns30.110]

BUOR, PIERRE, a Major in Colonel Alexander's Regiment, a planter in St Kitts in 1726. [SPAWI.1726.236]

BURGIS, HELEN, in St Kitts, probate, 1636, PCC. [TNA]

BURKE, JEFFREY, aboard the sloop True Friendship, master Charles Callahan, from Barbados bound for Antigua on 30 December 1679. [TNA]

BURKE, JOHN, born 1758, a planter, via London aboard the Turnbull bound for Tortola in 1774. [TNA.T47.9/11]

BURKE, JOHN, Solicitor General of the Leeward Islands, witness to a deed, 6 April 1792. [NRS.RD2.255.122]

BURLACE, WALTER, from Luggom, a husbandman aged 22, who emigrated via Plymouth aboard the Margaret bound for St Kitts in 1634. [TNA.E157.18]

BURLEY, WILLIAM, in Nevis, probate, 1658, PCC. [TNA]

BURN, GEORGE, late of St Kitts, third son of George Burn a coach proprietor in Glasgow, died in Greenock on 1 February 1849. [EEC.21769]

BURNETT, WILLIAM, in Antigua in 1758. [DA.Ogilvie pp.26]

BURNS, PATRICK, born February 1807 in St Andrews, Fife, Auditor General of the Leeward Islands, died 2 July 1875. [St Andrews gravestone]

BURRELL, PETER, from Antigua, died in London on 4 June 1766. [GM.36.294]

BURROWES, ANTHONY, from Jacobstow, a husbandman aged 20, who emigrated via Plymouth aboard the Margaret bound for St Kitts in 1634. [TNA.E157.18]

BURROUGHS, ELIZABETH, born 1708, died in Antigua on 1 December 1767. [St Stephen's]

BURROUGHS, NICHOLAS, in Nevis, probate, 1725, PCC. [TNA]

BURROWE, JANE, aged 17, bound aboard the Mathew of London, master Richard Goodladd, for St Kitts on 21 May 1635. [TNA.E157.20]

BURT, CHARLES PYM, on St John plantation, St Croix, in 1755, in St Croix in 1768, [SSF], probate, 1788, PCC. [TNA]

BURT, LOUISA, daughter of William Mathew Burt, died 1780. [Goat Hill gravestone. Antigua]

BURT, WILLIAM MATHEW, died 1780. [Goat Hill gravestone, Antigua]; Governor of the Leeward Islands, letter book, 1777-1780. [Glamorgan Record Office: Hick pp]

BURT, ..., daughter of Archdeacon P. Burt, was born in St Kitts on 9 September 1865. [GM.ns2.19.635]

BURT, ...,son of A. P. Burt, Queen's Counsel, was born in St Kitts on 18 March 1867. [GM.ns3.3.804][S.7396]

BURTON, Mr, born 1736, a gentleman, returning to St Kitts aboard the Pemberton via Whitehaven in 1774. [TNA.T47.9/11]

BUSHBY, WILLIAM, born 8 August 1824 in St Croix, son of Joseph Bushby. [EA.21.614]; died there on 20 February 1825. [S.548.232]

THE PEOPLE OF THE LEEWARD ISLANDS, 1620 - 1860

BUSHELL, WILLIAM, a time served indentured servant, aboard the Pearl, bound from Barbados to Antigua on 17 April 1679. [TNA]

BUTLER, DUKE, a planter in Nevis, a deed, Bermuda, 10 July 1693, executor of will of Captain Thomas Butler probate, Bermuda, 30 October 1693. [Mercer.26]

BUTLER, PACIS, a spinster, bound from Bristol to Nevis in 1660. [BRO]

BUTLER, Captain THOMAS, a planter in Nevis, probate, 1689, PCC. [TNA]

BUTLER, THOMAS, in Nevis, 1725. [RSM]; in Nevis, probate, 1744, PCC. [TNA]

BUTLER, TOBIAS, in the parish of Sandy Point, St Kitts on 7 February 1678. [TNA.COl.42]

BUTLER, WILLIAM, a planter in Nevis, a deed, Bermuda, 10 July 1693, executor of will of Captain Thomas Butler probate, Bermuda, 30 October 1693. [Mercer.26]

BYAM, EDWARD, Lieutenant Governor of Antigua, 26 September, 1721. [PCCol.App.ii.821]

BYAM, EDWARD, born 1766, of Cedarhill, Antigua, an Assemblyman, died in Antigua in 1795. [GM.65.794]

BYAM, EDWARD, born 1740, Judge of the Vice Admiralty Court, died in Antigua on 8 February 1817. [GM.87.374]

BYAM, M., from Antigua, died in Kew, London, on 22 April 1836. [GM.ns5.676]

BYAM, WILLIAM, a Councillor of Antigua, 26 September, 1721. [PCCol.App.ii.821]

BYAM, Mrs, born 1750, widow of William Byam of Cedarhill, Antigua, died in London on 28 January 1794. [GM.64.183]

BYAM, WILLIAM, born 1828, second son of William Byam, a barrister, died in Antigua on 30 June 1853. [GM.ns40.537]

BYAM, Reverend Dr., of Antigua, died at sea in 1757. [GM.27.435]

CABB, RICHARD, editor and proprietor of the 'St Kitts Advertiser', died in St Kitts in February 1830. [GM.100.382]

CABEL, JAMES, born 1779, died in St Thomas on 6 July 1816. [Howff gravestone, Dundee]

CABIBEL, PETER, senior, a planter in St Kitts, 1717. [JCTP.1717.26]

CABIBEL, STEPHEN, master of the frigate La Junon before the Admiralty Court of the Leeward Islands on 3 January 1719. [PCCol.1719.1316]

CALDER, ARCHIBALD, Commissary of Stores in Antigua, was admitted as a burgess of Banff in 1768. [BBR]

CALDWELL, JAMES ALEXANDER, died 27 July 1766, probate Christiansted. [RAK.1761-1768.262]

CALHOUN, Dr DAVID, probate 8 September 1779, Christiansted. [RAK.314.126]

CALHOUN, WILLIAM, an Assemblyman in St Kitts, 1677. [SPAWI.1678.741]

CALHOUN, Captain WILLIAM, 'dead on the coast of Guinea', probate 22 July 1760, Christiansted. [RAK]

CALLAHAN, DENNIS in Halfwaytree Division, St Kitts on 7 February 1678. [TNA.COI.42]

THE PEOPLE OF THE LEEWARD ISLANDS, 1620 - 1860

CALLAHAN, DERMOND in Halfwaytree Division, St Kitts on 7 February 1678. [TNA.COI.42]

CAMERON, DUNCAN, a Jacobite transported to St Kitts in 1716. [CTB.31.207][SPAWI.1716.312]

CAMERON, HUGH, a servant of Edward Garvine a merchant in St Kitts, was admitted as a burgess and guilds-brother of Ayr on 3 October 1737. [ABR]

CAMERON, J., born 1763 in Paisley, Renfrewshire, a planter in Antigua from 1782 until 1812, died in Whitehaven, England, on 25 August 1812. [GM.82.298]

CAMERON, ..., son of John Black Cameron, was born in St Thomas on 2 February 1862. [EEC.23689]

CAMPBELL, ALEXANDER, a surgeon in St Croix, testament, 21 September 1782, Comm. Edinburgh. [NRS]

CAMPBELL, ANN, wife of James McNeilledge in St Croix, died in New York on 24 August 1803. [DPCA.66][EEC]

CAMPBELL, ARCHIBALD, husband of Tabitha J. Downing, probate 3 July 1769, Christiansted. [RAK]

CAMPBELL, JAMES, a Jacobite transported to Antigua in 1716. [SPAWI.1716.310][CTB.31.204]

CAMPBELL, JOHN, a petitioner in Antigua on 20 September 1664. [SPAWI.1664.234]

CAMPBELL, DUNCAN, died in Antigua on 1 February 1764. [St John's Cathedral]

CAMPBELL, JOHN, a merchant in St Croix, later in Greenock, testament, 7 April 1769, Comm. Glasgow. [NRS]

CAMPBELL, JOHN, probate 3 November 1779, Christiansted. [RAK.103.313]

CAMPBELL, JOHN, probate 16 August 1780, Christiansted. [RAK.335.189]

CAMPBELL, NEILL, in Antigua in 1753. [NRS.CS96.644]

CAMPBELL, ROBERT STEVENSON, fifth son of Reverend John Campbell minister of the Secession Church in Nicholson Street, Lauriston, died in Nevis on 23 September 1839. [SG.8.820]

CAMPBELL, SOPHIA, born 1730, died 25 November 1798. [St Paul's, Antigua]

CAMPBELL, WILLIAM, born 1727 in Kirkinner, Wigtownshire, son of Reverend William Campbell and his wife Margaret Reid, a physician in Antigua, died in 1798. [F.3.365]

CAMPBELL, WILLIAM, Captain of the 96th Regiment of Foot, youngest son of John Campbell of Lochend, died in Antigua on 23 October 1805. [EEC][AJ.3032]

CANARAN, TEIGE, in the parish of Sandy Point, St Kitts on 7 February 1678. [TNA.COI.42]

CANAVANE, DAVID, in the parish of Sandy Point, St Kitts on 7 February 1678. [TNA.COI.42]

CANAVAN, JOHN, in the parish of Sandy Point, St Kitts on 7 February 1678. [TNA.COI.42]

CANNON, JOHN, a Jacobite banished to Jamaica, landed on Montserrat in 1716. [SPAWI.1716.313][CTP.CC43]

CANT, JOHN, a Jacobite transported to Antigua in 1716. [CTB.31.204]

THE PEOPLE OF THE LEEWARD ISLANDS, 1620 - 1860

CANT,....., a minister sent to the Leeward Islands in 1692. [EMA.19]

CARGILL, JOHN, a minister sent to the Leeward Islands in 1708, [EMA.19]; possibly later in Southwark, Surrey County, Virginia. [FPA.174]

CARKILLE, WILLIAM, born 1613, a sail-maker from Plymouth, bound from Dartmouth to St Kitts in 1634. [TNA]

CARLYLE, JOHN, probate 30 August 1767, Christiansted. [RAK.40.7]

CARLISLE, Mrs, of Woodford Bridge and Antigua, married John Gray of London and Jamaica, in July 1752. [GM.22.336]

CARMELL, JAMES, a Jacobite banished to Jamaica, landed on Montserrat in 1716. [SPAWI.1716.313][CTP.CC43]

CARMICHAEL, ALEXANDER, a surgeon in St Croix, died 5 January 1782, testament, 1782, Comm. Edinburgh. [NRS]

CARMICK, JAMES, probate 22 May 1767, Christiansted. [RAK]

CARMICK, JOHN, a planter in Montserrat in 1678. [TNA.CO1.22.17]

CARPENTER, HENRY, in Nevis, probate, 1704, PCC. [TNA]

CARRIER, JOHN, bound from Bristol to Nevis in 1660. [BRO]

CARRINGTON, ROBERT, a merchant in Antigua, probate 30 October 1734, Antigua.

CARRUTHERS, JOHN, settled in Antigua, died 1700, probate, 5/740; 11/449, PCC. [TNA]

CARSTENS, JOHAN LORENZ, a planter at Mosquito Bay, St Thomas, in 1739.

CARTER, CHRISTOPHER, aged 45, from St Gilt, emigrated via Plymouth aboard the Robert Bonaventure bound for St Kitts in February 1633. [TNA.E157.18]

CARTER, JAMES, aged 25, aboard the Paul of London, master Jo. Acklin, bound from Gravesend to St Kitts on 3 April 1635. [TNA.E157.20]

CARTER, JOSHUA, on Saba, petitioned the Dutch West India Company in Amsterdam in 1772. [DNA.Inv.1151]

CARTER, PETER, on Saba, petitioned the Dutch West India Company in Amsterdam in 1772. [DNA.Inv.1151]

CARTER, Mrs, widow of Lieutenant Colonel Carter, died in St John's, Antigua, on 24 June 1807. [GM.77.888]

CARTY, DANIEL, in St Thomas, Middle Island, St Kitts on 7 February 1678. [TNA.COI.42]

CARTY, DENNIS in St Thomas, Middle Island, St Kitts on 7 February 1678. [TNA.COI.42]

CARWAL, JAMES ALEXANDER, probate 29 May 1767, Christiansted. [RAK]

CARY, RICHARD, aboard the pink Sea Venture, master George Battersby, from Barbados to Antigua on 10 March 1679. [TNA]

CARTY, TYMOTHY, in the parish of St John Capistar, St Kitts, on 28 January 1678. [TNA.COI.42]

CASEY, JOHN in Halfwaytree Division, St Kitts on 7 February 1678. [TNA.COI.42]

CASEY, SIMON, in Halfwaytree Division, St Kitts on 7 February 1678. [TNA.COI.42]

THE PEOPLE OF THE LEEWARD ISLANDS, 1620 - 1860

CASSART, ..., led a raid on Montserrat in 1714. [SPAWI.1714.1]

CASSIN, HENRY R., MD, married Mrs Catherine Watts, widow of Thomas Watts of the Honorable East India Company Service, in Antigua on 30 May 1819. [GM.89.271]

CASSIN, MARY CAROLINE, eldest daughter of the late Henry R. Cassin M D in Nevis, married Reverend Samuel Whitbread in Islington, London, on 24 March 1852. [GM.ns37.512]

CATHCART, WILLIAM, fourth son of James Cathcart of Carbiston, died in Antigua on 1 November 1821. [BM.40.263][EEC.17255] [AJ.3866]

CATLOW, ALEXANDER, husband of Mary ....., probate 10 May 1747, St Croix. [RAK]

CAVE, JO., aged 34, bound aboard the Mathew of London, master Richard Goodladd, for St Kitts on 21 May 1635. [TNA.E157.20]

CAVERLIE, CHARLES, aged 17, bound aboard the Mathew of London, master Richard Goodladd, for St Kitts on 21 May 1635. [TNA.E157.20]

CHABERT, ANDREW, in the Island of St Croix, will, 1801. [PWI]

CHADS, AUGUSTA CORNELL, fourth daughter of Lieutenant Colonel Chads in the Virgin Islands, married James Watson Dunlop, son of the late James Dunlop in Glasgow, on Tortula on 13 March 1854. [GM.ns41.636]

CHADS, ELIZA WEST, youngest daughter of Lieutenant Colonel Chads in the Virgin Islands, married Charles Girdlestone, son of Reverend H. Girdlestone of Langford, in Tortula on 13 March 1854. [GM.ns41.636]

CHADS, Lieutenant Colonel JOHN CORNELL, born 1794, President of the British Virgin Islands, died on Tortula on 28 February 1854. [GM.ns41.444]

CHAFFART, ..., in St Kitts in 1673. [SPAWI.1673.1036]

CHAIRS, AUGUSTA CORNELL, fourth daughter of Lieutenant Colonel Chairs the President of the Virgin Islands, married James Watson Dunlop, son of James Dunlop in Glasgow, in Tortula on 13 March 1854. [GM.ns41.636]

CHALMERS, ALEXANDER, born 1730, eldest son of Provost William Chalmers of Aberdeen, late of Antigua, died in Peterhead, Aberdeenshire, on 9 January 1778. [AJ.1567]

CHALMERS, JAMES, a merchant in St Kitts, was admitted as a burgess and guilds-brother of Ayr on 20 December 1665. [ABR]

CHALMERS, JOHN, from Belfast, settled in Antigua, a letter, 1731. [PRONI.D162.24]

CHALMERS, JOHN, died in Antigua in 1757. [GM.27.189]

CHAMBERS, ALICIA W., died 16 October 1851. [St Anthony's mi, Montserrat]

CHAMBERS, Mrs SARAH, born 1727, died 28 January 1812, mother of John Chambers, born 1748, died 25 November 1796. [St Anthony's mi, Montserrat]

CHAMBERS, WILLIAM, in Montserrat, probate 1762, PCC. [TNA]

CHAPAN, JAMES, in Nevis in 1776. [NLS.Acc.8793]

CHARPENTIER, ..., in St Croix in 1802. [RDAG.I/2]

CHARTERIS, LAWRENCE, a Jacobite transported to St Kitts in 1716. [SPAWI.1716.312][CTB.31.207]

CHEAPE, HENRY, to the Leeward Islands in 1714. [SAL.ms36929/4/178]

CHENEZ, CHARLES, master of the sloop Catherine seized at Montserrat in 1736. [SPAWI.1737.61i]

THE PEOPLE OF THE LEEWARD ISLANDS, 1620 - 1860

CHERRIOT, GEORGE, a planter in Nevis in 1712. [JCTP.1712.395]

CHESEBOROUGH, JONATHAN, eldest son of Johnathan Cheseborough, died in Antigua on 18 February 1764. [St John's Cathedral]

CHESTER, EDWARD, a merchant in St John's, Antigua, agent for the Royal Africa Company, in 1704. [CTB.XIX.214]

CHESTERMAN, ADAM, aged 19, bound aboard the Mathew of London, for St Kitts on 21 May 1635. [TNA.E157.20]

CHEVALIER, LOUIS, a merchant planter in Antigua, who was denizised in 1665. [SPAWI.1665.376]

CHEVUS, BENJAMIN, on Nevis in 1708. [TNA.CO152-157]

CHILD, ANNE, a spinster, an indentured servant bound from Bristol to Nevis in 1660. [BRO]

CHILD, WILLIAM, a yeoman in Bristol, an indentured servant bound from Bristol to Nevis in 1660. [BRO]

CHISHOLM, Captain HUMPHREY, probate 24 March 1779, Christiansted. [RAK.338.198]

CHISHOLM, JOHN, born in Ross-shire, to America as a soldier of the 77th Regiment in 1757, in 1763 he settled in Camden, South Carolina, as a merchant, a Loyalist in 1776, moved to St Eustatia in 1778, then to St Kitts, and finally to Jamaica. [TNA.AO12.49.417]

CHRISTIAN, MARGARET, died in Antigua on 7 March 1745, daughter of Robert Christian and his wife Mary. [St John's Cathedral, Antigua]

CHRISTIE, THOMAS, in Antigua in 1759. [DA.Ogilvie pp.p36]

CHURCH, WILLIAM, aged 21, aboard the Paul of London, master Jo. Acklin, bound from Gravesend to St Kitts on 3 April 1635. [TNA.E157.20]

CLARE, GEORGE, in Nevis, probate, 1708, PCC. [TNA]

CLARK, GILBERT, aged 19, aboard the John of London, master James Waymoth, bound for St Kitts on 2 October 1635. [TNA.E157.20]

CLARKE, MARTHA, in St Kitts, probate 1774, PCC. [TNA]

CLARKE, MARTHA, daughter of Thomas Clarke in Antigua, married Captain Robilliard of the Royal Navy, on 12 July 1820. [GM.90.84]

CLARKE, Captain SAMUEL, a planter and Commander of the Militia of Nevis, 17.... [Caribbeana]

CLARKE, WILLIAM, aged 20, from Truro, emigrated via Plymouth aboard the Robert Bonaventure bound for St Kitts in February 1633. [TNA.E157.18]

CLARKE, WILLIAM, in Nevis, probate, 1746, PCC. [TNA]

CLAXTON, ROBERT, born 1792, late Customs Collector of Antigua, died in Bristol in 1841. [GM.ns16.664]

CLAXTON, ROBERT, born 1796, Chief Justice of St Kitts, died in London on 18 March 1849. [GM.ns31.551]

CLAXTON, Dr, in St Croix in 1802. [RDAG.I/2]

CLAYTON, ROBERT, a merchant in St Kitts, was admitted as a burgess of Glasgow on 6 September 1720. [GBR]

CLEGG, ROBERT, a merchant in St John's, Antigua, a witness, 24 March 1797. [NRS.RD2.271.419]

CLEGHORN, ADAM, probate 11 October 1736. [RAK]

THE PEOPLE OF THE LEEWARD ISLANDS, 1620 - 1860

CLEGHORN, MATHEW COLE, born 1832, died 4 November 1852. [St George gravestone, Basse Terre, St Kitts]

CLEGHORN, RALPH BUSH, the President of Nevis, died 17 March 1842. [St George gravestone, Basse Terre, St Kitts]

CLEMENT, HENRY, third son of Thomas Clement a solicitor in Alton, the Customs Collector of Tortula, died there on 21 August 1821. [GM.191.475]

CLEMENT, NATHANIEL, in St Kitts, probate, 1692, PCC. [TNA]

CLIFTON, JAMES, born 1725, a gentleman, from London aboard the Generous Planter bound for St Kitts in 1775. [TNA.T47.9/11]

CLINTON, JO., aged 19, bound aboard the Mathew of London, master Richard Goodladd, for St Kitts on 21 May 1635. [TNA.E157.20]

CLOGSTOUN, Mrs LETITIA, widow of Robert Clogstoun, late in Antigua, died in London on 11 April 1810. [GM.80.494]

CLOUGH, EDWARD, born 1748, purser aboard HMS Favourite, died 7 December 1777. [St Paul's mi, Antigua]

CLOVAN, THOMAS, aboard the sloop True Friendship, master Charles Callahan, bound from Barbados to Nevis on 31 May 1679. [TNA]; on 2 October 1679 he was on the same vessel bond for Antigua. [TNA]

CLUTH, NICHOLAS, bound from Bristol to Nevis in 1660. [BRO]

CLYMER, JO., aged 30, aboard the John of London, master James Waymoth, bound for St Kitts on 2 October 1635. [TNA]E157.20]

COATES, ALEXANDER, a shipwright in Antigua, husband of Dorothy [who died on 25 November 1777], their children – Thomas, Alexander, Francis, Rhoda, Dorothy and Rebecca – all died in infancy, [St John's burial register, Antigua], Alexander died in Antigua on 12 November 1807. [GM.78.1188];

COATES, R., son of Alexander Coates in Antigua, died in Towcaser in 1810. [GM.80.676]

COBB, RICHARD, a baker, and his wife Prudence Cobb, indentured servants, bound from Bristol to Nevis in 1660. [BRO]

COCHRANE, Lieutenant ARCHIBALD, a Representative in Antigua in 1678. [SPAWI.1678.741]; a Councillor of Antigua in 1684. [SPAWI.1684.1879]

COCHRANE, ARCHIBALD, a Councillor of Antigua, 26 September, 1721. [PCCol.App.ii.821]

COCHRAN, JOHN, died in Montserrat, probate, 1699, PCC. [TNA]

COCHRANE, PETER, master of the Linnet of Antigua a sloop, a petition in 1779. [PCCol.1780.478]

COCHRANE, RICHARD, in Antigua in 1709. [St John's Town Library Antigua, ms]; in Antigua in 1719. [NLS.ms5375.1-9]

COCHRANE, ROBERT, died on 3 April 1755, probate St Croix. [RAK.1751-1766.fo.129]

COCHRANE, ROBERT, second son of John Cochrane in Paisley, a surgeon, died in Antigua on 20 July 1816. [DPCA.743]

COCKE, RICHARD, aged 33, from Wincklye, emigrated via Plymouth aboard the Robert Bonaventure bound for St Kitts in February 1633. [TNA.E157.18]

COCK, Dr WILLIAM HENRY, died in St Kitts on 20 June 1843. [EEC.20641]

THE PEOPLE OF THE LEEWARD ISLANDS, 1620 - 1860

COCKBURN, ARCHIBALD, a minister sent to the Leeward Islands in 1710, minister of St Mary's Cayon, St Kitts, and of Christchurch, Nicholas Town, St John's Cape, St Kitts, in 1711. [FPA]; a minister in St Kitts from 1722 to 1737. [CFR.260][EMA.20][FPA.275][SPAWI.1728.494.i/ii]

COCKFIELD, THOMAS NELSON, born 1822, eldest son of Edward Cockfield in Dunbar, a merchant in St Kitts, died there on 27 October 1853. [EEC.22514]; testament, 1869, [NRS.SC70.1.142.861]

CODRINGTON, WILLIAM, a Councillor of Antigua, 26 September, 1721. [PCCol.App.ii.821]

COGAN, JOHN, in the parish of Sandy Point, St Kitts on 7 February 1678. [TNA.COI.42]

COGHALL, THOMAS, in the parish of Sandy Point, St Kitts on 7 February 1678. [TNA.COI.42]

COKE, ROBERT, aged 32, bound aboard the Mathew of London, master Richard Goodladd, for St Kitts on 21 May 1635. [TNA.E157.20]

COLE, JAMES, aboard the sloop John and Frances, master John Howard, bound from Barbados to Antigua on 2 September 1679. [TNA]

COLE, SAMUEL. in Nevis, probate, 16, PCC. [TNA]

COLE, THOMAS, in Nevis, probate, 1711, PCC. [TNA]

COLHOUN, or COLQUHOUN, ROBERT, in St Kitts in 1757. [NRS.GD237.12.47]; reference in James Stormonth's testament of 1761.

COLLINS, JOHN N., born 1803, died 19 August 1857. [St Anthony's mi, Montserrat]

COLLINS, Reverend J.C., born 1807, pastor in Montserrat, died in Antigua on 25 March 1844, buried in St John's Cathedral, Antigua. [St Anthony's mi, Montserrat]

COLLINS, LUCAS, son of Thomas Collins in St Croix, was apprenticed to John McKinlay a merchant in Edinburgh on 17 October 1799. [REA]

COLLINS, MARGARET MOTH, daughter of Thomas Collins in St Croix, married [1] Thomas Vaughan a painter in Edinburgh, in Canongait on 22 December 1797, [CMR]; married [2] Ebenezer Prentice, a merchant in Glasgow, there on 18 August 1801. [SM.63.587]

COLLINS, WALTER, aged 18, bound aboard the *Mathew of London*, master Richard Goodladd, for St Kitts on 21 May 1635. [TNA.E157.20]

COLLINSON, ROBERT, son of William Collinson, a gentleman in St Kitts, was admitted as a burgess and guilds-brother of Ayr on 20 December 1685. [ABR]

COLLY, FRANCIS, born in Peterculter, Aberdeenshire, emigrated to Antigua in 1770, a builder and architect, died in St John's, Antigua, in 1781. [AJ: 21.1.1782][ANQ.2.251]

COLQUHOUN, JANET, daughter of Richard Colquhoun in St Kitts, wife of John Wallace, late of Jamaica, now of Neilstonswell, Renfrewshire, 1765. [NRS.NRAS.0623.T-MJ.424]

COLQUHOUN, ROBERT, in St Kitts, letters, 1757. [NRS.GD237.12.47]

THE PEOPLE OF THE LEEWARD ISLANDS, 1620 - 1860

COLQUHOUN, ROBERT, born in Antigua, eldest son of Walter Colquhoun of Camstraddan, matriculated at Glasgow University in 1791, dead by 1826. [MAGU.165]; reference in Robert Graham's testament of 1780. [NRS]

COLQUHOUN, WALTER, of Camstradden, mason, died in Antigua on 12 February 1802. [GM.72.374][SM.44.446]

COLQUHOUN, WILLIAM, a planter in Antigua, a deed, 4 March 1778. [NRS.RD4.278.326]

COLVILLE, GEORGE, second son of George Colville a book-binder in Glasgow, died in Nevis on 30 December 1838. [SG.743]

COMBES, ADAM, in Nevis, probate, 1692, PCC. [TNA]

COMBE, CHARLES, youngest son of Dr Combe in London, died in Tortula on 29 September 1808. [GM.78.1039]

COMBES, ELIZABETH, in Nevis, probate, 1685, PCC. [TNA]

COMBES, MARY, wife of a tailor in Charlestown, Nevis, 1725. [TNA.CO186.1]

COMIN, JAMES, a schoolmaster, to the Leeward Islands in 1695. [EMA.21]

CONDEN, MORRIS in Halfwaytree Division, St Kitts on 7 February 1678. [TNA.COI.42]

CONEADE, TEIGE, in the parish of Sandy Point, St Kitts on 7 February 1678. [TNA.COI.42]

CONGLETON, JAMES, a Jacobite, transported to St Kitts in 1716. [SPAWI.1716.312][CTB.31.207]

CONNELL, TEIGE, in Kayon Division, St Kitts on 7 February 1678. [TNA.COI.42]

CONNER, ARTHUR, in the parish of Sandy Point, St Kitts on 7 February 1678. [TNA.COl.42]

CONNER, PATRICK in St Thomas, Middle Island, St Kitts on 7 February 1678. [TNA.COl.42]

CONNER, TEIGE, in Kayon Division, St Kitts on 7 February 1678. [TNA.COl.42]

CONNERY, WILLIAM, in the parish of St John Capistar, St Kitts, on 28 January 1678. [TNA.COl.42]

CONSIDENT, JOHN, a planter in St Kitts in 1712. [JCTP.1712.394]

CONSIDENT, SUSANNAH, in St Kitts in 1712. [JCTP.1712.395]

CONSTABLE, JACOB, in St Croix in 1790. [Caribbeana.5.265]

CONSTABLE, JOHN, in St Kitts in 1776. [NLS.Acc.8793.40]

CONSYDEN, DERMOND, in the parish of Sandy Point, St Kitts on 7 February 1678. [TNA.COl.42]

CONSYDEN, JOHN, in the parish of Sandy Point, St Kitts on 7 February 1678. [TNA.COl.42]

COOKE, EDWARD, aged 22, aboard the John of London, master James Waymoth, bound for St Kitts on 2 October 1635. [TNA.157.20]

COOPER, ANDREW DEAISEX, born 1666, died in Antigua on 18 May 1743. [St John's Cathedral, Antigua]

COOPER, ANN, youngest daughter of Arthur Cooper, died in St Croix on 2 September 1802. [EA.4053.02]

THE PEOPLE OF THE LEEWARD ISLANDS, 1620 - 1860

COOPER, ELIZABETH, daughter of John Cooper in St Kitts, married Dr Chisholm from Grenada, in Inverness on 22 December 1794. [EA.3235.422]

COOPER, ELIZABETH, daughter of Arthur Cooper in St Croix, married Charles Wightman of Tobago, in Canongait on 19 April 1800. [GC.1356][CMR]

COOPER, FRANCES, in Christiansted, St Croix, in 1771. [RDAG]

COOPER, GEORGE, a merchant in St Croix, a deed, 13 April 1821. [NRS.RD5.204.550]; died in Edinburgh on 16 January 1822. [DPCA.1017][AJ.3864]

COOPER, HENRY, a merchant in St Croix, husband of Mrs Henrietta Cooper, sometime in St Kitts then in Inverness in 1795. [NRS.GD23.5.353]

COOPER, JOANE, in St Kitts, probate, 1672, PCC. [TNA]

COOPER, MARGARET, daughter of Arthur Cooper in St Croix, married Dr Charles Kennedy, a physician in St Croix, in Eyemouth, Berwickshire, in October 1797. [EEC.392]

COOPER, MARY, daughter of John Cooper in St Kitts, died in 1812. [EA.5117.13]

COOPER, SIGISMOND, Deputy Receiver General of Montserrat in 1702. [CTB.XIX.213]

COOSE, SARA, born 1616, a spinster from Exeter, bound from Dartmouth to St Kitts in 1634. [TNA]

COPELAND, PETER, died in Nevis on 4 August 1767. [GM.37.430]

CORBET, HUGH, a witness in St Kitts in 1700. [NRS.GD84.Sec.1/22/9b]

CORBETT, WILLIAM, at Halfway Tree, St Kitts in 1667. [TNA.CO1.42/193]

CORBETT, WILLIAM, aboard the sloop Katherine, master Andrew Gall, bound from Barbados to Antigua on 27 November 1679. [TNA]

CORNEW, BARTHOLEMEW, from Crediton, a husbandman aged 18, who emigrated via Plymouth aboard the Margaret bound for St Kitts in 1634. [TNA.E157.18]

CORR, EBENEZER, probate 26 September 1751, St Croix. [RAK]

CORRIE, JOSEPH, a merchant in St Thomas, services of heirs, 1783. [NRS]

COSGRAVE, JAMES, in Antigua, will, 1765. [PWI]

COSSART, ……., commander of the French who attacked Montserrat in 1712. [SPAWI.1728.651]

COSSLY, JAMES, in the parish of Sandy Point, St Kitts on 7 February 1678. [TNA.COI.42]

COTES, JAMES, aged 21, bound aboard the Mathew of London, master Richard Goodladd, for St Kitts on 21 May 1635. [TNA.E157.20]

COTTERALL, Mr, died in St Kitts in January 1768. [GM.36.103]

COTTLE, GRACE CAMILLA, daughter of the late Thomas Cottle in Nevis, married James Selfe of Trewbridge, Wiltshire, in Camberwell, London, on 14 November 1797. [GM.67.1126]

COTTLE, THOMAS JOHN, born 1761, Councillor of Nevis, died at Round Hill, Nevis, on 1 February 1828. [GM.98.382]

COUGHLAND, DERMOND, in the parish of Sandy Point, St Kitts on 7 February 1678. [TNA.COI.42]

THE PEOPLE OF THE LEEWARD ISLANDS, 1620 - 1860

COULL, JAMES, a minister sent to Antigua in 1773. [EMA.22]

COURPONT, ..., a planter in St Kitts before 1717. [JCTP.1717.260]

COURTNEY, JAMES, born 1611, a blacksmith from Exeter, bound from Dartmouth to St Kitts in 1634. [TNA]

COURTNEY, WILLIAM, aboard the sloop Hopewell, master William Murphy, bound from Barbados to Antigua in 1679. [TNA]

COVENTRIE, MILES, aged 18, bound aboard the Mathew of London, master Richard Goodladd, for St Kitts on 21 May 1635. [TNA.E157.20]

COVENTRY, WILLIAM, born 1671, a merchant in the parish of St Thomas, Middle Island, St Kitts, died 16 August 1734. [St Thomas, St Kitts gravestone]

COX, JACOB, on Saba, petitioned the Dutch West India Company in Amsterdam in 1772. [DNA.Inv.1151]

COX, SAMUEL, a cleric, bound for the Leeward Islands in 1689. [BL.Rawl.ms.A306/66]

COX, WILLIAM, on Saba, petitioned the Dutch West India Company in Amsterdam in 1772. [DNA.Inv.1151]

COXSON, THOMAS, aged 21, bound aboard the Mathew of London, master Richard Goodladd, for St Kitts on 21 May 1635. [TNA.E157.20]

CRAFFORD, ALEXANDER, in Antigua, died aboard the Queen's frigate at sea in 1707, probate, PCC. [TNA]

CRAFFORD, ALEXANDER, a gentleman in Antigua, will, 1730. [PWI]

CRAIGIE, Captain WILLIAM, husband of Anna ......, probate 26 February 1773, Fredericksted. [RAK]

CRANSTOUN, Lord JAMES EDWARD, died in St Kitts on 5 September 1818. [AJ.3695]

CRAWFORD, ALEXANDER, in St Eustatia in 1779. [NRS.CS16.1.175]

CRAWFORD, DAVID, eldest son of David Crawford a merchant in Dublin, a deed, 15 May 1773, [NRS.RD4.213.1232]; in St Eustatia, 1779. [NRS.CS16.1.175]

CRAWFORD, JAMES, probate 30 June 1779, Christiansted. [RAK.372.268]

CRAWFORD, JOHN FRAME, born 1750 in Antigua, died at Kilburn Wells on 10 April 1800. [GM.70.397]

CRAWFORD, MARGARET, married George Steineth Harding from St Croix, in Fairfield, Ayrshire, on 26 August 1811. [DPCA.476]; she died in St Croix in October 1835. [Logie, Stirling, gravestone]

CRAWFORD, PATRICK, of Hisleside, Provost Marshal of the Leeward Islands, brother of Hugh Crawford of Garrive in 1734. [NRS.GD94.216]; services of heirs, 1733. [NRS]

CRAWFORD, ROBERT, a merchant in St Kitts, 1783, a partner in Crawford, Johnston and Company there, [NRS.CS18.714.25]; in 1784. [NRS.AC7.61]; services of heirs, 1784, [NRS]; a deed, 21 January 1784. [NRS.RD3.243.146]; testament, 5 April 1792, Comm. Edinburgh. [NRS]

CRAWFORD, Miss, was buried in St Eustatia on 13 February 1773. [ASS]

CRESSWELL, ROBERT, a Jacobite transported to St Kitts in 1716. [SPAWI.1716.312][CTB.31.207]

THE PEOPLE OF THE LEEWARD ISLANDS, 1620 - 1860

CRIGHTON, GEORGE, in Antigua, executor of Thomas Turnbull's testament, 1817.

CRILLICK, JANE, a servant belonging to John Follit, aboard the Old Head of Kingsale, master Robert Barker, bound from Barbados to the Leeward Islands on 4 January 1679. [TNA]

CRISP, Mrs MARY, born 1692, wife of Joseph Crisp of St Kitts, died 27 January 1730. [Christ Church mi, Nichola Town, St Kitts]

CRONEBERG, Captain, White Hook, Strand Street, in St Croix in 1802. [RDAG.I/2]

CRONEEN, JOHN in Halfwaytree Division, St Kitts on 7 February 1678. [TNA.COI.42]

CROOKE, FRANCES, in St Kitts, probate, 1798, PCC. [TNA]

CROOK, JEAN, widow of Robert Dewar a merchant in Antigua, married William Howieson a writer in Edinburgh, there on 7 April 1779. [EMR]

CROOKE, SAMUEL, a Councillor in St Kitts, died on 17 March 1772. [GM.42.151]

CROOKE, SARAH, born 1748, a lady in London, from London aboard the Dorsetshire bound for St Kitts in 1773. [TNA.T47.9.11]

CROOKSHANKS, WILLIAM, an overseer in St Kitts, testament, Comm. Edinburgh. [NRS]

CROWDER, RICHARD, aged 28, aboard the Paul of London, master Jo. Acklin, bound from Gravesend to St Kitts on 3 April 1635. [TNA.E157.20]

CROZIER, WILLIAM, probate 3 July 1769, Christiansted. [RAK]

CRUICKSHANK, ALEXANDER, a merchant from Aberdeen, died in Antigua in 1713. [APB.2.111]

CRUICKSHANK, JAMES, a chaplain bound for the Leeward Islands on 28 February 1694. [CTB.X.1.514]; minister of St George's on Montserrat, from April 1694 to 1724. [FPA]; an Anglican minister in Montserrat, a letter, 1731. [FPA.2.87]; a Councillor of Montserrat in 1734. [SPAWI.1734.140; 1737.55iii]

CRUMP, GEORGE, died in Antigua in July 1773. [Cocoa Nut Hall Plantation, Antigua]

CRUMP, GEORGE, born 1745, died in Antigua on 23 October 1793. [Cocoa Nut Hall Plantation, Antigua]

CRUMP, NATHANIEL, a Councillor of Antigua, 26 September, 1721. [PCCol.App.ii.821]

CRUMP, ..., Governor of Guadaloupe, died 1760. [NRS.GD126, box 28]

CULLEN, ROBERT, in Antigua in 1753. [NRS.CS96.644]

CULLEN, Miss, daughter of ..... Cullen of Parkhead, married Henry Fairley of Antigua, in Edinburgh on 28 October 1777. [EMR]

CUMBERBATCH, GEORGE, a yeoman, an indentured servant bound from Bristol to Nevis in 1660. [BRO]

CUMMIN, PETER, a Jacobite banished to Antigua in 1716. [SPAWI.1716.310][CTB.31.204]

CUMMING, ARCHIBALD, in St Kitts, probate 1741, PCC. [TNA]

CUMMING, GEORGE, a minister bound for the Leeward Islands in 1709. [EMA.22]

CUMMINGS, PATRICK, died in St John's, Antigua, in June 1795. [GM.65.703]

CUMING, RALPH, MD, late of Romsey, Hampshire, a surgeon at H.M. Naval Hospital, at English Harbour, Antigua, and his son Ralph, died in Antigua on 24 June 1808. [GM.78.851][SM.70.718]

CUNNINGHAM, ANDREW, in Antigua in 1788. [NRS.GD21.632]

CUNNINGHAM, CHARLES, in St Kitts, 1730s [HS.7.6/29]

CUNNINGHAM, CHARLES, in Antigua in 1761. [DA.Ogilvie.ms.p56]

CUNNINGHAM, DANIEL, of Cayon, St Kitts, married Elizabeth Hodges in 1733. [HS.7.6/29]; in St Kitts, son of the late Robert Cunningham of Cayonne in St Kitts, in 1745. [NRS.CS16.1.75]; probate 1777, PCC. [TNA]

CUNNINGHAM, JAMES, probate 31 October 1768, Fredericksted. [RAK]

CUNNINGHAM, JOHN, a surgeon in St Kitts, services of heirs, 1740. [NRS]

CUNNINGHAM, JOHN, probate, 1745, St Croix. [RAK]

CUNNINGHAM, MARY, in St Kitts, probate 1758, PCC. [TNA]

CUNNINGHAM, ROBERT, in St Kitts, born 1669 son of Robert Cunningham of Glengarnock, settled in St Kitts ca1690, married Judith Elizabeth de Bonnefant a Huguenot there, parents of Richard, Elizabeth, Daniel, and Robert, returned to Scotland in 1737, buried in Greyfriars, Edinburgh, 1743. [HS.7.6/29]; a planter in Montserrat and St Kitts in 1715, 1733; testament, Glasgow, 1745, [NRS] [NRS.CS230.Misc.15.17][BM.Add.ms18683]

CUNNINGHAM, ROBERT, in Cayan, St Kitts, then in Leith, and Mary Gainer, former servant to Captain James Dalrymple, a

THE PEOPLE OF THE LEEWARD ISLANDS, 1620 - 1860

Process of Scandal, Comm. Edinburgh, 1740. [NRS]; died in St Kitts in 1762. [GM.32.45]; probate 1766, PCC. [TNA]

CUNNINGHAM, WILLIAM, a merchant in St Kitts, was admitted as a burgess of Glasgow on 6 September 1720. [GBR]

CUNNINGHAM, WILLIAM, died 8 December 1768, probate St Jan. [RAK.1758-1775.fo.64-67]

CURKE, WILLIAM, aged 24, from Monteratt, emigrated via Plymouth aboard the Robert Bonaventure bound for St Kitts in February 1633. [TNA.E157.18]

CURRIE, DAVID, from Newlaw, died in St Thomas on 28 February 1782. [SM.44.221]

CURRIE, JAMES, a Jacobite banished to St Kitts in 1716. [SPAWI.1716.312][CTB.31.207]

CUSHEN, THOMAS, in the parish of St John Capistar, St Kitts, on 28 January 1678. [TNA.COI.42]

CUTLER, CLINTON, aged 20, bound aboard the Mathew of London, master Richard Goodladd, for St Kitts on 21 May 1635. [TNA.E157.20]

DABBIN, NICHOLAS, aged 40, from St Stephen's, emigrated via Plymouth aboard the Robert Bonaventure bound for St Kitts in February 1633. [TNA.157.18]

DABRAM, ..., Irish, a militiaman in Montserrat in 1654. [Remonstrances ...., London, 1654]

DALGLEISH, SAMUEL, in Basse Terre, Guadaloupe, services of heirs, 1815. [NRS]

DALMAHOY, THOMAS, a Jacobite transported to St Kitts in 1716. [SPAWI.1716.312][CTB.31.207]

DALRYMPLE, Colonel CAMPBELL, late Governor of Guadaloupe, was granted the lands of Gruigfoot on 3 July 1764. [NRS.RGS.107.119; RS27.166.335]

DALRYMPLE, Dr DAVID, from St Kitts then in Methil, Fife, in 1766, [NRS.SC20.36.12]; in St Kitts was granted the lands of Ladifron on 23 February 1767, [NRS.RGS.109.160]; in in St Kitts, 1780. [NRS.CS16.1.181/185]

DALY, DENNIS, in Plymouth, Montserrat, 1719. [TNA.CO152.13]

DALY, JOSEPH, born 1791, died 9 July 1867. [St Anthony's mi, Montserrat]

DALZELL, Mrs ANN, in St Kitts in 1776. [NLS.Acc.8793.33]

D'AMBLEMONT, Marquis, in St Kitts, 1697-1698. [SPAWI.1697.639/715/859/978; 1698.1089]

DANES, RICHARD, aged 20, aboard the Paul of London, master Jo. Acklin, bound from Gravesend to St Kitts on 3 April 1635. [TNA.E157.20]

DANG, MARGARET, aboard the sloop Resolution, master John Ingleby, bound from Barbados to Nevis, on 14 February 1678. [TNA]

DANIELL, JAMES, in Nevis, a bond, 23 April 1818. [NRS.RD5.301.19]

DANIELL, JOHN, aboard the barque John's Adventure, master John Welch, bound from Barbados to Antigua on 9 April 1679. [TNA]

DANIELL, JOHN, in the parish of Sandy Point, St Kitts on 7 February 1678. [TNA.COI.42]

DANIELL, JOSEPH, from Nevis, graduated MD from Edinburgh University in 1809. [EMG.41]; married Eliza, daughter of William and Elizabeth Pemberton on 2 October 1823. [St John's, Figtree, Nevis]

DANIELL, Mrs J W, was buried 28 June 1824. [St George's, Gingerland, Nevis]

DANIELL, JOSIAH WEBBE, a widower, and Eliza Catherine Lyons, spinster, both of St Paul's, Charlestown, Nevis, were married on 9 February 1837.

DANIELLSEN, ..., tavern keeper, in St Croix in 1802. [RDAG.I/2]

DANNY, WILLIAM, born 1798, only son of the late Dr William Danny, died in St Kitts on 10 September 1818. [GM.88.270]

DAPWELL, ELIZABETH, died in Antigua in 1750. [Belfast Estate gravestone, Antigua]

DARBY, SAMUEL, in Fredericksted, St Croix, in 1770. [RDAG.I.50]

DARE. LOUISA CAROLINE, born 1763, daughter of William Julius of Mansion Estate, St Kitts, widow of Pholion Dare in Long Ashton, died in London on 22 September 1845. [GM.ns24.544]

DARIUS, AUGUST, in St Croix in 1768. [SSF]

DASART, JOHN, Chief Justice of Antigua in 1724. [TNA.CO18.1]

DAVID, JOHN, a yeoman from Cadoxton, Glamorgan, an indentured servant bound from Bristol to Nevis in 1660. [BRO]

DAVID, THOMAS, an indentured servant aboard the Laurell, master John West, bound for Nevis, Jamaica or New England in 1671. [BRO]

THE PEOPLE OF THE LEEWARD ISLANDS, 1620 - 1860

DAVIDSON, CHARLES, probate, 12 May 1779, Christiansted. [RAK.31.278]

DAVIDSON, ROBERT, a minister of St Paul's, Cabaccaterre, St Kitts, in 1734; minister of St Paul's, Falmouth, Antigua in 1742. [FPA.280/282][SPAWI.1735.602vii]

DAVIE, HENRY, a planter in St Kitts, probate, 1654, PCC. [TNA]

DAVIES, EDMOND, aged 21, aboard the Paul of London, master Jo. Acklin, bound from Gravesend to St Kitts on 3 April 1635. [TNA.E157.20]

DAVIES, GABRIEL, aged 38, bound aboard the Mathew of London, master Richard Goodladd, for St Kitts on 21 May 1635. [TNA.E157.20]

DAVIES, WILLIAM, from Belfast, an indentured servant aboard the Elisabeth and Ann master William Benn, bound from Liverpool to Montserrat in March 1700. [LRO]

DAVIS, DANIEL, on Saba, petitioned the Dutch West India Company in Amsterdam in 1772. [DNA.Inv.1151]

DAVIS, Reverend DANIEL GATEWARD, born in St Kitts in 1788, son of Reverend W. Davis the Bishop of Antigua, died in London on 25 October 1857. [GM.ns2.3.675]

DAVIS, FRANCES JANE, daughter of B. Brown Davis in St Kitts, married C Hamilton Mills, eldest son of G. Galway Mills, in St Kitts on 21 July 1820. [GM.90.272]

DAVIS, GATEWARD COLERIDGE, a barrister, eldest son of the late Daniel G. Davis, late Bishop of Antigua, married Elizabeth Gordon Jackson, fourth daughter of William Walrond Jackson the Bishop of Antigua, in St John's, Antigua, on 21 January 1864. [GM.ns2.16.520]

DAVIS, Colonel JOHN, President of the Council of St Kitts, died 1725, probate 1725, PCC. [TNA]; buried in Westminster Abbey.

DAVIES, WILLIAM, a merchant, died in Nevis, probate, 1690, PCC. [TNA]

DAVY, JOHN, bound from Bristol to Nevis in 1660. [BRO]

DAWLEY, DANIEL, a planter in Montserrat in 1678. [TNA.CO1.22.17]

DAWSON, CHARLES, MD, surgeon to the 54th Regiment, died in Antigua on 13 November 1849. [AJ.5322]

DAWSON, ELIZABETH, relict of Robert French late of Tortula, testament, 23 January 1821, Comm. Lauder. [NRS]

DAWSON, JAMES, in Tortula, graduated MD from King's College, Aberdeen, on 24 October 1767. [KCA.132]

DAWSON, SAMUEL, born 1788, son of the late Elliot Dawson in Hinckley, Leicestershire, died in St Bartholemew on 23 October 1809. [GM.80.87]

DAY, Miss, daughter of the late John Day in Antigua, married Thomas Loddington, of the Court of Common Pleas, on 22 September 1791. [GM.61.873]

DEACON, CHARLES, a Jacobite rebel who was transported via London aboard the *Prince George*, master James Nairn, bound for Antigua on 14 January 1746, landed there on 16 March 1748. [TNA.T53.44]

DEAN, ALEXANDER, in Antigua in 1753. [NRS.CS96.644]

DEANE, MARY, a single woman, an indentured servant bound from Bristol to St Kitts in 1660. [BRO]

DEANS, JAMES, born 22 August 1757, son of William Deans a merchant in Old Meldrum, was educated at Marischal College, Aberdeen, 1778-1780, a clergyman in Basseterre, St Kitts, in1790. [FPA]

DE BONNEMERE, DANIEL, a Huguenot and a planter in the Pentecoste Division of St Kitts, later in Jamaica, before 1715. [PCCol.1715.1225][SPAWI.1714.630VII/IX; 1715.375/431]

DE BONNEMERE, PAUL MINVIELLE, a Huguenot, son of Daniel de Bonnemere in St Kitts, had his estates restored in 1715. [PCCol.1715.1225][SPAWI.1714.630VII/IX; 1715.375/431]

DE BRETON, Baron FREDERICK, in St Croix in 1768. [SSF]

DE BRETTON, JUDITH, eldest daughter of Baron Frederick de Bretton in St Croix, married a Lieutenant Cuming in Guadaloupe on 26 January 1811. [GM.81.188][SM.73.557]

DE BRISAC, Captain, in St Kitts in 1717. [JCTP.1717.261]

DE BRISSON, PAUL, a planter in Nevis, 1712. [JCTP]

DE BUCK, JAN SYMONSZOON, in St Eustatia, 1646. [GAR.ONA.334.110.289]

DE CHAMBRE, ..., a planter in St Kitts, 1665, 1672, 1701. [SPAWI.1672.903; 1701.1091/1130/1133][PCCol.1702.49]

DE COSTA, DAVID, a cavalryman of the Leeward Regiment in 1679. [TNA.CO1.44.47]

D'ESNAMBUE, ..., in St Kitts in 1625. [SPAWI.1734.314ii]

DE GEORGE, SOLOMAN, at 26 King's Cross Street, Christinstaed, 1789. [RDAG]

DE GRAEFS, PETER, in St Kitts, a deposition, 1682. [SPAWI.1682.602xviii]

DE GRAND, FRANCIS, pastor of a French church in St Kitts in 1727. [FPA.276]

DE GRUYTER, BALTASAR, a planter on St Eustatia, 1644. [GAR.MA.206.225.363]

DE HAMELL, ……, in St Kitts, 1672. [SPAWI.1672.903]

DE LA COUSAYE, ALETTA, daughter of the late Captain Van Del Bourgh a Huguenot planter in St Kitts prior to 1715, who fled to the British sector to avoid persecution, their estates were restored in 1715. [PCCol.1715.1225][SPAWI.1714.639iv; 1715.375]

DE LA FERTE, ABRAHAM PICARD, in Antigua, 1730. [PCCol.1730.177]

DE LA FREILLE. …., a Huguenot in St Kitts in 1716. [JCTP.1716.197]

DELANEY, RICHARD MAR, born 1753, son of Daniel M. Delaney and his wife Mary, died 31 March 1755, also son Daniel born 1753, died 26 November 1757, and the above Mrs Mary Delaney, born 1720, died 9 May 1783. [St George gravestone, Basse Terre, St Kitts]

DELANEY, Mr, a tavern-keeper in Christianstaed, St Croix, in 1770. [RDAG.I.3]

DELAP, ELIZABETH, died in Antigua on 25 September 1744, wife of Francis Delap. [Willoughby Church]

DE LA POITERIE, Le Chevalier, in Nevis in 1674. [SPAWI.1674.1333]

DE LAURENS, ……., in St Kitts in 1689. [SPAWI.1689.193]

DE LEON, DAVID, a merchant in St Kitts, 1765. [see Haim Abinum's will]

THE PEOPLE OF THE LEEWARD ISLANDS, 1620 - 1860

DE LEUZE, Captain, in St Kitts in 1718. [JCTP.1718.369]

DE LILLY, JAMES, a servant of the Governor of St Kitts in 1654. [CSPCol.1654.xii]

DE LIMA, HAM ABINUM, a merchant in Nevis, died in London, probate 1765, PCC. [TNA]

DE LOMPRE DU CHEMIN, DANIEL, a Huguenot planter in St Kitts who fled to the British sector to avoid persecution prior to 1714. [SPAWI.1714.630xiii/xv]

DE MARSHALL, PAUL, born 1701, died 21 September 1758. [St George gravestone, Basse Terre, St Kitts]

DE MESQUITA, ABRAHAM BUENO, in Nevis in 1708, [TNA.CO152-157]; resettled in Nevis in 1712. [JCTP.1709-1715.383]

DE MARSALL, LOUIS, a planter on St Kitts in 1712. [JCTP]

DE MIMIE, ...in St Kitts in 1672. [SPAWI,1672.903]

DE MOUCHET, ..., in St Kitts in 1673. [SPAWI.1674.1273]

D'ENAMBUE, ..., settled in St Kitts or St Lucia in 1626. [SPAWI.1730.324]

DE NAMPONE, MARGARET, a Huguenot planter at Cabesterre, St Kitts, 1695-1714, lands were restored in 1715. [PCCol.1715.1225] [SPAWI.1714.630x; 1715.375]

DE NAMPONE, Dr, a planter in St Kitts before 1714. [SPAWI.1714.630xii]

DE NAYAC, LOUIS WILLIAM DUREPAIRE, a Huguenot, formerly in the military service of the King of Prussia, petitioned for estates in St Kitts by right of his wife the widow of .....Maigne, in 1715. [SPAWI.1715.643]

THE PEOPLE OF THE LEEWARD ISLANDS, 1620 - 1860

DENING, SARAH, died in Antigua on 13 June 1744 aged 6 months. [St John's Cathedral, Antigua]

DENNIE, ……, in St Kitts in 1672. [SPAWI.1672.903]

DENNIN, CHARLES, in the parish of Sandy Point, St Kitts on 7 February 1678. [TNA.COI.42]

DENNISTOUN, ROBERT, from Glasgow, was admitted as a burgess of St Eustatia on 16 September 1780. [TNA.CO318.8.83]

DE NOGEL, Frere PHILLIPE, in St Kitts, 1670s. [SPAWI.1671.583; 1673.1036]

DENTEN, ROBERT, aged 26, bound aboard the Mathew of London, master Richard Goodladd, for St Kitts on 21 May 1635. [TNA.E157.20]

DE PAQUERAY, LOUIS, a planter in St Kitts, dead by 1701. [SPAWI.1701.1091]

DE POINCY, Chevalier, Governor of St Kitts and Lieutenant General of the French Leeward Islands in 1640, 1654. [SPAWI.1730.324][SPCol.1654.XII]

DE POYETT, ……, in St Kitts in 1673. [SPAWI.1674.1273]

DE PRAILLE, …., in Guadaloupe in 1674. [SPAWI.1674.1333]

DE PRAYLE, ….., in St Kitts in 1672. [SPAWI.1672.903]

DE PRESIMON, …….., in St Kitts in 1672. [SPAWI.1672.903]

DERETHEUILLE, BINOIST, in Guadaloupe in 1703. [SPAWI.1705.1025ii]

DE RO, ….., in St Kitts in 1672. [SPAW.1672.903]

DERRITT, PETER, a Jacobite banished to Antigua in 1716. [SPAWI.1716.310][CTB.31.204]

DE RUAN PALLU, ..., in St Kitts in 1671. [SPAWI.1671.583]

DE SAINT LAURENT, Chevalier, in St Kitts in 1671, 1678. [SPAWI.1671.583; 1678.763]

DE SALENAVE, JORDAIN, husband of Elizabeth de Salenave, Huguenots on St Kitts ca1700 [HS.6.7/32]

DE STALPERT, JACOB, Commander of St Eustatia from 1719 to 1720.

DEWAR, DAVID, in St Kitts, probate 1794, PCC. [TNA]

DEWAR, EDWARD, from Clapham, Surrey, died in St Thomas on 16 June 1800. [GM.70.694]

DEWAR, GEORGE, in St Kitts, probate 17876, PCC. [TNA]

DEWAR, JAMES, in Antigua in 1757. [DA.Ogilvie pp.14]; born 1718, died in Antigua on 26 December 1764. [St John's Cathedral]

DEWAR, MARY, a daughter of Robert Dewar a merchant in Antigua, was granted the lands of Drumcross on 23 February 1768. [NRS.RGS.110.95; RS27.180.276]; services of heirs, 1768. [NRS]; daughter of Robert Dewar, a merchant in St Eustatia, services of heirs, 1772. [NRS];1778. [NRS.CS16.1.173/305]; married William Nisbet a physician in Edinburgh on 31 July 1786. [EMR]

DEWAR, ROBERT, a merchant in Antigua, a sasine, 1768. [NRS.RS27.180.276]

DEWER, STEPHEN, aboard the barque Resolution, master Thomas Gilbert, at Barbados bound for Antigua on 15 November 1679. [TNA]

DE WINDT, JAN, sr., on Saba, 17.. [NWIC#619.18]

THE PEOPLE OF THE LEEWARD ISLANDS, 1620 - 1860

DE WINDT, JAN, born 1717, son of Jan de Windt, Commander of St Eustatia, died in January 1775.

DE WINT, GEURT SPRE, in St Croix in 1768. [SSF][Wintberg Plantation gravestone]

DE WINT, JOHN JACOB, in St Croix, 1768. [SSF]

DE WINT, JOHN, in St Thomas, 1783. [HMC.A.IV.63]

DE WITT, GEORGE, a planter in Antigua, 1710. [SPAWI.1710.674]

DE WITT, PHILLIP, a planter in Nevis in 1712. [JCTP.P224]

DE WITT, THOMAS, a planter in Antigua in 1709. [SPAWI.1709.487]

DICK, THOMAS, a clerk in Antigua, testament, 1867, Comm. Edinburgh. [NRS]

DICKIE, JAMES, from Ayrshire, was admitted as a burgess of St Eustatia on 13 November 1780. [TNA.CO318.8.84]

DICKSON, Dr D.J.H., a physician in the Leeward Islands, married Miss Tracy in 1812. [GM.82.188]

DINGLE, JAMES, in the parish of Sandy Point, St Kitts on 7 February 1678. [TNA.COI.42]

DISHINGTON, Captain JACOB, died 9 May 1776, probate Christiansted. [RAK.1773-1777.216]

DITTIE, THOMAS, in Nevis, probate, 1697, PCC. [TNA]

DODD, GEORGE, aged 17, bound aboard the Mathew of London, master Richard Goodladd, for St Kitts on 21 May 1635. [TNA.E157.20]

THE PEOPLE OF THE LEEWARD ISLANDS, 1620 - 1860

DODSON, EDWARD, aged 21, aboard the John of London, master James Waymoth, bound for St Kitts on 2 October 1635. [TNA.E157.20]

DOE, JO., aged 22, bound aboard the Mathew of London, master Richard Goodladd, for St Kitts on 21 May 1635. [TNA.E157.20]

DOIG, ANNE, only child of William Doig in Antigua, 1783. [NRS.CS17.1.2]

DOIG, JAMES, younger brother of David Doig the Provost of Montrose, in Antigua in 1753, [NRS.CS96.644]; was admitted as a burgess of Edinburgh on 30 September 1757, [EBR]; died in Antigua on 14 July 1759. [SM.21.557]; subscribed to his will in Antigua on 30 July 1759. [NRS.NRAS.0792.7.5]

DOIG, JAMES, son of James Doig in Antigua, was admitted as a burgess of Montrose in 1758. [MBR]; services of heirs, 1791. [NRS]

DOIG, JOHN, son of James Doig in Antigua, was admitted as a burgess of Montrose in 1763. [MBR]

DOIG, PATRICK, MD, born 1763, from Antigua, married Jane Austin, daughter of John Austin a merchant in Glasgow, on 15 February 1808. [SM.70.237]; Colonel of the Militia in Antigua, died in Stirling on 9 May 1833, his wife, Jane Austin, died in Stirling on 14 March 1849. [Stirling, Holy Rude, gravestone]

DOIG, ROBERT, in Antigua in 1757. [DA.Ogilvie pp.14]

DOIG, WILLIAM HENRY, son of James Doig in Antigua, was admitted as a burgess of Montrose in 1748, and of Edinburgh in 1757, [MBR][EBR]; was granted the lands of Crookston on 23 February 1765. [NRS.RGS.107.168]; a will dated 1765. [NRS.NRAS.0792.7.5]

DONALDSON, JAMES, in Antigua, services of heirs, 1785. [NRS]

DONCKER, JAN SIMONZOON, sr., on the Dutch Leeward Islands in 1689, Commander there from 1704 until his death in 1717.

DONNEL, JAMES, probate 6 December 1780, Christiansted. [RAK.441.35]

DONOVAN, DERMOND, in Kayon Division, St Kitts on 7 February 1678. [TNA.COI.42]

DONOVAN, RICHARD, a barrister from Tibberton Court in Gloucestershire, died in Antigua in 1816. [GM.86.571]

DORIE, DANIEL, a Jacobite transported to Antigua in 1716. [CTB.31.204]

DORN, WILLIAM, aged 22, bound aboard the *Mathew of London*, master Richard Goodladd, for St Kitts on 21 May 1635. [TNA.E157.20]

DOUGAL, PHILIP, a Scot, was admitted as a burgher of St Eustatia on 8 August 1781. [TNA.CO318.8.83]

DOUGLAS, ALEXANDER, son of Reverend Alexander Douglas and his wife Isabella Houston in Edinburgh, a merchant in St Kitts in 17... [F.1.175]

DOUGLAS, Captain DUNBAR, son of the Earl of Selkirk, died in St Kitts in November 1796. [GM.67.80]

DOUGLAS, HENRY, born 1683, died in Antigua on 19 February 1753, his wife Mary, born 1688, died 22 September 1744. [St John's Cathedral, Antigua]

DOUGLAS, HUGH, a witness in the Virgin Islands in 1790. [NRS.RD2.252.1038]

DOUGLAS, JAMES, probate, 12 November 1776, Fredericksted. [RAK.177]

DOUGLAS, JAMES GEORGE, in St Kitts, probate 1768, PCC. [TNA]

THE PEOPLE OF THE LEEWARD ISLANDS, 1620 - 1860

DOUGLAS, Sir JAMES, in St Kitts, probate, 1795, PCC. [TNA]

DOUGLAS, JEAN, daughter of Reverend Alexander Douglas and his wife Isabella Houston in Edinburgh, married Aretas B. Akers, in 17..., and settled in St Kitts. [F.I.175]

DOUGLAS, JOHN, in Antigua in 1713. [BM.Sloane.4065.121]

DOUGLAS, JOHN, a minister sent to Antigua in 1732, minister of St George's, Antigua, to Nevis in 1751. [EMA.24][FPA.280/284]

DOUGLAS, JOHN, in St Kitts, father of James Douglas who matriculated at Glasgow University in 1748. [MAGU]; in St Kitts, probate 1783, PCC. [TNA]

DOUGLAS, ROBERT, son of Alexander Douglas and his wife Isabella Houston in Edinburgh, a planter in St Kitts in 17.... [F.I.175]

DOUGLAS, ROBERT, Governor of St Kitts, died on 24 October 1780. [GM.50.50][SM.42.54]; in 1776. [NLS.Acc.8793]

DOUGLAS, WALTER, Governor of St Kitts and the Leeward Islands, was admitted as a burgess of Glasgow on 17 November 1712. [GBR]

DOUGLAS, WILLIAM, indentured in Bristol for 4 years' service in Nevis in 1670. [BRO]

DOW, EDWARD LESLIE, a surgeon who died in St John's, Antigua, on 30 August 1839. [SG.8.814]

DOW, WILLIAM, son of Reverend Dow in Blairgowrie, Perthshire, died in Antigua on 7 July 1803. [GM.73.882][EEC.14316]

DOWNING, JOHN, aboard the Laurel, master Robert Ox, bound from Barbados to Nevis on 22 December 1679. [TNA]

DOWSE, JOHN, in Nevis, probate, 1733, PCC. [TNA]

DRAN, MAREN, aboard the ketch Dove, master Jacob Le Roux, bound from Barbados to Antigua on 29 July 1679. [TNA]

DOWNING, JAMES, born 1754, a surgeon, via London aboard the Turnbull bound for Tortola in 1774. [TNA.T47.9/11]

DOWNING, NICHOLAS, a mariner from Bristol, died in Nevis, probate 1691, PCC. [TNA]

DRISCOLL, DENNIS, in Plymouth, Montserrat, 1719. [TNA.CO152.13]

DRIVER, WILLIAM, a missionary from Shrewsbury, died in St Eustatia in 1813. [GM.83.505]

DU BERRY, THOMAS, died in Montserrat in 1764. [GM.34.46]

DU BERRY, M., a Councillor of Montserrat in 1729. [JCTP.86.234]

DU BOIS, JOHN, master of the St Anne of Guadaloupe was seized for smuggling in Antigua in 1730. [PCCol.1730.201]

DUFFUS, DANIEL, a Jacobite a prisoner transported to Antigua in 1716. [SPAWI.1716.310]

DU LIGNON, Abbe, a priest in Guadaloupe, in 1761. [NRS.GD126]

DU MAINE, Madame, a planter in Fig Tree Quarter, St Kitts, before 1717. [JCTP.1717.261]

DU MOUCHE, ……, in St Kitts in 1671. [SPAWI.1671.583]

DUN, WILLIAM, aged 16, from Perino, emigrated via Plymouth aboard the Robert Bonaventure bound for St Kitts in February 1633. [TNA.E157.18]

DUNBAR, CHARLES, from Ireland, settled in Antigua by 1731. [PRONI.D162.24]

DUNBAR, CHARLES, in Antigua, father of John Dunbar in 1778, [NRS.CS16.1.173/155][NRS.RS.Dumfries.xx.211]

DUNBAR, GRACE, daughter of Charles Dunbar in Antigua, and spouse of John Hart a counsellor at law there in 1779. [NRS.CS16.1.175]

DUNBAR, JAMES, master of the Amherst of St Kitts at Savanna, Georgia, on 31 March 1762. [TNA.CO5.709]

DUNBAR, JOHN, a physician in Antigua, only son of Charles Dunbar in Antigua and his wife Gratianas Hart, only child of John Hart a counsellor-at-law in Antigua and his wife Grace Dunbar, daughter of the said Charles Dunbar, versus Charles Warner Dunbar, 1779. [NRS.CS16.1.175]

DUNBAR, JOHN, formerly a merchant in Antigua, a bond, 14 March 1796. [NRS.CS97.111.132]

DUNBAR, ROBERT, master of the Tidewell galley, died in Nevis, probate 1700, PCC. [TNA][DP.335]

DUNBAR, THOMAS, in Antigua in 1770. [NRS.RS.Dumfries.xx.211]

DUNBAR, WILLIAM, son of C. Dunbar, in Antigua, services of heirs, 1762, [NRS]; of Machriemore, in Antigua 1765. [NRS.AC7.51]; in Antigua in 1759. [DA.Ogilvie pp.33]

DUNCAN, ALEXANDER, a Jacobite a prisoner transported to Montserrat in 1716. [SPAWI.1716.313][CTB.31.205]

DUNCAN, ANNIE, born in Glasgow on 10 March 1838, wife of Henry Leckie, died in St Thomas, DWI, on 6 December 1864. [St Thomas gravestone]

DUNCAN, DAVID, a minister sent to the Leeward Islands in 1712. [EMA.25]

DUNCAN, JOHN, a Jacobite a prisoner transported to Montserrat in 1716. [SPAWI.1716.313][CTB.31.205]

DUNCAN, NINIAN, born 1826, son of James Duncan and his wife Mary Brown, died in St John's, Antigua, in February 1843. [Rothesay gravestone]

DUNLOP, ANNA, daughter of John Dunlop in St Croix, married John Edgar, a surgeon in Ayr, in Irvine on 9 November 1821. [S.253.374][AJ.3854]

DUNLOP, JOHN, a merchant in St Croix, 1790, [Caribbeana.5.265]; a merchant in St Croix in 1791, [RDAG];a deed, 2 November 1805, [NRS.RD3.317.530]; died in St Croix on 25 July 1805. [GM.75.881]

DUNN, THOMAS, second son of the late William Dunn a baker in Dublin, died in St Croix in 1798. [GM.68.724]

DUNN, WILLIAM, from Scotland, settled in St Eustatia, a widower who married Sarah Godet, widow of Henricus Benners, in St Eustatia on 14 November 1733. [Afscriften huwelijksakten van St Eustatia van 1710-1750]]

DUNOVAN, DENNIS, in St Thomas, Middle Island, St Kitts on 7 February 1678. [TNA.COI.42]

DU PAS, ..., a civil and criminal judge in St Kitts in 1679. [SPAWI.1679.963]

DU PORT, STEPHEN, in St Kitts in 1698, 1707, 1714. [SPAWI.1698.675; 1714.630] [PCCol.1714.1069][JCTP.1707.467]

DU PUY, ISAAC, died 21 September 1829. [St George gravestone, Basse Terre, St Kitts]

DURBAN, CATHERINE, in St Kitts, probate 1792, PCC. [TNA]

DU REPAIRE, ..., and his wife, the widow of M. Maigne, planters of Le Jardin, La Solovette, and Le Frontiere, in St Kitts in 1715. [JCTP.1715.85]

DU ROY, ANTHONY, a planter in St Kitts in 1712. [JCTP.1712]

DUSTAN, JOHN, from St Cullom, aged 26, a husbandman who emigrated via Plymouth aboard the Margaret bound for St Kitts in 1634. [TNA.E157.18]

DUZART, RICHARD, a yeoman, an indentured servant bound from Bristol to Nevis in 1660. [BRO]

DYER, HENRY, died 2 February 179-. [St Anthony's mi, Montserrat]

DYER, M., born 1749, from Tortula, died in Alphington, Devon, on 15 October 1832. [GM.102.483]

DYETT, JOSHUA, died 19 October 1793. [St Anthony's mi, Montserrat]

DYETT, MARY, wife of Robert Dyett, died 2 January 1815. [St Anthony's mi, Montserrat]

DYETT, RICHARD, born 4 September 1775, son of Henry Dyett in London, died 11 January 1808, husband of Frances, born 30 November 1777, died 17 August 1822, parents of Mary and Ann. [St Anthony's mi, Montserrat]

DYSON, Reverend HENRY JEREMIAH, from Barking, Essex, died in St Kitts on 27 March 1854. [GM.ns41.663]

DYSON, MATILDA, wife of Reverend H.J.Dyson, died in St Kitts on 26 March 1854. [GM.ns41.663]

EARLE, TIMOTHY, in St Kitts, probate 1787, PCC. [TNA]

EASDALE, JAMES, a merchant in St Kitts, 1765. [NRS.CS16.1.122]

EATON, GEORGE, aged 27, bound aboard the Mathew of London, master Richard Goodladd, for St Kitts on 21 May 1635. [TNA.E157.20]

EBBESEN, LAURENS, a merchant in St Croix in 1770, [RDAG.I.50]

EBERLEY, MICHAEL, a sugar baker, died 26 October, 1765. [St George mi, Basse Terre, St Kitts]

EDDY, Captain JOHN, died 2 April 1682. [St John's, Fig Tree, Nevis, gravestone]

EDE, JOB, from Southampton, died in Nevis on 1 July 1844. [GM.ns22.334]

EDMONDS, MARY, from South Petherton, an indentured servant bound from Bristol to Nevis in 1660. [BRO]

EDWARD, HUGH, from Antigua, died in London on 31 May 1856. [GM.ns2.1.125]

EDWARD, RICHARD, from St Virian, a husbandman aged 28, who emigrated via Plymouth aboard the Margaret bound for St Kitts in 1634. [TNA.E157.18]

EDWARDS, WILLIAM, a merchant from Bristol, died in St Vincent in January 1810. [GM.80.384]

EDYE, RAWLEIGH, aged 15, from Bodmyn, emigrated via Plymouth aboard the Robert Bonaventure bound for St Kitts in February 1633. [TNA.E157.18]

EEKE, GEORGE, aged 26, bound aboard the Mathew of London, master Richard Goodladd, for St Kitts on 21 May 1635. [TNA.E157.20]

THE PEOPLE OF THE LEEWARD ISLANDS, 1620 - 1860

EELES, EDWARD, aged 20, bound aboard the Mathew of London, master Richard Goodladd, for St Kitts on 21 May 1635. [TNA.E157.20]

EDGCOMBE, KATHLEEN, born 4 April 1695, daughter of Thomas and Martha Edgcombe, died 11 September 1776. [St Paul's gravestone, Antigua]

EDGCOMBE, PAUL, born 31 March 1692, died 17 October 1774, son of Thomas and Martha Edgcombe. [St Paul's gravestone, Antigua]

EDWARDS, JOSEPH, in St Kitts, probate 1785, PCC. [TNA]

EILSCOW, FRIIS, in St Croix in 1770. [RDAG.I.50]

EILSCOW, PETER MATTHIAS FRIIS, on Constitution Hill plantation, St Croix around 1755 also 1768. [SSF]

EIVERS, OWEN, a merchant in St Thomas, records, 1809-1829. [NRS.CS96.4488]

ELDRIDGE, RICHARD BURROUGHES, born in Great Yarmouth, an Assemblyman, died in St John's, Antigua, on 18 September 1852. [GM.ns38.655]

ELIZABETH, MARIA, in Kongens Tvergade, St Croix, in 1768. [SSF]

ELLERY. C., formerly a planter in Nevis, later a wine-merchant in London, died on 19 August 1811. [GM.81.286]

ELLIOT, Miss, third daughter of Samuel Elliot, married William Hay Carr, brother of the Earl of Errol, in Antigua on 27 July 1796. [GM.66.701]

ELLIOT, HENRY, aboard the sloop True Friendship, master Charles Callahan, at Barbados bound for Antigua on 2 October 1679. [TNA]

ELLIOT, JOHN, in St Kitts in 1776. [NLS.Acc.8793]

ELLIOT, MARY, youngest daughter of Samuel Elliot in Antigua, and sister of the Countess of Errol, married Lieutenant Cope of Loughall, on 10 June 1811. [SM.73.557][GM.66.701]

ELLIS, JOHN, from Ledbury, Herefordshire, bound from Bristol to Nevis in 1660. [BRO]

ELMES, RICHARD, aged 21, aboard the John of London, master James Waymoth, bound for St Kitts on 2 October 1635. [TNA.E157.20]

ELSEGOOD, EDMOND, born 1749, a merchant in London, bound via London aboard the Dorsetshire bound for St Kitts in 1773, to be a planter there. [TNA.T47.9/11]

ELVYN, WILLIAM, aged 23, bound aboard the Mathew of London, master Richard Goodladd, for St Kitts on 21 May 1635. [TNA.E157.20]

ENDERBEE, OLIVER, aboard the Ann and Mary, master John Johnson, at Barbados bound for Antigua on 13 March 1679. [TNA]

ENGLER, GEORGE, born 1725, died in Antigua on 2 June 1775. [St John's Cathedral]

ENTWISTLE, ERNIE, born 1733, died in Antigua in April 1803. [GM.73.691]

ERSKINE, THOMAS, a planter in Nevis, a witness to a deed, 8 December 1788. [NRS.RD4.245.702]; son of James Erskine of Finlaton, died in Nevis on 14 January 1792. [EEC.11518]

ERWINN, CHARLES, a Jacobite a prisoner transported to Antigua in 1716. [SPAWI.1716.310][CTB.31.204]

THE PEOPLE OF THE LEEWARD ISLANDS, 1620 - 1860

ESDAILE, ARCHIBALD, President of St Kitts, Master in Chancery, and the Admiralty Judge, died in St Kitts on 25 October 1796. [GM.67.164]

ESDAIL, JAMES, a merchant in Basseterre, St Kitts in 1778. [NRS.CS16.1.173/322]

ESTRIDGE, JOHN, a Councillor in St Kitts, died in Weymouth on 3 October 1773, in St Kitts, probate 1778, PCC. [TNA] [GM.48.495]

EVANS, DAVID, aged 22, aboard the Paul of London, master Jo. Acklin, bound from Gravesend to St Kitts on 3 April 1635. [TNA.E157.20]

EVANS, LEWIS, aged 25, aboard the John of London, master James Waymoth, bound for St Kitts on 2 October 1635. [TNA.E157.20]

EVANS, RICHARD, aged 21, aboard the John of London, master James Waymoth, bound for St Kitts on 2 October 1635. [TNA.E157.20]

EVANS, WALTER, bound from Bristol to St Kitts in 1660. [BRO]

EVERY, ANTHONY, on Saba, petitioned the Dutch West India Company in Amsterdam in 1772. [DNA.Inv.1151]

EVERY, JAMES, on Saba, petitioned the Dutch West India Company in Amsterdam in 1772. [DNA.Inv.1151]

EVERY, JOHN, on Saba, petitioned the Dutch West India Company in Amsterdam in 1772. [DNA.Inv.1151]

EVERY, PETER, on Saba, petitioned the Dutch West India Company in Amsterdam in 1772. [DNA.Inv.1151]

EWART, DAVID, born 1810, son of George Ewart a saddler and iron-monger in Duns, Berwickshire, and his wife Catherine Hogg, died in Antigua on 2 August 1835. [Duns gravestone]

EWART, JOHN, from Nevis, died in London in 1821. [GM.91.572]

EWING, WILLIAM, in Antigua in 1760. [DA.Ogilvie pp43]

EYLITZ, FRID., in St Croix in 1802. [RDAG.I/2]

FAESCH, ISAAC, Governor of the Dutch Leeward Islands from 1737-1740. [NWIC#585.49]

FAHIE, JOHN, son of Anthony Fahie and his wife Elizabeth Molineux in Montserrat, a Judge of the Vice Admiralty Court of St Kitts in 1779. [PCCol.1780.478]

FAHIE, RICHARD, in St Kitts, probate 1767, PCC. [TNA]

FAIRBAIRN, HENRY, MD, in Saunderston, Antigua, a letter, 1794, [NRS.RD3.275.573]; died in Antigua on 15 November 1795. [GM.65.166]

FAIRBAIRN, THOMAS, in Antigua, son of Dr James Fairbairn of Hopewell, a deed, 5 December 1789. [NRS.RD3.259.635]

FAIRER, JOHN, born 1757, a clerk in London, bound from Bristol aboard the London Merchant to Nevis in 1773. [TNA.T47.9/11]

FAIRFAX, THOMAS, aged 22, aboard the Paul of London, master Jo. Acklin, bound from Gravesend to St Kitts on 3 April 1635. [TNA.E157.20]

FAIRNIE, ALEXANDER, a merchant in St Martins, 1784. [NRS.AC7.61]

FARLEY, FRANCIS, born 1719, Assistant Judge of Antigua, died at sea on 31 March 1779. [St Anthony's mi, Montserrat]

FARRELL, DOMINICK, in St Croix in 1802. [RDAG.I/2]

FARRELL, JAMES, born 1732, a planter returning to St Kitts aboard the Pemberton via Whitehaven in 1774. [TNA.T47.9/11]

THE PEOPLE OF THE LEEWARD ISLANDS, 1620 - 1860

FARQUHAR, ALEXANDER, born 27 October 1761, son of Alexander Farquhar in Kintore, educated at Marischal College in Aberdeen, around 1781, a surgeon who settled in Antigua, died 19 October 1792, buried in St Mary's, Antigua. [MCA.II.357][St John's Wood Chapel gravestone, London]

FARQUHAR, ROBERT, born 19 June 1755, late of Antigua and Grenada, died 29 January 1836 in Keswick, Cumberland. [St John's Wood Chapel gravestone, London]

FARRELL, HUGH, aboard the barque Dove, master Antony Jenour, at Barbados bound for Nevis on 29 October 1679. [TNA]

FARRELL, ROGER, aboard the sloop Katherine, master Andrew Gall, at Barbados bound for Antigua on 26 November 1679. [TNA]

FAUCER, ROBERT, aged 40, bound aboard the Mathew of London, master Richard Goodladd, for St Kitts on 21 May 1635. [TNA.E157.20]

FAUCHER, ..., in Montserrat in 1736. [SPAWI.1736.460]

FAVEY, LUCY JANE, third daughter of the late Charles Favey a merchant, married Francis Horatio Pryce, fourth son of Captain Henry Pryce of the Royal Navy, in Antigua on 13 January 1848. [GM.ns29.421]

FENTON, WILLIAM, in Nevis, probate, 1754, PCC. [TNA]

FENWICK, ANDREW, in Antigua in 1753. [NRS.CS96.645]

FERGUS, LUCY, born 1744, daughter of Patrick Fergus in Montserrat, died in Bury on 24 March 1824. [GM.94.381]

FERGUSON, HUGH, in Antigua in 1757. [DA.Ogilvie pp.21]

FERGUSON, PETER, a Jacobite, a prisoner transported to Montserrat in 1716. [SPAWI.1716.313][CTB.31.206]

FERGUSON, Dr THOMAS, born 12 September 1799, eldest son of Reverend Ferguson and his wife Marion Murray, in Inch, Wigtownshire, educated at Glasgow University around 1817, died in St John's, Antigua, on 21 May 1845.
[SG.14.1416][F.2.337][MAGU.272]

FERNANDEZ, DAVID, from Lambeth, died in St Thomas in 1810. [GM.80.281]

FERNE, JOHN, in St Kitts, probate, 1638, PCC. [TNA]

FERRALL, MATHIAS, a planter on the island of St Croix, will, 1787. [PWI]

FERRIER, ROBERT, a merchant, died in Nevis on 7 September 1839. [SG.8.812]

FEUILLETEAU, ELEANOR, in St Kitts, probate 1781, PCC. [TNA]

FEUILLETEAU, LEWIS, in St Kitts, probate 1775, PCC. [TNA]

FIDLER, WILLIAM, born 1733 in Aberdeen, emigrated to Antigua, returned to Scotland, died 22 March 1809. [St Nicholas gravestone, Aberdeen]

FIELD, HENRY, aged 25, aboard the John of London, master James Waymoth, bound for St Kitts on 2 October 1635. [TNA.E157.20]

FIELDS, JAMES, and SARAH, probate, 17 September 1760, Christiansted. [RAK]

FINDLAY, CHARLES, a planter in Nevis, a witness to a deed, 8 December 1788. [NRS.RD4.245.702]

FINLAY, THOMAS, in St Croix in 1790. [Caribeanna.5.265]

FINN, THOMAS, in St Croix, probate, 1773, PCC. [TNA]

FISHER, EDWARD, aged 27, aboard the Paul of London, master Jo. Acklin, bound from Gravesend to St Kitts on 3 April 1635. [TNA.E157.20]

FITZGARRALD, MAURICE, in the parish of Sandy Point, St Kitts on 7 February 1678. [TNA.COl.42]

FLEETWOOD, ALEXANDER, aged 19, aboard the John of London, master James Waymoth, bound for St Kitts on 2 October 1635. [TNA.E157.20]

FLEMING, ANN, in St Kitts, probate 1769, PCC. [TNA]

FLEMING, GILBERT, a minister in Antigua in 1751. [FPA.284]

FLEMING, GILBERT FANE, in St Kitts, probate 1777, PCC. [TNA]

FLEMING, JAMES, master of the Lucretia of St Kitts trading between Scotland and St Kitts in 1748. [NRS.E504.28.3]

FLEMING, LAURA AMANDA, only daughter of the late J.H.Fleming in Anguilla, married Berkeley Johnson, eldest son of Adolphus Pugh Johnson in London on 17 June 1847. [GM.ns28.312]

FLETCHER, JOHN JAMES, son of Richard Fletcher and his wife Jane Mary, died 17.... [St George gravestone, Basse Terre, St Kitts]

FLETCHER, ANTHONY, in Antigua in 1753. [NRS.CS96.644]

FLOWER, FRANCIS, born 1783, from Hammersmith, died in St Croix on 26 June 1811. [GM.81.285]

FLOYD, HUGH, a yeoman from Cardigan, an indentured servant bound from Bristol to Nevis in 1660. [BRO]

FOGERTON, DANIEL, in the parish of Sandy Point, St Kitts on 7 February 1678. [TNA.COl.42]

FOGO, DAVID, a merchant in Antigua, services of heirs, 1749, [NRS]; in Antigua in 1753 and 1759. [NRS.CS96.644][DA.Ogilvie.ms.34]

FOLKARD, P., born 1746, an ironmonger in London, via London aboard the Pemberton bound for St Kitts in 1774. [TNA.T47.9/11]

FOOT, JOHN FREELAND, born 1717, died 13 November 1789. [Vernon's Estate, Antigua]

FORBES, ANTONY GEORGE, from St Kitts, graduated MD from Edinburgh University in 1788. [EMG.21]

FORBES, FRANCIS, in Barbuda, married Miss Lindsay on 30 April 1764. [GM.34.250]

FORBES, GEORGE, born 1801, a barrister, died in St Kitts on 3 November 1825. [GM.94.647]

FORBES, HUGH, in Montserrat, probate, 1796, PCC. [TNA]

FORBES, JAMES, in St Croix, later in the Old Manse of Glass, testament, 6 March 1810, Comm. Moray. [NRS.CC16.9.10/271]

FORBES, JANET, born 1735, third daughter of Thomas Forbes of Waterton and his wife Margaret Montgomerie, died in Antigua. [Forbes of Waterton pedigree II, Aberdeen, 1857]

FORBES, JEAN, born 1737, fourth daughter of Thomas Forbes of Waterton and his wife Margaret Montgomerie, married Walter Thibou a physician in Antigua. [Forbes of Waterton pedigree II, Aberdeen, 1857]

FORBES, Miss JESSIE, died 10 December 1778. [St John's burial register, Antigua]

FORBES, JOSEPH, a wright from Antigua, was buried in St Nicholas churchyard, Aberdeen, in 1764. [ACA]

THE PEOPLE OF THE LEEWARD ISLANDS, 1620 - 1860

FORBES, Mrs JUDITH, in Nevis, 1699. [SPAWI.1699.714]

FORBES, Lord, Commander in Chief of the Leeward Islands in 1731. [HMC.I.Granard.212]

FORD, GEORGE, aged 30, from Exeter, emigrated via Plymouth aboard the Robert Bonaventure bound for St Kitts in February 1633. [TNA.E157.18]

FOREMAN, JOHN, born 1820, son of J. Foreman in Belfast, a merchant and assemblyman, died in Antigua on 14 June 1866. [GM.ns3.2.269]

FORGINE, SAMUEL, from Wallen Lizard, a husbandman aged 26, who emigrated via Plymouth aboard the Margaret bound for St Kitts in 1634. [TNA.E157.18]

FORREST, ELIZABETH, only child of Robert Forrest a skipper in St Croix, testament, 28 April 1774, Comm. Edinburgh. [NRS]

FORREST, HENRY, born 1741, a mariner from Bristol bound for Nevis in 1774. [TNA.T47.9/11]

FORSAN, JAMES, in the Leeward Islands, died on 20 October 1758. [GM.28.556]

FORSYTH, HUGH, a Jacobite a prisoner transported to Antigua in 1716. [SPAWI.1716.310][CTB.31.204]

FOUDIRNIER, PAUL, a merchant in St Kitts, died on 1 August 1770. [GM.40.393]

FOWLIS, WILLIAM, in St Kitts in 1776. [NLS.Acc.8793]

FRAISE, CATHERINE, a Huguenot planter at Cabisterre, St Kitts, around 1695, daughter of Daniel de Lompre, a petition in 1714; estate restored in 1715. [PCCol.1715.1225][SPAWI.1714.630xiii; 1715.375]

FRANCE, HAROLD, born 1772, Assistant Commissary General, died in Montserrat on 20 June 1820. [St Anthony's mi, Montserrat]

FRANK, MANSEL, was resettled in Nevis in 1712. [JCTP.1709-1715.392]

FRANCKLIN, GILBERT, in St Kitts, probate, 1799, PCC. [TNA]

FRASER, ALEXANDER, probate, 30 April 1770, Christiansted. [RAK.205.65]

FRASER, ALEXANDER, son of Thomas Fraser, [1747-1789] a tacksman, and his wife Catherine ….., settled in Tortula. [Boleskine gravestone]

FRAZER, ALEXANDER, on St John's Island, Danish West Indies, in 1841. [1841 Census]

FRASER, CHARLES, second son of Dr Thomas Fraser in Antigua, a sasine, 10 October 1775. [NRS.RS38.13.250-310]

FRASER, EDWARD, a merchant from Glasgow, died in St Croix in September 1802. [EA.4074.03]

FRASER, GEORGE, son of the late Lord George Saltoun, died in Nevis on 8 January 1799. [GM.69.254][GC.1179][SM.61.210]

FRASER, HUGH, Collector of Customs in Parkham, Antigua, died in St John's, Antigua, in May 1750, testament, 1752, Comm. Edinburgh. [NRS]

FRASER, HUGH, probate, 30 April 1770, Christiansted. [RAK.205.65]

FRASER, JAMES, in St Croix in 1790. [Caribbeana.5.265]

FRASER, JAMES, a merchant in St Kitts, 1792. [NRS.GD23.10.607]

FRASER, JAMES, of Kingask, died in St Kitts on 28 May 1813. [EA.5173.13][AJ.3422]

FRASER, JOHN, a Jacobite a prisoner transported to Antigua in 1716. [SPAWI.1716.310][CTB.31.204]

FRASER, JOHN, from Inverness, was admitted as a burgher of St Eustatia on 20 August 1780. [TNA.CO318.8.83]

FRASER, JOHN, in St Croix in 1790. [Caribbeana.5.265]

FRASER, Mr, born 1753, a gentleman from Scotland, via Portsmouth aboard the Charles Shayse bound for St Kitts, to visit his brother in St Vincent, in 1774. [NRS.T47.9/1]

FRASER, SIMON, born 1757, a clerk from London aboard the Mathew bound for St Kitts in 1774. [TNA.T47.9/11]

FRASER, Dr THOMAS, in Antigua in 1753. [NRS.CS96.645]

FRASER, WILLIAM MACKINNEN, from Antigua, graduated MD from Edinburgh University in 1775. [EMG.12]

FRASER, WILLIAM, a merchant in St Kitts, 1792. [NRS.GD23.10.607]

FREEMAN, ELIZABETH, aged 18, aboard the John of London, master James Waymoth, bound for St Kitts on 2 October 1635. [TNA.E157.20]

FREEMAN, HARRIET, daughter of Mr Freeman in Antigua, and wife of Thomas Oliver former Governor of Massachusetts, died in Bristol on 16 July 1808. [GM.78.662]

FREEMAN, MELUSINA WARBURTON, daughter of the late Arthur Freeman in Antigua, married Nathaniel Bayley, in Bath on 24 August 1795. [GM.65.703]

FREEMAN, THOMAS, in Antigua, will, 1736. [PWI]

FREEMAN, THOMAS, in Antigua, father of Thomas Freeman, services of heirs, 1802. [NRS]

FREEMAN, WILLIAM, inherited the manor of Godwyn in Antigua from his father and by letters patent on 8 August 1699, complaint 1702. [PCCol.1702.49]

FRENCH, EDWARD A., born 1798, eldest son of John Lynch French in St Kitts, and his wife Elizabeth Darrell, daughter of Harry Darrell of Calehill, Kent, and brother of Andrew Lynch French in St Kitts, died in St Kitts on 9 October 1859. [GM.ns2.7.654]

FRENCH, GEORGE, in Plymouth, Montserrat, 1719. [TNA.CO152.13]

FRENCH, JOHN, from Washford, Ireland, aged 26, from emigrated via Dartmouth bound for St Kitts in 20 February 1634. [TNA

FRENCH, JO, aged 18, aboard the Paul of London, master Jo. Acklin, bound from Gravesend to St Kitts on 3 April 1635. [TNA.E157.20]

FRENCH, LAWRENCE, born 1674, from Galway, an indentured servant, bound from Liverpool aboard the Elizabeth and Ann, bound for Montserrat in 1700. [LRO]

FRENCH, MARTIN, in Plymouth, Montserrat, 1719. [TNA.CO152.13]; a planter in Montserrat in 1712. [TNA.CO152.16]

FRENCH, Miss, daughter of Nathaniel French in Antigua, married Captain Palmer of the Guards Regiment, son of Sir Charles Palmer, on 25 October 1752. [GM.22.478]

FRENCH, Mrs, born 1740, daughter of the late Thomas Nicholas in Antigua, great-grand-daughter of Sir Edward Nicholas the Secretary of State under King Charles II, died in Cavendish, Suffolk, in 1815. [GM.85.378]

FRENCH, Mrs, born 1746, widow of William French in Montserrat, died in London in 1818. [GM.88.644]

FRETHY, THOMAS, aged 24, from Perintho, emigrated via Plymouth aboard the Robert Bonaventure bound for St Kitts in February 1633. [TNA.E157.18]

FROST, REGINALD, aged 15, from Totness, emigrated via Plymouth aboard the Robert Bonaventure bound for St Kitts in February 1633. [TNA.E157.18]

FROST, THOMAS, aged 28, aboard the John of London, master James Waymoth, bound for St Kitts on 2 October 1635. [TNA.E157.20]

FRYE, JOHN, a Councillor of Antigua, 26 September, 1721. [PCCol.App.ii.821]; born 1669, died in Antigua on 6 March 1747. [Bridgetown mi]

FRYE, SARAH, born 1775, daughter of the late John Revel Frye in Montserrat, died in London on 8 March 1844. [GM.ns21.440]

FRYE, WILLIAM, President of Montserrat, died on 17 May 1736. [GM.6.423]

FULFORD, JO., aged 18, bound aboard the Mathew of London, master Richard Goodladd, for St Kitts on 21 May 1635. [TNA.E157.20]

FULLARTON, ARCHIBALD, Lieutenant of the Militia of St Croix in 1790. [Caribbeana.5.265]

FULLARTON, GEORGE, in Montserrat in 1696. [TNA.Association Oath Rolls]

FURLONGE, WILLIAM, jr., born 1761, a Councillor in Montserrat, died there on 7 April 1813, husband of Elizabeth Mary Dardis, born 1775, died 31 July 1823. [GM.83.660][St Anthony's mi]

GAINER, MARY, widow of R. Cunningham in Cayon, St Kitts, services of heirs, 1761. [NRS]

GALBRAITH, ARCHIBALD, died in St Thomas on 1 March 1826. [BM.19.765]

GALE, JOHN, from Bristol, died aboard the Seaphiar at Nevis, probate, 1691, PCC. [TNA]

GALLOWAY, Mrs CHRISTIAN, widow of John Galloway, died 14 October 1782. [St John's Cathedral burial register]

GALLAWAY, TOBIAS WALL, a planter in St Kitts, died 2 December 1767. [GM.37.611]

GALLIE, ALEXANDER, born 1839, second son of Thomas Gallie in East Linton, Haddington, died in Basseterre, St Kitts, on 16 November 1868. [S.7919]

GALWAY, DAVID, a planter in Montserrat, in the 1660s, Major of the Militia in Montserrat, a member of the Council of Montserrat in the 1670s

GALWAY, JOHN, son of David Galway of Galway's Plantation, in Plymouth, Montserrat, 1719. [TNA.CO152.13]

GALLWEY, JOHN, died 13 April 1775. [St John's Cathedral burial register, Antigua]

THE PEOPLE OF THE LEEWARD ISLANDS, 1620 - 1860

GAMBLE, ANN, died in Antigua on 24 December 1745. [St John's Cathedral, Antigua]

GAMBLE, DOROTHY STEVENS, died in Antigua on 9 February 1763. [St John's Cathedral]

GAMBLE, EDWARD, died 11 October 1779. [St John's Cathedral burial register, Antigua]

GAMBLE, GABRIEL, died in Antigua on 5 June 1743. [St John's Cathedral, Antigua]

GAMBLE, Captain JAMES, died in Antigua on 30 April 1753. [St John's Cathedral, Antigua]

GAMBLE, JOHN, a Councillor of Antigua, 26 September, 1721. [PCCol.App.ii.821]

GAMBLE, LOUISA, a child, died in Five Islands, Antigua, on 31 January 1766. [St John's Cathedral]

GAMBLE, MARY, daughter of Edward Gamble, died in Antigua on 16 October 1745. [St John's Cathedral, Antigua]

GAMBLE, RACHEL, died at Five Islands on 5 July 1655. [St John's Cathedral, Antigua]

GAMBLE, RACHEL, born 1736, died in Antigua on 8 October 1772. [St John's Cathedral, Antigua]

GAMES, EDWARD, a yeoman, an indentured servant bound from Bristol to Nevis in 1660. [BRO]

GARDELIN, PHILIP, Governor of St Croix in 1733. [SSF]

GARDNER, JOHN, in St Kitts, probate, 1649, PCC. [TNA]

GARIGNE, MATTHEW, in St Kitts in 1712. [JCTP.1712.395]

GARNET, THOMAS, deceased by 1665, a planter in St Kitts, father of John Garnet, later in Ireland, a petition in 1674. [PCCol.1674.1000]

GARRALD, EDMOND, in the parish of Sandy Point, St Kitts on 7 February 1678. [TNA.COl.42]

GARRETT, ANTHONY, died in Antigua on 9 February 1754. [St John's Cathedral, Antigua]

GARRETT, ELIZABETH, died in Antigua on 22 August 1761. [St Philips]

GARRETT, FRANCES, died in Antigua on 5 February 1747. [St John's Cathedral, Antigua]

GARRETT, RIORSON, died in Antigua on 15 September 1744. [St John's Cathedral, Antigua]

GARRETT, SARAH, daughter of William Garrett, died in Antigua on 8 February 1739. [St John's Cathedral, Antigua]

GARRET, STEPHEN, aged 19, aboard the Paul of London, master Jo. Acklin, bound from Gravesend to St Kitts on 3 April 1635. [TNA.E157.20]

GARRETT, SUSANNAH, died in Antigua on 12 June 1747. [St John's Cathedral, Antigua]

GARRETT, THOMAS, aged 20, bound aboard the Mathew of London, master Richard Goodladd, for St Kitts on 21 May 1635. [TNA.E157.20]

GARRETT, WILLIAM, born 1666, died in Antigua on 18 May 1743. [St John's Cathedral, Antigua]

GARRET, ……., in Guadaloupe in 1724-1725. [SPAWI.1724.400; 1728.65]

THE PEOPLE OF THE LEEWARD ISLANDS, 1620 - 1860

GARTY, GEORGE, a Jacobite, a prisoner transported to Antigua in 1716. [SPAWI.1716.310]

GARVEY, WILLIAM, in St Kitts, probate 1780, PCC. [TNA]

GARVINE, EDWARD, a merchant in St Kitts, was admitted as a burgess and guilds-brother of Ayr on 3 October 1737. [ABR]

GASS, EDWARD, aged 20, aboard the Paul of London, master Jo. Acklin, bound from Gravesend to St Kitts on 3 April 1635. [TNA.E157.20]

GAVETT, LAURENCE, born on Jersey, a mariner aboard HMS Assistance, died at Guadaloupe, probate, 1692, PCC. [TNA]

GAYNOR, MARY, born 1730, daughter of Patrick Gaynor in Antigua, wife of Sir George Colebrook, died in Hampstead, London, on 13 August 1818. [GM.88.282]

GEORGE, ELIZABETH, wife of William Cunningham, died 27 February 1768, probate St Jan. [RAK.1749-1770.356]

GERRISH, WILLIAM, a merchant in Montserrat, a petition, 1718. [TNA.CO152.12]; in Plymouth, Montserrat, in 1719. [TNA.CO152.13]

GIBB, CHARLEY, probate, 1769, Christiansted. [RAK.80.192]

GIBBES, JOHN, a comber, bound from Bristol to Nevis in 1660. [BRO]

GIBBONS, DAVID, in the parish of St John Capistar, St Kitts, on 28 January 1678. [TNA.COI.42]

GIBSON, ..., a planter in Nevis in 1683. [PCCol.118]

GIBSON, EDWARD INMAN, son of Reverend J. G. Gibson in Holybourne, Hampshire, died in Antigua in 1828. [GM.98.286]

GIBSON, WILLIAM, a merchant in St Thomas, died 14 June 1841, testament, 1842. [NRS.SC70.I.61]

GIDEON, ROWLAND, aboard the sloop True Friendship, master Charles Callaghan, at Barbados on 7 October 1679 bound for Antigua. [TNA]

GIFFARD, JOHN, a schoolmaster, educated at Edinburgh University, emigrated to the Leeward Islands in 1703. [EMA.29]

GILBERT, GRACE, wife of Reverend T. M. Chambers, died 5 April 1856. [St George gravestone, Basse Terre, St Kitts]

GILBERT, Mrs MARY, born 17 September 1725 in London, died in Antigua on 18 July 1747, wife of Nathaniel Gilbert. [St John's Cathedral, Antigua]

GILCHRIST, GEORGINA BECKWITH, youngest daughter of William Gilchrist in Antigua, died in Teignmouth on 15 July 1829. [S.997.490]

GILLICH, G.E., in St Croix in 1802. [RDAG.I/2]

GILLINGHAM, HENRY, in Nevis, probate, 1664, PCC. [TNA]

GILLON, JAMES, from Inverness, a planter in St John's parish, Antigua, pre-1797. [ANY.I.148]

GILLESPIE, JOHN, probate 1768, Christiansted. [RAK.57.139]

GILMAN, RICHARD, a merchant in Nevis, probate, 1687, PCC. [TNA]

GLASGOW, JOHN, a minister, bound to Antigua in 1707. [EMA.30]

GLASS, JOHN, a Jacobite, a prisoner transported to Antigua in 1716. [SPAWI.1716.310][CTB.31.204]

THE PEOPLE OF THE LEEWARD ISLANDS, 1620 - 1860

GLASS, WILLIAM, in St Croix, eldest son of Reverend Hugh Glass in Kettle, Fife, and his wife Elizabeth Arnot, a deed. 21 December 1784. [NRS.RD3.244.530]

GLASSFORD, ROBERT, a merchant in Glasgow, late in St Kitts, purchased Montreal Estate in Grenada in 1761. [GA.T-MJ]

GLESSEN, JOHN, a Jacobite a prisoner transported to Antigua in 1716. [SPAWI.1716.310]

GLOSTER, ARCHIBALD, in St John, Antigua, witness to a deed, 6 April 1792. [NRS.RD2.255.122]

GLOSTER, RUSSEL, widow of Archibald Gloster MD in Antigua, died in London on 2 July 1808. [GM.78.661]

GLOVER, ROGER, in Nevis, probate, 1637, PCC. [TNA]

GOBLE, SAMUEL WICKHAM, born 28 August 1751, died 7 January 1753, and John Goble, born 4 June 1749, died 12 March 1756, sons of Martin and Mary Goble in Antigua. [St John's Cathedral, Antigua]

GOLD, ANNE, a spinster, bound from Bristol to Nevis in 1660. [BRO]

GOODWYN, JANE, aged 20, aboard the John of London, master James Waymoth, bound for St Kitts on 2 October 1635. [TNA.E157.20]

GOODWIN, MARY, aged 18, aboard the John of London, master James Waymoth, bound for St Kitts on 2 October 1635. [TNA.E157.20]

GOODWIN, MATTHEW, from St Kitts, died in London in 1773. [GM.43.622]

GOODWIN, THOMAS, aged 30, bound aboard the Mathew of London, master Richard Goodladd, for St Kitts on 21 May 1635. [TNA.E157.20]

GOOLD, PATRICK, in Plymouth, Montserrat, 1719. [TNA.CO152.13]

GORDON, ALBINIA, widow of William Gordon a stipendiary magistrate and Member of the Council of Tortula, died in St Kitts on 3 July 1840. [AJ.4834][W.66]

GORDON, ALEXANDER, born 1730, a planter returning to St Kitts aboard the Pemberton via Whitehaven in 1774. [TNA.T47.9/11]

GORDON, ALEXANDER, of Kingsgrange, born 1738, died 16 June 1790, [St Anthony's mi, Montserrat]; Customs collector in Montserrat, 1783. [NRS.CS17.1.2]; services of heirs, 1777. [NRS]

GORDON, ALEXANDER, in Montserrat, probate, 1795, PCC. [TNA]

GORDON, ALEXANDER, in St Croix in 1790, [Caribbeana.5.265]; will, 10 October 1800. [NRS.RD3.310.761]; died 24 January 1805, testament, 26 July 1806, Comm. Edinburgh. [NRS]

GORDON, ARCHIBALD, died 16 June 1736, husband of Elizabeth, probate, St Croix. [RAK.1735-1742.10]

GORDON, COSMO, died in St Croix on 26 August 1827. [AJ.4163]

GORDON, EDWARD, born 1728, returning to St Kitts from London aboard the Pemberton in February 1774. [TNA.T47.9/11]

GORDON, ELISABETH, daughter of Dr George Gordon in St Kitts, married Dr William Stedman a physician in St Croix, in Glasgow on 2 February 1795. [SM.57.132]

GORDON, Dr GEORGE, son of William Gordon, was admitted as a burgess of Banff in 1767, later in St Croix, graduated MD from

King's College, Aberdeen, on 18 August 1770, probate 29 January 1772, Christiansted. [RAK.139.22][BBR][KCA.133]

GORDON, GEORGE, MD in St Kitts, father of John Gordon who matriculated at Glasgow University in 1770 and graduated MA and MD in 1775. [RGG.227]

GORDON, Dr GEORGE, a planter, died 27 September 1797, husband of Mary, probate St Jan. [RAK.1797-1807.2/88]

GORDON, GEORGE, in St Croix in 1790. [Caribbeana.5.265]

GORDON, HANNAH, daughter of Francis Gordon in New York, late of Huntly, Aberdeenshire, died in St Kitts on 8 September 1862. [AJ.29/10/1862]

GORDON, HENRY, in Montserrat, probate 1793, PCC. [TNA]

GORDON, JAMES, in St Kitts, 1726. [RSM]; a planter in St Kitts 1723-1730. [NRS.GD237.12.50]

GORDON, JAMES, a merchant in St Kitts, was granted the lands of Tippersie on 23 February 1767. [NRS.RGS.109.165]

GORDON, JOHN, ['Jan Gording'], a widower, born in Scotland, settled in St Kitts, married Judith Markoe, daughter of Johannes Markoe and his wife Maria Gerrits in St Eustatia, there on 31 December 1735. [Afscrifen huwelijksakten van St Eustatius van 1710-1750]

GORDON, JOHN, MD, physician to the King of Denmark for the Danish West Indies, died in Bath on 16 February 1807. [SM.69.159][AJ.3085][Bath Abbey gravestone]

GORDON, JOHN, born 1740, died in Cane Valley, St Croix, on 22 July 1824. [BM.16.734]; in St Croix in 1790. [Caribbean.5.265]

GORDON, JOHN, born 1809, a Major of the 47th Regiment, died in St Kitts on 16 March 1843. [EEC.20596]

GORDON, ROBERT MELVILLE, in St Croix in 1790. [Caribbeana.5.265]

GORDON, WILLIAM, from Aberdeenshire, a physician in Antigua, 17...

GORDON, WILLIAM, a stipendiary magistrate and Member of the Council of Tortula, died in St Kitts when bound for Tortula on 18 June 1840; his wife Albinia died in St Kitts on 3 July 1840. [AJ.4832/4834][EEC.20091/20096]

GORDON, WILLIAM, a merchant in Antigua, died in St John's, Antigua, on 27 July 1847. [EEC.21543]

GORE, JOHN, died in February 1770, son of John Gore. [James Watson's plantation gravestone, Antigua]

GORTIE, GEORGE, a Jacobite, a prisoner transported to Antigua in 1716. [CTB.31.204]

GOSLIN, JO., aged 20, bound aboard the Mathew of London, master Richard Goodladd, for St Kitts on 21 May 1635. [TNA.E157.20]

GOSLING, THOMAS, aged 22, bound aboard the Mathew of London, master Richard Goodladd, for St Kitts on 21 May 1635. [TNA.E157.20]

GOSSE, PHILIP, in Nevis, probate, 1664, PCC. [TNA]

GOULDING, JANE, born 1618, from St Thomas the Apostle in Devon, bound from Dartmouth to St Kitts in 1634. [TNA]

GOVETT, Mrs J., died in St Kitts on 23 January 1794. [GM.64.385]

GOW, WILLIAM, a watchmaker in Glasgow, later in St Kitts, 1783.
[NRS.CS17.1.2]

GRADY, JAMES, in the parish of Sandy Point, St Kitts on 7
February 1678. [TNA.COI.42]

GRAHAM, GEORGE, formerly a merchant in Copenhagen, later a
planter in St Croix, now in Glasgow in 1798. [HCR.21B3]; died in
Glasgow on 13 June 1798. [GM.68.542][AJ.2630]; probate 1800
PCC. [TNA]

GRAHAM, HUGH, late of Antigua, died in Meadow Place,
Edinburgh, on 1 May 1826. [EEC.17888]

GRAHAM, JOHN, in Antigua in 1757. [DA.Ogilvy pp.15]

GRAHAM, ROBERT, a planter in Antigua, a deed, 4 March 1778.
[NRS.RD4.278.326]

GRAHAM, WILLIAM, died on 30 November 1750, husband of
Mary, probate, St Croix. [RAK.1747-1754.320]

GRAHAM, WILLIAM LECKIE, a merchant from Glasgow, died in St
Thomas on 6 June 1843. [EEC.20635]

GRAINGER, AGNES, daughter of Dr James Grainger in St Kitts,
1772. [NRS.CS16.1.151]

GRAINGER, HELEN, daughter of James Grainger a physician in St
Kitts, 1782. [NRS.CS17.1.1]; services of heirs, 1781. [NRS]

GRAINGER, Dr JAMES, in St Kitts, an MD of Edinburgh University,
applied for admittance to the Royal College of Physicians of
Edinburgh in 1763. [NRS.NRAS.726]; services of hers, 1766, [NRS];
father of Louisa, Agnes, and Ellen in St Kitts in 1772.
[NRS.CS96.1.151]; testament, 1790, Comm. Edinburgh. [NRS]

GRAINGER, LOUISA, daughter of Dr James Grainger in St Kitts, 1772. [NRS.CS16.1.151]

GRANT, ALEXANDER, a teacher in Antigua who converted to Anglicanism, via London to Antigua in 1749, settled in Tortula, dead by 1750. [EMA.30][FPA.284/289]

GRANT, ALEXANDER, in St Croix in 1790, [Caribbeana.5.265]; in 1809. [NRS.GD23.6.459]

GRANT, ALEXANDER, son of Alexander Grant in St Croix, was educated at King's College, Aberdeen, from 1795, graduated MA in 1800. [KCA.2.379-380]

GRANT, COLIN, in St Croix in 1790. [Caribbeana.5.265]

GRANT, DUNCAN, in Antigua in 1753, [NRS.CS96.644]; in Antigua in 1758, [DA.Ogilvy pp.28]; a merchant in Antigua, was admitted as a burgess of Edinburgh on 2 July 1760. [EBR]; a planter who died on passage from Antigua to Britain on 26 April 1770. [SM.32.342]

GRANT, FRANCIS BELL, born 1811, Rector of the Parish of Parham, Antigua, and from 1859 to 1869 was Rector of Christ Church in Barbados, died in England on 29 September 1888.

GRANT, HUMPHREY, in Antigua in 1753. [NRS.CS96.645]

GRANT, JAMES, born in Abernethy, Strathspey, late of St Thomas in the Vale, Jamaica, died in St Croix on 28 October 1830. [AJ.4351]

GRANT, JOHN, died 1760. [Antigua gravestone]

GRANT, JOSHUA, eldest son of Duncan Grant a merchant in Inverness and his wife Anne Grant, a deed of attorney subscribed in Basseterre, St Kitts, on 3 February 1766, witnessed by John

THE PEOPLE OF THE LEEWARD ISLANDS, 1620 - 1860

Fraser and Alexander Fraser clerks to Smith and Baillie, merchants in St Kitts. [NRS.SC29.55.11.331]

GRANT, PATRICK, in Antigua in 1753. [NRS.CS96.644]; in Antigua from 1741 to 1762. [NRS.GD248.48.1/2]

GRANT, PATRICK, a physician, uncle of James Grant of Curron, died in Antigua on 26 December 1770. [SM.33.331] [NRS.NRAS.771.bundle 295]

GRANT, RICHARD, from Edinburgh, emigrated via Bristol to St Kitts in 1660. [BRO]

GRANT, SAMUEL, in Antigua in 1753. [NRS.CS96.644]

GRANT, WILLIAM, born in Arbroath before 1780, son of George Grant and his wife Agnes Mitchell, settled in Antigua by 1815. [Arbroath gravestone]

GRAVEN, JOHN, born 1734, a gentleman from London, via London aboard the Catherine bound for St Kitts in 1774. [TNA.T47.9/11]

GRAY, EDWARD, aged 32, aboard the Paul of London, master Jo. Acklin, bound from Gravesend to St Kitts on 3 April 1635. [TNA.E157.20]

GRAY, ROBERT, in Antigua in 1757. [DA.Ogilvie pp.21]

GRAY, SAMUEL, a minister sent to Maryland in 1705, from there to Antigua in 1710. [EMA.31]

GRAY, T., in St Kitts, eldest daughter of the Marquis of Tweedale, died in 1757. [GM.27.338]

GREATHEAD, CRAISTER, Commander in Chief of the Leeward Islands, a letter, 5 June 1776. [JCTP.20.9.1776]

GREATHEAD, Lady MARY, in St Kitts, probate 1774, PCC. [TNA]

THE PEOPLE OF THE LEEWARD ISLANDS, 1620 - 1860

GREATHEAD, MARY, in St Kitts, probate 1790, PCC. [TNA]

GREATHEAD, RICHARD, and his wife, in St Kitts, died on 23 December 1763. [GM.33.619]

GREATHEAD, SAMUEL, in St Kitts, probate 1766, PCC. [TNA]

GREENE, HENRY CHARLES, born 1821, fourth son of Benjamin Greene in Bury St Edmund, died in St Kitts on 7 August 1840. [GM.ns.14.446]

GREENE, JO., aged 29, bound aboard the Mathew of London, master Richard Goodladd, for St Kitts on 21 May 1635. [TNA.E157.20]

GREEN, PATRICK, in the parish of Sandy Point, St Kitts on 7 February 1678. [TNA.COI.42]

GREENSLATT, THOMAS, aboard the sloop True Friendship, master Charles Callaghan, at Barbados bound for Antigua on 7 October 1679. [TNA]

GREENWAY, ELIZABETH, died in Antigua on 22 January 1741. [St George's]

GREENWAY, JOHN, died in Antigua in February 1766. [St Peter's, Antigua]

GREENWAY, MATTHEW WILLIAM, died in Antigua on 5 December 1765. [St George's, Antigua]

GREGG, JAMES, a minister sent to St Kitts in 1711. [EMA.31]

GRIFFIN, DENNIS, aboard the sloop John and Francis, master John Howard, at Barbados bound for Antigua on 2 September 1679. [TNA]

THE PEOPLE OF THE LEEWARD ISLANDS, 1620 - 1860

GRIFFIN, GEORGE, from Marazion, a husbandman aged 18, a husbandman who emigrated via Plymouth aboard the Margaret bound for St Kitts in 1634. [TNA.E157.18]

GRIFFITHS, EDWARD, the Solicitor General of the 'Ceded Islands', died in Antigua on 24 January 1766. [GM.36.47]

GRIGGSON, RICHARD, aged 34, bound aboard the Mathew of London, master Richard Goodladd, for St Kitts on 21 May 1635. [TNA.E157.20]

GRUNWALD, ISAAC, a Dutch Reformed Church pastor on St Thomas from 1716. [RAK.WIC.430]

GUICHARD, FRANCIS, and other children of Francis Guichard, Huguenots in St Kitts, a petition, 1714-1715. [SPAWI.1714.74][JCTP.1715.17]

GUICHARD, FRANCIS, and other children of Arouet Guichard, Huguenots in St Kitts, a petition, 1714-1715. [SPAWI.1714.74]

GUICHINOT, HENRY, in Antigua in 1723. PCCol.1725.87]

GUIGNARD, MATHURIN, in Nevis in 1719, formerly in St Kitts. [SPAWI.1719.466i]

GUINARD, LOUISA, in St Kitts, probate, 1798, PCC. [TNA]

GUION, Captain, in Bassend, St Croix, in 1777-. [RDAG]

GUITTEAU, ..., in St Kitts in 1689-1690. [SPAWI.1689.193; 1690.789i/988/1004i]

GULD, ROBERT, born 1753, a clerk in London, via London aboard the Catherine bound for St Kitts in 1774. [TNA.T47.9/11]

GUNN, JOHN, at Halfway Tree, St Kitts, in 1667. [TNA.CO1.42/193]

GURGE, WILLIAM, born 1614, a shoe-maker from Exeter, bound from Dartmouth to St Kitts in 1634. [TNA]

GURNEY, JOHN, in Nevis, probate, 1705, PCC. [TNA]

GUYHARD, FRANCIS, in St Kitts in 1714. [PCCol.1714.1069]

HACKETT, WILLIAM PATRICK, died 17... [St George gravestone, Basse Terre, St Kitts]

HADBIE, THOMAS, aged 22, bound aboard the Mathew of London, master Richard Goodladd, for St Kitts on 21 May 1635. [TNA.E157.20]

HADDOCK, JOHN, on Saba, petitioned the Dutch West India Company in Amsterdam in 1772. [DNA.Inv.1151]

HAGGART, CHARLES, in St Thomas, 1789. [NRS.NRAS.0623.T-MJ.427.36]

HAGGART, CHARLES, jr., from St Thomas, died in London on 12 December 1812. [GM.82.672]

HAIG, WILLIAM, born 20 June 1670, son of Anthony Haig of Bemersyde, a merchant in Antigua. [Haigs of Bemersyde, Edinburgh, 1881, p.443]

HAINES, CHARLES SAMUEL, a witness at Cap Basseterre, St Kitts on 18 February 1797. [NRS.RD2.270.347]

HAIES, WILLIAM, aged 24, aboard the Paul of London, master Jo. Acklin, bound from Gravesend to St Kitts on 3 April 1635. [TNA.E157.20]

HALDANE, Miss, daughter of John Haldane in St Kitts, married Thomas Foster a Member of Parliament on 2 June 1741. [GM.11.331]

HALE, BARNABIE, aboard the barque Dove, master Anthony Jenour, at Barbados on 29 October 1679 bound for Nevis. [TNA]

THE PEOPLE OF THE LEEWARD ISLANDS, 1620 - 1860

HALE, JAMES, in Nevis, probate, 1674, PCC. [TNA]

HALFHIDE, PHILLIP, in St Kitts, probate, 1657, PCC. [TNA]

HALIBURTON, THOMAS, a merchant in St Eustatia, services of heirs, 1787, [NRS]; testament, 1795, Comm. Edinburgh. [NRS]

HALL, EDWARD, the Attorney General of the Grenades, died in Antigua in 1766. [GM.36.247][SM.28.335]

HALL, Dr JAMES, from Dumfries, died in St Croix on 11 June 1824. [EA]

HALL, RICHARD, son of James and Eleanor Hall, died in September 179- aged 6 years. [St George gravestone, Basse Terre, St Kitts]

HALL, THOMAS, aged 25, bound aboard the Mathew of London, master Richard Goodladd, for St Kitts on 21 May 1635. [TNA.E157.20]

HALL, WILLIAM, a Jacobite, a prisoner transported to Antigua in 1716. [SPAWI.1716.310][CTB.31.204]

HALLEY, ABRAHAM, on Saba, petitioned the Dutch West India Company in Amsterdam in 1772. [DNA.Inv.1151]

HALLEY, PETER, on Saba, petitioned the Dutch West India Company in Amsterdam in 1772. [DNA.Inv.1151]

HALLIDAY, ALEXANDER, born 1731, a merchant in St Kitts, died on 1 October 1754 – brother of John and William. [St George gravestone, Basse Terre, St Kitts]

HALLIDAY, JOHN, in Antigua in 1757. [DA.Ogilvie pp.17]

HALLIDAY, WILLIAM, in St Kitts, died in 1759. [GM.29.497]

HALLIDAY, Mrs, widow of William Halliday in St Kitts, died in London on 7 October 1810. [GM.80.493]

HALLOWELL, HUGH, aged 22, bound aboard the Mathew of London, master Richard Goodladd, for St Kitts on 21 May 1635. [TNA.E157.20]

HAMBLETON, JANE, a spinster, bound from Bristol to Nevis in 1660. [BRO]

HAMILTON, ALEXANDER, in Montserrat in 1696. [TNA.Association Oath Rolls]

HAMILTON, ALEXANDER, settled in Nevis before 1700. [DP.308]

HAMILTON, ALEXANDER, born 1757 in Nevis, son of James Hamilton, a physician, and Mrs Rachel Faucette Levine from St Kitts, moved to St Croix in 1765, educated at King's College in New York, a Revolutionary War hero, a lawyer and politician, husband of Elizabeth Schuyler, killed in a duel in New York on 11 July 1804.

HAMILTON, ALEXANDER, born 12 December 1767, son of the Earl of Selkirk, an army officer, died in Guadaloupe in June 1794. [SP.7.522]

HAMILTON, ANDREW, died 3 April 1808. [St John's, Fig Tree, Nevis, gravestone]

HAMILTON, CHARLES, late surgeon in Nevis, son of John Hamilton of Gilkerscleugh, a deed, 8 July 1738. [NRS.RD4.176.1.181]

HAMILTON, CHARLES, born 1757, a servant of James Irwin a physician, from London to Antigua on the Nancy in December 1773. [TNA.T47.9/11]

HAMILTON, DUNBAR, born 9 July 1766, son of the Earl of Selkirk, an officer of the Royal Navy, died at St Kitts on 29 October 1796. [SP.7.522]

HAMILTON, HUGH, Captain of the 96th Regiment in St Croix, son of John Hamilton of Sundrum, 1809-1810. [NRS.GD51.6.693.1/2; GD51.6.700]

HAMILTON, JOHN, in Antigua in 1696. [TNA.Association Oath Rolls]; a representative in Antigua, was appointed a Councillor of Antigua in August 1699, [SPAWI.1678.741; 1699.658] [PCCol.]

HAMILTON, JOHN, a Councillor of Antigua, 26 September, 1721. [PCCol.App.ii.821]; dead by 18 April 1726.

HAMILTON, JOHN, in Antigua in 1753. [NRS.CS96.644]

HAMILTON, JUDITH, in St Kitts, probate 1763, PCC. [TNA]

HAMILTON, Colonel WALTER, in Nevis in 1696. [TNA.Association Oath Rolls]; in Nevis by 1699, [SPAWI.1699.714]; was appointed as a Councillor of Nevis on 22 August 1699. [PCCol]

HAMILTON, WILLIAM, in St Kitts, probate, 1698, PCC. [TNA]

HAMILTON, WILLIAM LESLIE, the Attorney General of the Leeward Islands, and a Councillor of St Kitts, died 9 October 1780. [GM.50.495]

HAMILTON, ..., a schoolmaster, emigrated to the Leeward Islands in 1701, in Nevis by 1716. [EMA.32][FPA.270]

HAMILTON, Mrs, born 1748, daughter of Benjamin Vaughan a prize-broker, wife of Mr Hamilton a merchant in St Kitts, died in Enfield on 14 March 1782. [GM.52.151]

HAMRAH, MICHAEL, in St Croix in 1768. [SSF]

HANCOCK, ALEXANDER, aboard the sloop True Friendship, master Charles Callaghan, at Barbados on 7 October 1679 bound for Antigua. [TNA]

HANDYSIDE, ROBERT, a Jacobite, a prisoner transported to Montserrat in 1716. [SPAWI.1716.313][CTB.31.206]

HANNAH, ANDREW, aboard the sloop Katherine, master Andrew Gall, at Barbados on27 November 1679 bound for Antigua. [TNA]

HANNAM, JANE, wife of Richard Hannam, died 28 Janaury 1867. [St Anthony's mi, Montserrat]

HANSON, FRANCIS, born 1721, died in Antigua on 23 November 1747. [St John's Cathedral, Antigua]

HARAGIN, DANIEL, in the parish of Sandy Point, St Kitts on 7 February 1678. [TNA.COl.42]

HARCUM, ANNE, born 18 January 1757, daughter of William Harcum and his wife Anne, died 14 February 1774. [St Anthony's mi, Montserrat]

HARCUM, ELIZABETH, born in 1744, wife of Thomas Harcum, died on 24 May 1774. [St Anthony's mi, Montserrat]

HARDCASTLE, JOHN, a notary public and Deputy Secretary of Antigua, 1784. [NRS.AC7.61]

HARDING, GEORGE STEINETH, from St Croix, married Margaret Crawford in Fairfield, Ayrshire, on 26 August 1811. [DPCA.476]

HARDING, JESSY, eldest daughter of the late Henry Harding of HM Customs in Nevis, married Reverend F L Lloyd of Aldworth, Berkshire, on 10 February 1859. [GM.ns.2.6.316]

THE PEOPLE OF THE LEEWARD ISLANDS, 1620 - 1860

HARDMAN, JOHN, emigrated from Ireland via Antigua to Pennsylvania before 1739. Sought there in 1738. [Pa.Gaz.6.7.1738]

HARDWICK, WILLIAM, a Jacobite, a prisoner transported to St Kitts in 1716. [SPAWI.1716.312][CTB.31.207]

HARE, HAMIL, in Falmouth parish, died in Antigua on 7 July 1701. [St Paul's]

HARLAW, JOHN, in Montserrat, son of Alexander Harlaw a merchant in Fraserburgh, services of heirs, 1789. [NRS]

HARLOWE, JO., aged 16, bound aboard the Mathew of London, master Richard Goodladd, for St Kitts on 21 May 1635. [TNA.E157.20]

HARMAN, Mrs, widow of Samuel Harman in Antigua, died in Cheltenham on 3 March 1820. [GM.90.284]

HARMAN, ANN ELIZABETH, daughter of William D. Harman a barrister in Montpelier, Antigua, married William Mure, MD, of the 42nd Regiment, in Bermuda on 2 January 1851. [FJ.944]

HARMAN, EMY, died in Antigua on 1 January 1769. [St Philip's]

HARMAN, JOHN, died in Antigua on 11 March 1768. [St Philip's]

HARMAN, SAMUEL, born 1696, died in Antigua on 22 November 1759, husband of Dorothy, born 1710, died 29 May 1754. [Montpelier gravestone, Antigua]

HARMAN, SAMUEL, born 16 November 1730, died in Antigua om 16 November 1767, husband of Mary, parents of Mrs Patricia Cusack, born 12 May 1744, died 11 December 1769. [Montpellier gravestone, Antigua]

HARPER, CORNELIA ELIZABETH, born 1783, wife of Thomas Harper the Secretary of St Kitts, died there on 16 February 1819. [GM.88.485]

HARPER, WILLIAM, born 1794, died 28 July 1834. [St Anthony's mi, Montserrat]

HARRIS, JAMES, born 1755, a surgeon in London, from London aboard the Betsey bound for St Kitts in 1775. [TNA.T47.9/11]

HARRIS, JAMES, a Stipendiary Magistrate in St Kitts, married Mary Augusta Hart, eldest daughter of Nathaniel Hart, the Colonial Treasurer, in Paris on 19 June 1851. [GM.ns36.315]

HARRIS, MARTHA, from Shrewsbury, Shropshire, bound from Bristol to St Kitts n 1660. [BRO]

HARRIES, MARY, born 1611, from Stoke Pomneroy in Devon, bound from Dartmouth to St Kitts in 1634. [TNA]

HARRIS, MARY ANN, born 1757, died in Antigua on 1 December 1763, daughter of William and Mary Harris. [Vernon's Estate mi]

HARRIS, RICHARD, a miller, bound from Bristol to Nevis in 1660. [BRO]

HARROW, DORMAN, in St Kitts, probate, 1650, PCC. [TNA]

HART, JOHN, Governor of the Leeward Islands in 1723. [TNA.CO152.14]

HARRY, NICHOLAS, a yeoman, an indentured servant bound from Bristol to Nevis in 1660. [BRO]

HART, JOAB, a merchant on Antigua, will, 1758. [PWI]

HART, JOHN JOHNSON, in St Kitts, probate 17875, PCC. [TNA]

THE PEOPLE OF THE LEEWARD ISLANDS, 1620 - 1860

HARTE, MARY, born 1616, a spinster from Lyme, bound from Dartmouth to St Kitts in 1634. [TNA]

HART, Dr., born 1753, late a physician in St Kitts, died in Walcot, Somerset, in 1813. [GM.83.668]

HARTMAN, ELIZABETH, in St Kitts, 1712. [JCTP.P243]

HARTMAN, JOAN, in Nevis, 1712. [JCTP.P245]

HARVIE, ALEXANDER, born 1725 in Midmar, Aberdeenshire, late of Antigua, in Aberdeen in 1760. [APB.2.204]

HARVIE, FRANCIS, of Antigua, died in Dominica on 29 January 1839. [SG.8.757]

HARVEY, THOMAS, a gentleman from Bristol, died in Nevis, probate, 1691, PCC. [TNA]

HARWOOD, MARGARET, born 1612, a spinster in Stoke Gabriel in Devon, bound from Dartmouth to St Kitts in 1634. [TNA.E157.18]

HASSELL, GEORGE, on Saba, petitioned the Dutch West India Company in Amsterdam in 1772. [DNA.Inv.1151]

HASSELL, HENRY, on Saba, petitioned the Dutch West India Company in Amsterdam in 1772. [DNA.Inv.1151]

HASSELL, HERCULES, on Saba, petitioned the Dutch West India Company in Amsterdam in 1772. [DNA.Inv.1151]

HASSELL, JOHN, on Saba, petitioned the Dutch West India Company in Amsterdam in 1772. [DNA.Inv.1151]

HASSELL, PETER, on Saba, petitioned the Dutch West India Company in Amsterdam in 1772. [DNA.Inv.1151]

HASSELL, RICHARD, on Saba, petitioned the Dutch West India Company in Amsterdam in 1772. [DNA.Inv.1151]

HASSELL, THOMAS, on Saba, petitioned the Dutch West India Company in Amsterdam in 1772. [DNA.Inv.1151]

HATHWAY, S., son of R. Hathway in Hereford, died in Nevis in 1800. [GM.70.1112]

HATTERTON, JO, aged 38, bound aboard the Mathew of London, master Richard Goodladd, for St Kitts on 21 May 1635. [TNA.E157.20]

HAUKINS, WILLIAM, born 1609, a glover from Exeter, bound from Dartmouth to St Kitts in 1634. [TNA]

HAWES, ELIZA HAWES, born 1805, died 1814. [Antigua gravestone]

HAY, ALEXANDER GEORGE, in Montserrat in 1795. [NRS.NRAS.0335]

HAY, CHARLES, from Nevis, married Georgina Augusta Mair, youngest daughter of the late Reverend W. Mair, in London on 10 March 1847. [GM.ns.27.648]

HAY, JAMES, formerly of the Customs in Anguilla, died there on 9 April 1829. [BM.26.268]; his son was born in Basseterre, St Kitts, on 17 August 1820. [BM.8.239]

HAYTON, JAMES, in Nevis, probate, 1720, PCC. [TNA]

HEALY, JOHN, in St Thomas, Middle Island, St Kitts on 7 February 1678. [TNA.COl.42]

HEATH, MAHER SHAHEL HASHBETH, was resettled in Nevis in 1712. [JCTP.1709-1715.383]

HEATHCOTE, Miss, eldest daughter of Sir William Heathcote, married Langford Lovell, in Antigua on 28 April 1798. [GM.68.441]

THE PEOPLE OF THE LEEWARD ISLANDS, 1620 - 1860

HEELIS, GEORGE, aged 19, aboard the John of London, master James Waymoth, bound for St Kitts on 2 October 1635. [TNA.E157.20]

HELAINE, WILLIAM, aged 21, bound aboard the Mathew of London, master Richard Goodladd, for St Kitts on 21 May 1635. [TNA.E157.20]

HELMES, SARAH, in Nevis, probate, 1690, PCC. [TNA]

HELOT, EDMUND, died in S Kitts in 1680. [SPAWI.1718.510]

HELOT, JOHN, born 1678 on St Kitts, mate of HM Galley Leeds in 1697. [TNA.HCA.Vol.82.11.5.1699]

HELY, MATHEW, aged 21, bound aboard the Mathew of London, master Richard Goodladd, for St Kitts on 21 May 1635. [TNA.E157.20]

HENDERSON, ALEXANDER, in Nevis in 1682. [SPAWI.1682.602]

HENDERSON, ALEXANDER, a merchant in St Kitts, was admitted as a burgess of Banff in 1770. [BBR]

HENDERSON, Captain ARCHIBALD, a planter in Antigua in the 1660s. [SPAWI.1672.806]

HENDERSON, JAMES, in St Croix in 1790. [Caribbeana.5.265]

HENDERSON, JOHN, a surgeon in Antigua, son of John Henderson of Cleughbrae, services of heirs, 1797. [NRS]

HENDERSON, WILLIAM, a Jacobite, a prisoner transported to St Kitts in 1716. [SPAWI.1716.312][CTB.31.207]

HENDRIE, DAVID, a merchant in St Martins, son of James Hendrie a merchant in St Kitts, 1782. [NRS.CS17.1.1]

HENDRICKSEN, LEONARD, a planter in Nevis in 1712. [JCTP.P224]

HENDRICKSON, WILLIAM, in Nevis, married Eleanor Fyfe, daughter of William Fyfe in Jamaica, in London on 7 January 1821. [EA]

HENMAN, JO., aged 19, aboard the <u>John of London</u>, master James Waymoth, bound for St Kitts on 2 October 1635. [TNA.E157.20]

HENNING, HEGIDIUS, in St Croix in 1768. [SSF]

HENNIS, DARBY, in the parish of Sandy Point, St Kitts on 7 February 1678. [TNA.COl.42]

HENRICHSEN, HENRICH, a Dutch Reformed Church minister in St Croix in 1742. [RAK.WIC.429]

HENRY, JAMES, probate 28 July 1773, Christiansted. [RAK.173.157]

HENRY, Dr JOHN, in St Croix, was admitted as a burgess of Arbroath, Angus, in 1791. [ArBR]

HENTEYNE, ANTHONY, in Antigua in 1709. [SPAWI.1709.487ii]

HERBERT, Mrs DOROTHY, born 1682, wife of Thomas Herbert, daughter of Major Henry Lytton of Nevis, died 16 January 1724. [St George gravestone, Nevis]

HERBERT, JOHN RICHARDSON, President of Nevis, died 18 January 1793, husband of Elizabeth born 1733, died 29 September 1769, parents of Martha Williams Hamilton. [St John's, Fig Tree, Nevis, gravestone][SM.55.153][GM.63.373]

HERBERT, JOSEPH, in Nevis, 1720s. [RSM]

HERBERT, JOSEPH, President of Nevis, died 13 October 1767. [GM.38.47][SM.30.54]

THE PEOPLE OF THE LEEWARD ISLANDS, 1620 - 1860

HERBERT, Mrs, wife of Joseph Herbert in Montserrat, died 3 December 1796. [GM.66.168]

HERBERT, MAGNUS MORTON, from Nevis, died in Brussels on 31 October 1834. [GM.105.446]

HERBERT, SARAH, born 1732, daughter of Thomas and Frances Herbert, died 5 September 1785. [St John's, Fig Tree, Nevis, gravestone]

HERON, PATRICK, born 4 December 1798, son of Reverend James Heron and his wife Mary Donaldson in Kirkgunzeon, died in St Kitts on 10 November 1824. [Kirkgunzeon gravestone] [F.2.280]

HESSELBERG, ENGELBRET, a bailiff in Christiansted,St Croix in 1768. [SSF]

HESSEN, JAN, in Nevis, 1678. [SPAWI.1678.849]

HESTER, Mrs AGNES HELM, born 1726 in Nevis, died in Walworth, Surrey, in 1806. [GM.76.90]

HETHERINGTON, H., daughter of R. Hetherington in Tortula, married Andrew Anderson from Tortula, in Durham on 25 April 1799. [GM.69.525][EA.3688.287]

HEWETT, Captain JAMES, a planter in Nevis, probate, 1656, PCC. [TNA]

HEWETT, THOMAS, from St Kitts, died in London on 23 June 1766. [GM.36.294]

HEWITSON, Mrs JUDITH, wife of C. Hewitson a merchant in Antigua, services of heirs, 1794. [NRS]

HEYLINGER, JOHAN, Commander of St Eustatius from 1730 to 1736. [NWIC][SPAWI.1737.318]

HEYLIGER, JOHN, in Prince's Quarter, St Croix, in 1770. [RDAG]

HEYLIGER, PETER, in St Croix in 1768. [SSF]

HEYS, JAMES, a Jacobite a prisoner transported to St Kitts in 1716. [SPAWI.1716.312][CTB.31.207]

HICKS, R. L., of Nevis, died on his passage from the West Indies on 22 March 1785. [GM.56.440]

HICKS, RICHARD LYTCOTT, born 1810, died 10 January 1836. [St George gravestone, Nevis]

HIDE, JAMES, aged 22, bound aboard the Mathew of London, master Richard Goodladd, for St Kitts on 21 May 1635. [TNA.E157.20]

HIGGINS, JOHN, died in Nevis in 1822 from wounds received in a duel with Walter Maynard the President of Nevis. [BM.12.522]

HILK, JOHN, aboard the sloop True Friendship, master Charles Callaghan, at Barbados on 7 October 1679 bound for Antigua. [TNA]

HILL, ABRAM CHALIVILL, in Tortula, witness to a deed, 18 September 1803. [NRS.RD3.303.743]

HILL, ADAM, probate October 1767, Christiansted. [RAK.37]

HILL, EDWARD, a cooper from Bristol, died in Nevis, probate, 1691, PCC. [TNA]

HILL, ELIZABETH, born 1610, from Brixham in Devon, bound from Dartmouth to St Kitts in 1634. [TNA]

HILL, Dr JAMES, from Dumfries, settled in St Croix, married Arabella Sherlock, daughter of Thomas Sherlock of Garrybritts, in London in 1810. [EA.4899.303]; died in St Croix on 11 June 1824. [BM.16.488]

THE PEOPLE OF THE LEEWARD ISLANDS, 1620 - 1860

HILL, JOAN, aged 21, aboard the John of London, master James Waymoth, bound for St Kitts on 2 October 1635. [TNA.E157.20]

HILL, JO., aged 18, bound aboard the Mathew of London, master Richard Goodladd, for St Kitts on 21 May 1635. [TNA.E157.20]

HILL, JOSEPH, probate August 1767, Christiansted. [RAK]

HILL, NICHOLAS, died on 8 June 1813 in Montserrat. [GM.83.194]

HILL, ROBERT, a burgher of St Croix, a deed, 6 November 1820. [NRS.RD5.251.310]

HILL, THOMAS, merchant in St Kitts, 1766. [NRS.CS16.1.125]

HILL, THOMAS, born 1785, a Councillor and Chief Judge of Montserrat, died there on 26 October 1825. [GM.96.191] [DPCA.1224]

HILL, Dr, from St Croix, married Arabela Sherlock, daughter of Thomas Sherlock of Garrybritts, in London in 1810. [EA.4899.303]

HILLIARD, JO. aged 35, bound aboard the Mathew of London, master Richard Goodladd, for St Kitts on 21 May 1635. [TNA.E157.20]

HINSELIN, ..., in Guadaloupe in 1674. [SPAWI.1674.1333]

HIX, WILLIAM, a yeoman, an indentured servant, from Bristol to Nevis in 1660. [BRO]

HOBBS, RICHARD, born 1740, with his sister Ann, emigrated via Plymouth bound for St Kitts in 1773, to be a planter there. [TNA.T47.9/11]

HOCKSLEY, JOHN, born 1606, a tailor from Stoke Cannon in Devon, bound from Dartmouth to St Kitts in 1634. [TNA]

HODDINS, JO., aged 50, bound aboard the Mathew of London, master Richard Goodladd, for St Kitts on 21 May 1635. [TNA.E157.20]

HODGES, ANTHONY, a planter and deputy governor of Montserrat, 17..... father of Elizabeth. [HS.7.6/29]

HODGE, LANGFORD LOVELL, a Councillor of Antigua, died in 1817. [GM.87.379]

HODGE, LANGFORD LOVELL, from Antigua, married Anne Elizabeth Hart, only daughter of William Hart in Madras, in Edinburgh on 2 April 1830. [BM.27.964]

HODGE, MICHAEL LOVELL, from Antigua, graduated MD from Edinburgh University in 1795. [EMG.26]

HODGES, THOMAS, aged 20, bound aboard the Mathew of London, master Richard Goodladd, for St Kitts on 21 May 1635. [TNA.E157.20]

HODGE, WILLIAM PACKWOOD, eldest son of Robert Hodge a merchant in St Eustatia, matriculated at the University of Glasgow in 1809, graduated MD from the University of Edinburgh in 1814. [MAGU.246][EMG.49]

HOFMAN, JOHAN LAMBERT URBAN BARCEL, a Dutch Reformed Church minister in St Croix in 1757. [RAK.WIC.429]

HOGAN, MATTHEW, in the parish of Sandy Point, St Kitts on 7 February 1678. [TNA.COI.42]

HOGG, GEORGE, a merchant in St Croix, died in Paisley on 28 February 1821. [EA]

HOLBORON, GEORGE, born 1857, President of the Council of Antigua, died 5 August 1891. [Antiguan Archives]

THE PEOPLE OF THE LEEWARD ISLANDS, 1620 - 1860

HOLEMAN, ROGER, aboard the sloop True Friendship, master Charles Callaghan, at Barbados on 24 December 1679 bound for Antigua. [TNA]

HOLLIS, NICHOLAS, aged 20, aboard the Paul of London, master Jo. Acklin, bound from Gravesend to St Kitts on 3 April 1635. [TNA.E157.20]

HOLMES, HUGH, a merchant in Antigua, will, 1762. [PWI]

HOLMES, JO., aged 22, aboard the Paul of London, master Jo. Acklin, bound from Gravesend to St Kitts on 3 April 1635. [TNA.E157.20]

HOLMES, RICHARD, in St Kitts, died in January 1757. [GM.27.92]

HOLMES, SARAH, in Nevis, probate, 1690, PCC. [TNA]

HOLT, JAMES, from the Leeward Islands, died on 1 June 1748. [GM.17.284]

HOLT, JOSEPH, aboard the Hopewell, master John Ayres, at Barbados on 29 October 1679 bound for Antigua. [TNA]

HOLT, THOMAS, in St Kitts, probate, 1799, PCC. [TNA]

HOME, ALEXANDER, from Berwickshire, settled in St Kitts, a sasine in 1769. [NRS.RS.18.15.371]; a merchant in St Kitts in 1782. [NRS.CS17.1.1.97]

HOME, ELIZABETH, wife of James Cook, died on Pond Estate, St Kitts on 23 June 1841. [EEC.20242]

HONE, MARY, a single-woman from Southwark, London, bound from Bristol to Nevis in 1660. [BRO]

HONIBYM, RICHARD, aged 31, bound aboard the Mathew of London, master Richard Goodladd, for St Kitts on 21 May 1635. [TNA.E157.20]

HOOD, Dr ALEXANDER, born 1737 in Scotland, Speaker of the House of Assembly, died in Montserrat on 7 July 1817. [GM.87.561] [S.41.17]; husband of Martha Iles. [St Anthony's mi, Montserrat]

HOPE, JOHN, a surgeon in Nevis, died in Demerara on 11 August 1804. [SM.66.973]

HOPPINE, MARY, born 1614, a spinster from Exminster, bound from Dartmouth to St Kitts in 1634. [TNA]

HORAN, WILLIAM, sr. in St Thomas, Middle Island, St Kitts on 7 February 1678. [TNA.COI.42]

HORAN, WILLIAM, jr. in St Thomas, Middle Island, St Kitts on 7 February 1678. [TNA.COI.42]

HORN, ARTHUR, a merchant in the Leeward Islands, died on 14 August 1753. [GM.23.372]

HORNE, JAMES CLUKIES, born 1848, fifth son of Alexander Horne of 27 Buccleuch Street, Edinburgh, died in Basseterre, St Kitts, on 23 October 1868. [S.7895]

HORNE, Mr, born 1747, a surgeon in London, emigrated via Portsmouth aboard the Charles Shayse bound for St Kitts in 1774. [TNA.T47.9/11]

HORNE, V M, a land grant in Antigua, a petition by C Spooner, 1766. [PCCol.1766.730]

HORSFORD, JOHN, born 1741, a Member of the Council of Antigua, died 29 January 1795. [Bath Abbey gravestone]

HORSFORD, PAUL, born 1771, Councillor and Chief Justice of Antigua, died there on 16 April 1850. [GM.ns.34.230]

THE PEOPLE OF THE LEEWARD ISLANDS, 1620 - 1860

HORSFORD, ….., son of Sir R. Horsford the Solicitor General of Antigua, was born there in 1843. [GM.ns.20.86]

HOSKINS, GEORGE, born 1725, died 13 January 1763 in Antigua. [St John's Cathedral]

HOTEN, MARGERY, aboard the sloop Africa, master Anthony Burgess, at Barbados on 7 October 1679 bound for the Leeward Islands. [TNA]

HOTSON, Mr, born 1748, a gentleman and planter, bound via Portsmouth aboard the William and Elizabeth bound for Antigua in 1774. [TNA.T47.9/11]

HOUSTON, ANDREW, probate 4 July 1772, Christiansted. [RAK.26.60]

HOUSTOUN, ROBERT, in St Kitts in 1776. [NLS.Acc.8793.22]

HOW, THOMAS, aboard the barque Dove, master Anthony Jenour, at Barbados on 29 October 1679 bound for Nevis. [TNA]

HOWARD, ELIZABETH, died 177-. [Mount William Estate gravestone, Antigua]

HOWARD, WILLIAM, a Jacobite, transported to Antigua in 1716. [SPAWI.1716.310][CTB.31.204]

HOWDEN, ANDREW HOWDEN, an apprentice writer in Christiansted, St Croix, 1821. [NRS.RD5.204.550]

HOWE, JOHN, born 1750, master aboard HMS Favourite, died 7 December 1777. [St Paul's mi, Antigua]

HOWISON, JAMES, a barber in Antigua, 1783. [NRS.CS17.1.2]

HUBBARD, Mrs FRANCES, born 1735, wife of William Hubbard, died 10 October 1768 [St John's Cathedral, Antigua].

THE PEOPLE OF THE LEEWARD ISLANDS, 1620 - 1860

HUBBARD, JAMES, aged 27, bound aboard the Mathew of London, master Richard Goodladd, for St Kitts on 21 May 1635. [TNA.E157.20]

HUBBARD, RICHARD, aged 18, bound aboard the Mathew of London, master Richard Goodladd, for St Kitts on 21 May 1635. [TNA.E157.20]

HUDE, PATRICK, a painter in St Kitts, dead by 5 December 1749. [NRS.RD4.175.2]

HUGGINS, EDWARD, born 1780, of Nevis, died in Newhaven, USA on 18 October 1840. [St George, gravestone, Nevis]

HUGGINS, ELIZABETH, born 1717, died 3 January 1818; Edward Huggins, born 1748, died 3 June 1822; John Huggins, son of

HUGGINS, EDWARD, born 1788, died 17 June 1822. [St George's gravestone, Nevis]

HUGGINS, GEORGIANA ELIZA, born 1814, wife of Richard Lytcott Hicks, died on 5 August 1835. [St George gravestone, Nevis]

HUGGINS, Mrs JANE, born 1792, wife of Edward Huggins, eldest daughter of Major Juxon, died 24 August 1840. [St George's gravestone, Nevis]

HUGGINS, JOHN, a planter in Nevis, 1734. [TNA.CO186.1]

HUGGINS, JOHN, a Councillor of Nevis, died 21 November 1855. [GM.ns.45.99]

HUGGINS, THOMAS, eldest son of P T Huggins in Nevis, married Annie Melville, third daughter of David Melville, in Nottingham on 17 November 1841. [GM.ns.17.92]

HUMPHREYS, Mrs DOROTHEA, widow of Reverend William Humphreys in Antigua, services of heirs, 1813. [NRS]

THE PEOPLE OF THE LEEWARD ISLANDS, 1620 - 1860

HUNT, EDWARD, a Jacobite, a prisoner transported to Antigua in 1716. [SPAWI.1716.310][CTB.31.204]

HUNT, JOHN, the Customs Collector of St Kitts, died in Basseterre, St Kitts, on 23 January 1790. [GM.60.274][SM.52.153]

HUNT, LEONARD, aged 38, bound aboard the Mathew of London, master Richard Goodladd, for St Kitts on 21 May 1635. [TNA.E157.20]

HUNTER, CHARLES, a merchant in St Kitts, graduated DL at Glasgow University on 6 February 1766. [GUL]

HUNTER, PETER, Secretary to the Commissioner for American Claims, died in St Kitts on 6 December 1787. [SM.50.257]

HUNTER, ROBERT, in Antigua in 1760. [DA.Ogilvie pp.30]

HUNTER, SAMUEL, a merchant planter, from London aboard the Dorsetshire bound for St Kitts in 1773. [TNA.T47.9/11]

HUNTER, ..., a merchant in Antigua, husband of Helen Mure, 1779. [NRS.CS16.1.175]

HUNTING, JOSEPH, born in New England, a carpenter in St Kitts in August 1727. [TNA.HCA.Vol.88.; 8.5.1728]

HUPTOW, MURTOW in St Thomas, Middle Island, St Kitts on 7 February 1678. [TNA.COI.42]

HURLIE, DARBY, aged 18, bound aboard the Mathew of London, master Richard Goodladd, for St Kitts on 21 May 1635. [TNA.E157.20]

HUSBAND, JOHN, a surgeon in Antigua in 1744. [NRS.RD4.176.2.326]

HUSSEY, PETER, a merchant in Montserrat, 1738. [PCCol.1739.474]

HUTCHESON, JAMES, in Antigua, testament, 6 June 1788, Comm. Edinburgh. [NRS]

HUTCHISON, Mrs MARY, daughter of the late M. Byam in Antigua, died in Durham on 16 September 1826. [GM.96.379]

HUTTON, CHARLES, in Nevis, probate, 1763, PCC. [TNA]

HUTTON, CHARLES, in Nevis in 1779, [NLS.ms8794]; from Nevis, died in Carlton-on-Trent on 11 October 1788. [GM.58.938]

HYDE, Dr JOHN, from Antigua, died in London on 21 February 1813. [GM.83.291]

HYNDE, MAXWELL, in St Kitts in 1776. [NLS.Acc.8793.28]

HYNDMAN, THOMAS, eldest son of Robert Hyndman a merchant in Antigua, matriculated at Glasgow University in 1806, [MAGU.218]; from Antigua, died at Glen Oak, County Antrim on 3 September 1815. [GM.85.376]

HYNDMAN, WILLIAM, from Greenock, a merchant in St Kitts in 1765, later in Grenada in 1767, sasines. [NRS.RS81.7.414; RS81.8.373], in Nevis, probate, 1770, PCC. [TNA]

INLIAN, DAVID, a merchant in St Croix, witness to a deed, 24 June 1819. [NRS.RD5.168.283]

INNES, ALEXANDER, a chaplain sent to the Leeward Islands on 28 February 1694. [CTB.X.1.514]

INNES, ALEXANDER, a surgeon in St Kitts, dead by 1779. [NRS.CS16.1.175]

INNES, FRANCES, daughter of Alexander Innes a surgeon in St Kitts, wife of Andrew Buchanan a merchant in Glasgow, died in January 1785, testament 22 September 1802, Comm. Glasgow. [NRS.CC9.7.75.452]

INNES, FRANCES, widow of Alexander Innes a surgeon in St Kitts, 1779. [NRS.CS16.1.175]; died on 27 July 1798. [EA.3610.79]

IRELAND, JOHN, master of the Two Friends of St Kitts trading between Scotland and North Carolina in 1764. [NRS.E504.11.5]

IRISH, GEORGE, born 1802, died 1841. [St Anthony's mi, Montserrat]

IRVINE, GEORGE, a planter in St Kitts, executor of Walter Pringle's testament of 1760.

IRVIN, JOHN, probate, 30 September 1770, Fredericksted. [RAK.56]

IRVIN, LINDSAY, probate, 7 April 1781, Fredericksted. [RAK.56]

IRVINE, RICHARD, in Antigua in 1753. [NRS.CS96.644]

IRVINE, RICHARD, probate, 31 May 1769, Christiansted. [RAK.20.33]

IRWIN, JAMES, born 1752, a physician in London, with his servant Charles Hamilton, emigrated via London aboard the Nancy bound for Antigua in 1773. [TNA.T47.9/11]

ISAACS, GEORGINA ANN, only daughter of the late John C Isaacs, the Colonial Secretary of Tortula, married Charles Osborne Baker, a Captain of the Royal Marines Light Infantry, in Cornwall on 12 October 1858. [GM.ns.2.5.629]

ISAACS, JANE, a planter on Nevis in 1708, [TNA.CO152-157]; was resettled in Nevis in 1712. [JCTP.1709-1715.384]

ISRAEL SHAKERLY, was resettled in Nevis in 1712. [JCTP.1709-1715.386]

ISRAEL, SOLOMON, on Nevis in 1678, [TNA.CO1]; on Nevis in 1708, [TNA.CO152-157]; resettled on Nevis in 1712, [JCTP.1709-1715, 386]; witness to the will of Azariah Pinney on Nevis in 1718. [TNA]

JACK, EVAN, senior, in Antigua in 1851, a sasine. [NRS,RS.Argyll.140]; his daughter was born in Helensburgh, Dunbartonshire, on 7 August 1839. [SG.8.793]

JACK, JAMES, a merchant on the island of St Thomas in 1816. [NRS.SC58.6.28]

JACKSON, ANNE JANE, born 1741, died in Antigua on 30 November 1765, wife of John Jackson. [St Stephen's]

JACKSON, ELIZABETH GORDON, fourth daughter of William Walrond Jackson the Bishop of Antigua, married Gateward Coleridge Davis a barrister, eldest son of the late Daniel G. Davis the Bishop of Antigua, in St John's, Antigua, on 21 January 1864. [GM.ns.2.16.520]

JACKSON, WILLIAM, aboard the Ann and Mary, master John Johnson, at Barbados on 13 March 1679 bound for Antigua. [TNA]

JACKSON, WILLIAM, in St Kitts, probate, 1768, PCC. [TNA]

JACOBS, JUDAH, born 1779, died in St Kitts on 5 July 1825. [Car.i.134]

JAMES, EDWARD, a barrister, second son of Edward James the Swedish Vice-Consul in Bristol, died in St Kitts in May 1829. [GM.99.94]

JAMES, EDWARD, a barrister, only son of J W James a solicitor in Devizes, died in St Kitts in May 1829. [GM.99.190][BM.26.412]

THE PEOPLE OF THE LEEWARD ISLANDS, 1620 - 1860

JAMES, JANE, a single woman, bound from Bristol to Nevis in 1660. [BRO]

JAMES, THOMAS, aged 25, aboard the John of London, master James Waymoth, bound for St Kitts on 2 October 1635. [TNA.E157.20]

JARDEN, WILLIAM, in Antigua, died 1705, probate PCC. [TNA]

JARVIS, BERTIE ENTWISTLE, Councillor of Antigua, married Lucy Brasier, youngest daughter of Kilner Brasier of Saffronhill, County Cork, on Watergrass Hill on 23 November 1843. [GM.ns.21.88]

JARVIS, B E, of Mount Joshua, Antigua, a Councillor there, married Martha Elliot Oliver, third daughter of the late L. Oliver in Bristol, in Antigua on 6 December 1859. [GM.ns.28.178]

JARVIS, BERTIE ENTWISTLE, born 1793, a Councillor of Antigua, died at sea on 15 October 1862. [GM.ns.2.13.789]

JARVIS, THOMAS, son of Thomas Jarvis a merchant in Antigua, matriculated at Glasgow University in 1736, graduated MA in 1741, [RGG.292]; later Chief Judge in Antigua, died there on 18 December 1785. [SM.48.51]

JARVIS, THOMAS, of Mount Joshua, St John's, Antigua, married Annie Hill, second daughter of Stephen J. Hill, Governor of the Leeward Islands, on 15 December 1863. [GM.ns.2.16.244]

JARVIS, Mrs, born 1763, wife of Thomas Jarvis, eldest daughter of the late William Whitehead, died in Antigua on 6 February 1797. [GM.67.435]

JARVIS, Miss, daughter of T. Jarvis, was born in Antigua on 17 March 1867. [GM.ns.3.3.804]

JEAFFARD, JEAN, in St Kitts, 1672, 1680. [SPAWI.1672.903; 1689.1312]

JEFFERS, GEORGE BRYAN, born 1781, died 24 July 1841. [St Anthony's mi, Montserrat]

JEFFERS, WILLIAM, born 1787, son of Thomas Jeffers, died 13 November 1810. [St Anthony's mi, Montserrat]

JEAFFRESON, CHRISTOPHER, in St Kitts, probate 1789, PCC. [TNA]

JEFFERSON, ROBERT, born 1753, a gentleman and planter, bound via Portsmouth aboard the William and Elizabeth bound for Antigua in 1774. [TNA.T47.9/11]

JEFFERSON, Sir ROBERT, a judge in Antigua, died in London on 25 June 1807. [GM.77.686]

JEFFRESON, JOHN, born 1710, died in February 1760, his widow Elizabeth, born 1713, died in November 1779, their daughter Sarah, born 1739, wife of Bertie Entwistle, died 22 May 1799. [St Stephen's gravestone, Antigua]

JEFFRESON, JOHN, in St Kitts, a letter, 9 August 1641. [NRS.GD34.935]

JENNINGS, Captain JOHN, a merchant in London, owner of the plantation 'Fig Tree Pond' in Nevis, probate 1655, PCC. [TNA]

JENNINGS, PHILLIP, aged 25, aboard the Paul of London, master Jo. Acklin, bound from Gravesend to St Kitts on 3 April 1635. [TNA.E157.20]

JENNINGS, WILLIAM, aboard the sloop True Friendship bound from Barbados on 7 October 1679 for Antigua. [TNA]

JERMAYNE, THOMAS, an ostler from Exeter, bound from Dartmouth to St Kitts in 1634. [TNA]

THE PEOPLE OF THE LEEWARD ISLANDS, 1620 - 1860

JERMYN, HUGH TURENNE, born 1849, second son of Archdeacon Jermyn, died in Basseterre, St Kitts, on 21 May 1855. [GM.ns.54.217]

JESSUP, EDWARD, a planter in St Kitts, a petition, 9 February 1737. [PCCol.1737.395]

JOHNSEN, JOHN, in St Croix in 1768. [SSF]

JOHNSON, CORNELIUS, in Halfwaytree Division, St Kitts on 7 February 1678. [TNA.COl.42]

JOHNSON, JOHN, on Saba, petitioned the Dutch West India Company in Amsterdam in 1772. [DNA.Inv.1151]

JOHNSON, Colonel JOHN, was appointed Lieutenant Governor of Nevis on 1 July 1703. [JCTP:13.7.1704]

JOHNSON, NATHANIEL, bound from Barbados aboard the Friends Adventure, master John Long, for Antigua on 19 April 1679; on 13 September 1679 he is recorded as being aboard the True Friendship, master Charles Callaghan bound for Antigua. [TNA]

JOHNSON, OLIVER, on Saba, petitioned the Dutch West India Company in Amsterdam in 1772. [DNA.Inv.1151]

JOHNSON, PETER, on Saba, petitioned the Dutch West India Company in Amsterdam in 1772. [DNA.Inv.1151]

JOHNSON, WILLIAM, aged 32, from London, emigrated via Plymouth aboard the Robert Bonaventure bound for St Kitts in February 1633. [TNA.E157.18]

JOHNSTON, ANNA, probate, 29 June 1774, Christiansted. [RAK.208.80]

JOHNSTON, HARRY, a planter in St Kitts, a sasine, 13 August 1791. [NRS.RS.Orkney.250]

JOHNSTON, JAMES, a merchant from Glasgow, died in Montserrat in 1684, 1691. [NRS.RDS2.104.958]

JOHNSTON, JAMES, a planter, died 12 October 1799, probate St Jan. [RAK.1797-1807.10]

JOHNSTON, JOHN, from Glasgow, was admitted as a burgher of St Eustatia on 13 August 1780. [TNA.CO318.8.83]

JOHNSTON, JOSEPH, a servant to Henry Doig in Antigua, was admitted as a burgess of Montrose, Angus, in 1754. [MBR]

JOHNSTON, LEWIS, a merchant in St Kitts, son of James Johnston a merchant in Edinburgh, services of heirs, 1756. [NRS]

JOHNSTON, MARGARET, eldest daughter of Hugh Johnston in Bellevue Crescent, Edinburgh, wife of Archibald Scott, died on Thibou Estate, Antigua, on 29 September 1862. [S.2300]

JOHNSTON, WILLIAM, in Antigua in 1753. [NRS.CS96.644]

JOHNSTON, WILLIAM, a planter, died 25 August 1802, husband of Mary Leonard Scatcliff, probate St Jan. [RAK.1797-1807.28]

JOHNSTON, WILLIAM, born 1803, died on St Bartholemew's on 21 November 1827. [St Michael's gravestone, Dumfries]

JOLLY, JOHN, born 1760, a merchant, son of T W Jolly a merchant in London, died in St Kitts in 1781. [GM.52.150]

JONES, ANDREW CUNNINGHAM, born 1850, son of Charles Cunningham Jones, died in Basseterre, St Kitts, on 17 February 1856. [GM.ns.45.545]

JONES, CHARLES CUNNINGHAM, born 1819, of the Colonial Bank, died in Basseterre, St Kitts, on 11 February 1856. [GM.ns.45.434]

JONES, EDWARD, of Esdaile and Jones merchants in Basseterre, St Kitts, 1778. [NRS.CS16,1.173]

JONES, EVAN, aged 19, bound aboard the Mathew of London, master Richard Goodladd, for St Kitts on 21 May 1635. [TNA.E157.20]

JONES, FRANCES, widow of Reverend William Jones in Nevis, died in Bristol on 12 July 1813. [GM.83.93]

JONES, HUGH, bound from Bristol to Antigua in 1660. [BRO]

JONES, MARY WILHELMINA, born 1849, daughter of Charles Cunningham Jones of the Colonial Bank, died in Basseterre, St Kitts, on 8 February 1856. [GM.ns45.434]

JONES, RICHARD, from Bury, Lancashire, an indentured servant aboard the Elisabeth and Ann master William Benn, bound from Liverpool to Montserrat in March 1700. [LRO]; in Nevis, probate, 1713, PCC. [TNA]

JORDAN, RICHARD, in St Kitts, probate, 1638, PCC. [TNA]

JOUBERT, ..., a French Catholic in St Kitts in 1686. [PCCol.1715.1225]

JOYCE, ROBERT, an indentured servant, from Tane, County Galway, Ireland, aboard the Elisabeth and Ann, master William Benn, bound for Montserrat in March 1699. [LRO]

JULIUS, WILLIAM, died in St Kitts on 19 February 1780. [GM.50.103]

KAY, JOHN, a tailor in St Eustatia, dead by 1782, husband of Agnes Boyle. [NRS.CS17.1.1]

KEDSLIE, MARGARET, wife of John Gittens, died in Guadaloupe in 1853. [S.14.1.1854]

KEENE, WILLIAM, sr., in Kayon Division, St Kitts on 7 February 1678. [TNA.COI.42]

KEENE, WILLIAM, jr, in Kayon Division, St Kitts on 7 February 1678. [TNA.COI.42]

KEEVE, JOHN, on Saba, petitioned the Dutch West India Company in Amsterdam in 1772. [DNA.Inv.1151]

KEEVE, THOMAS, on Saba, petitioned the Dutch West India Company in Amsterdam in 1772. [DNA.Inv.1151]

KEEVE, WILLIAM, on Saba, petitioned the Dutch West India Company in Amsterdam in 1772. [DNA.Inv.1151]

KELLY, DANIEL, in the parish of Sandy Point, St Kitts on 7 February 1678. [TNA.COI.42]

KELLY, DENNIS, in the parish of Sandy Point, St Kitts on 7 February 1678. [TNA.COI.42]

KELLY, EDMOND, in Christiansted, St Croix in 1770. [RDAG]

KELLY, EDMOND, sr., on Saba, petitioned the Dutch West India Company in Amsterdam in 1772. [DNA.Inv.1151]

KELLY, EDMOND, jr., on Saba, petitioned the Dutch West India Company in Amsterdam in 1772. [DNA.Inv.1151]

KELLY, JOHN, on Saba, petitioned the Dutch West India Company in Amsterdam in 1772. [DNA.Inv.1151]

KEMP, JOHN, a merchant in Antigua, 1782. [NRS.CS17.1.1]

KENNEDY, ALEXANDER, a Jacobite, a prisoner transported to Montserrat in 1716. [SPAWI.1716.313][CTB.31.205]

KENNEDY, Dr CHARLES, a physician in St Croix, married Margaret Cooper, daughter of Arthur Cooper in St Croix, in Eyemouth in October 1797. [EEC.392]

THE PEOPLE OF THE LEEWARD ISLANDS, 1620 - 1860

KENNEDY, JAMES, in St Croix in 1768. [SSF]

KENNEDY, JOHN, a Jacobite, a prisoner transported to Antigua in 1716. [SPAWI.1716.310][CTB.31.204]

KENNEDY, Captain JOHN, probate 26 May 1779, Christiansted. [RAK.317.132]

KENNEDY, MARGARET, wife of Gun More the Customs Collector, died in Tortula on 17 December 1843. [AJ.5012]

KENNEDY, MARY, a washerwoman from Glengarry, a Jacobite banished to the Leeward Islands, liberated by the French and landed on Martinique in 1747. [TNA.SP36.102][P.2.314]

KENNEDY, ROBERT, a surgeon in St Eustatia, 1766. [NRS.CS16.1.125/72]

KENNY, ANDREW, from St Croix, graduated MD from Edinburgh University in 1812. [EMG.45]

KENNY, JOHN, probate, 23 December 1772, Christiansted. [RAK.148.45]

KENNY, Mrs MARY, born 1817, wife of Charles Kenny late Captain of the 52nd Regiment, died in Nevis on 16 December 1840. [GM.ns.15.558]

KENSLEY, Mr, born 1738, a gentleman and planter, bound via Portsmouth aboard the William and Elizabeth bound for Antigua in 1774. [TNA.T47.9/11]

KERBY, THOMAS NORBURY, in St John's, Antigua, reference in John Pew's will of 1800, PCC. [TNA]; Commander-in-Chief of Antigua and Montserrat, died in Antigua during November 1819. [F.J.4.2.1820]

KERR, CHARLES, a merchant, died in Antigua on 11 December 1796. [GM.66.168][SM.58.143]

KERR, JAMES, a merchant in Antigua, was granted the lands of East Grange on 3 July 1765, [NRS.RGS.108.34]; of Kerr and Burles merchants in Antigua, 1772. [NRS.CS16.1.151/319]

KERR, JOHN, a Jacobite, a prisoner transported to Antigua in 1716. [SPAWI.1716.310][CTB.31.204]

KERR, Dr WILLIAM, in St Croix, died in St Kitts on 8 December 1837. [AJ.4700]

KERRY, T N, the Commander in Chief of Antigua and Montserrat, died in Antigua on 18 November 1819. [GM.90.186]

KEUTSCH, HENRY, in St Croix in 1802. [RDAG.I/2]

KEY, JOHN, a tailor in St Eustatia, 1781. [NRS.CS16.1.183]

KIBIE, JO., aged 21, bound aboard the Mathew of London, master Richard Goodladd, for St Kitts on 21 May 1635. [TNA.E157.20]

KIDWILLAR, JANE, a spinster, bound from Bristol to Nevis in 1660. [BRO]

KIDMILLAR, JOHN, a yeoman, bound from Bristol to Nevis in 1660. [BRO]

KING, ANNE, only daughter of David King, married D A Yetts, in St John's, Antigua on 28 October 1809. [DPCA.394]

KING, GEORGE, from Southampton, died in Antigua in 1813. [GM.83.595]

KING, JAMES, in Antigua in 1760. [DA.Ogilvie.ms.43]

KING, JANE, a spinster, an indentured servant bound from Bristol to Antigua to serve Edmund Ellis a planter in 1660. [BRO]

THE PEOPLE OF THE LEEWARD ISLANDS, 1620 - 1860

KING, JOSEPH, married Miss Giles from London, in St Kitts in January 1772. [GM.42.46]

KING, NATHANIEL, in Nevis, probate, 1687, PCC. [TNA]

KING, WILLIAM, aged 18, aboard the Paul of London, master Jo. Acklin, bound from Gravesend to St Kitts on 3 April 1635. [TNA.E157.20]

KING, WILLIAM, a merchant in St Kitts, co-owner of the Polly of Greenock in 1792. [NRS.CE60.11.3.54]

KINNAIRD, Sir ALEXANDER, of Culbin, an overseer, a witness in St Kitts in 1700. [NRS.GD84.Sec.1/22/9b]

KIN……., CHRIS……, born 1731, died 1809. [Antigua gravestone]

KIRKBY, JOHN MALMSBURY, born 1826, eldest son of the late Reverend J M Kirby in Stourbridge, died in St Thomas on 29 September 1848. [GM.ns31.222]

KIRKPATRICK, HENRY ERSKINE, a minister sent to the Leeward Islands in 1768. [EMA.39]

KIRKPATRICK, WILLIAM, of Raeberry, in Antigua in 1775. [NRS.CS16.1.165/409]

KIRKPATRICK, WILLIAM, a planter in St Kitts, appealed re the condemnation of the Peggy by the Vice Admiralty Court of Antigua on 21 December 1767. [PCCol.1768.174]; of Raeberry, late of St Kitts, in December 1775. [NRS.CS16.1.165/409]

KIRWAN, JOHN, a planter in Montserrat in 1712. [TNA.CO152.16]; in Plymouth, Montserrat, 1719. [TNA.CO152.13]

KIRWAN, JOHN, in St Croix in 1770. [RDAG.I.50]

KIRWAN, MARK, in Plymouth, Montserrat, 1719. [TNA.CO152.13]

KIRWAN, PATRICK, died in Antigua, 1819. [GM.89.91]

KITTOE, Mrs, widow of G Kittoe in Antigua, died in Barnstaple on 8 October 1811. [GM.81.487]

KNEVE, JOHANN WERMER, a Dutch Reformed Church minister in St Croix in 1757. [RAK.WIC.429]

KNIGHT, THOMAS, aged 21, bound aboard the Mathew of London, master Richard Goodladd, for St Kitts on 21 May 1635. [TNA.E157.20]

KNIGHT, WILLIAM, aged 13, bound aboard the Mathew of London, master Richard Goodladd, for St Kitts on 21 May 1635. [TNA.E157.20]

KNOX, HUGH, a Presbyterian minister Saba from 1752 to 1772, thereafter in St Croix, was awarded an honorary degree of Doctor of Divinity by Marischal College, Aberdeen, on 25 November 1773, [MCA]; in 1776, [NLS.Acc.8793.26]; husband of Mary, daughter of Governor Peter Simmons and his wife Rebecca.

KNOX, JAMES, born in Edinburgh during 1690s, son of Reverend Henry Knox once in Bowden, a minister of St Mary's, Antigua, in 1726 St Kitts, [F.2.172]; services of heirs, 1719, [NRS]; a cleric in Antigua, probate 2 January 1740, PCC. [TNA] [FPA.276][EMA.39]

KNOX, PETER JOHN, son of Hugh Knox in St Croix, was educated at Marischal College, Aberdeen, from 1777 to 1781. [MCA.II.353]

KOEFOED, GEORG ALBRECHT, a Danish Judge in the West Indies and Recorder for Christiansted, St Croix, 1825. [NRS.RD5.301.447]

KORTRIGHT and CRUGER, slave traders at Cruger's Yard, St Croix, in 1771. [RDAG]

KRAUSE, M. L., in 19 King Street, in St Croix in 1802. [RDAG.I/2]

KRAUSE, Miss, daughter of Colonel Krause in Danish service, married James Brown a merchant in St Croix, there on 23 May 1820. [BM.7.583]

LACIE, ROBERT, aged 21, bound aboard the Mathew of London, master Richard Goodladd, for St Kitts on 21 May 1635. [TNA.E157.20]

LA COUSAY, PHILIPE, a planter in Nevis in 1712. [JCTP.1712]

LADD, CORNELIUS, sr., in Kayon Division, St Kitts on 7 February 1678. [TNA.COl.42]

LADD, CORNELIUS, jr, in Kayon Division, St Kitts on 7 February 1678. [TNA.COl.42]

LA FERTEY, SAMUEL PICARD, in Antigua in 1709. [SPAWI.1709.487ii]

LAFFON, ..., a planter in Capisterre Quarter, St Kitts, before 1717. [JCTP.1717.261]

LA FOON, CHARLES, son of Charles and Mary Lafoon, died 11 January 1789. [St Anthony's mi, Montserrat]

LA FOON, JOHN, son of Charles and Mary Lafoon, died 16 January 1785. [St Anthony's mi, Montserrat]

LA FOON, SARAH ANNE ALLEN, daughter of Charles and Mary Lafoon, died 1 June 1772. [St Anthony's mi, Montserrat]

LA FOON, THOMAS, son of Charles and Mary Lafoon, died 1 December 1787. [St Anthony's mi, Montserrat]

LA FORTUNE, ..., in St Kitts in 1672. [SPAWI.1672.903]

LA GUARIGNE, ..., in St Kitts in 1673. [SPAWI.1674.1273]

LAING, JOHN, a planter in St Croix, died on 24 August 1851, testament, 1852. [NRS.SC70.1.74]

LAMBE, TOBIAS, in St Kitts, probate, 1684, PCC. [TNA]

LAMONT, ISAAC, Commander of St Eustatius from 1700 to 1704.

LAMYN, WILLIAM, aged 21, aboard the Paul of London, master Jo. Acklin, bound from Gravesend to St Kitts on 3 April 1635. [TNA.E157.20]

LAND, JOHN, a yeoman, bound from Bristol to Nevis in 1660. [BRO]

LANDELL, JOHN, brother of Reverend James Landell minister at Coldingham, Berwickshire, died in St Thomas in October 1809. [EA]

LANE, ELIZA HARRIET, only daughter of Thomas Lane the Colonial Secretary, married Richard Paget Campbell Jones of the Royal Artillery, in Antigua on 23 November 1850. [GM.ns.3.196]

LANE, RICHARD, aged 28, bound aboard the Mathew of London, master Richard Goodladd, for St Kitts on 21 May 1635. [TNA.E157.20]

LANG, JESSIE MORRIS, youngest daughter of Robert Lang in Largs, Ayrshire, died in St Croix on 14 September 1842. [SG.XI.1080][GSP.779]

LANG, JOHN, of St Croix, residing in Blackdales, Largs, was granted the lands of Knockewart on 17 March 1851. [NRS.RGS.247.4.8]

LANG, ROBERT, in St Croix in 1790. [Caribbeana.5.265]

LANG, WILLIAM, in St Croix in 1790. [Caribbeana.5.265]

LANGE, JO., aged 22, bound aboard the Mathew of London, master Richard Goodladd, for St Kitts on 21 May 1635. [TNA.E157.20]

THE PEOPLE OF THE LEEWARD ISLANDS, 1620 - 1860

LANGFORD, JONAS, a Quaker merchant and planter in Antigua, settled in 1660, died 1712. [St John's mi, Antigua]

LAPSLEY, WILLIAM, born in St Kitts, only son of James Lapsley, matriculated at Glasgow University in 1792. [MAGU.168]

LATIMORE, FRANCES, a yeoman, bound from Bristol to Nevis in 1660. [BRO]

LATOYIONEN, JOHN, in St Croix in 1768. [SSF]

LAUERE, JOAN, born 1615, from Modbury in Devon, bound from Dartmouth to St Kitts in 1634. [TNA]

LAURIE, PETER, a merchant in Guadaloupe, 1782. [NRS.CS17.1.1]

LA VAUX, Captain ALEXANDRE, an engineer in St Kitts, possibly a French spy. [PCCol.1742.529]

LAVEROCK, CHARLES SIMMONS, on Saba, petitioned the Dutch West India Company in Amsterdam in 1772. [DNA.Inv.1151]

LAVEROCK, JAMES, on Saba, petitioned the Dutch West India Company in Amsterdam in 1772. [DNA.Inv.1151]

LAVEROCK, MOSES, on Saba, petitioned the Dutch West India Company in Amsterdam in 1772. [DNA.Inv.1151]

LAVEROCK, RICHARD, on Saba, petitioned the Dutch West India Company in Amsterdam in 1772. [DNA.Inv.1151]

LAVEROCK, WILLIAM, on Saba, petitioned the Dutch West India Company in Amsterdam in 1772. [DNA.Inv.1151]

LAVINGTON, Lord RALPH, Knight of the Bath, Governor General of the West Indies, died in Antigua on 1 August 1807. [SM.64.958]

LA VICOMPTE, JOHN, a planter in Antigua in 1718. [SPAWI.1718.729]

LAWDER, GEORGE, in St Thomas, Middle Island, St Kitts, in 1667. [TNA.CO1.42/193]

LAWLER, STEPHEN, a merchant from Plymouth, died in Antigua, probate, 1686, PCC. [TNA]

LAWLOR, WILLIAM DIGBY, in St Kitts, graduated MD from King's College, Aberdeen, on 2 May 1796. [KCA.141]

LAWRIE, JAMES, from Edinburgh to St Kitts in 1742. [NRS.GD461.8]

LAWSON, JOSHUA, in St Kitts, probate 1775, PCC. [TNA]

LAWSON, ROBERT, son of Robert Lawson of Knockhorrock [1728-1800] and his wife Helen Hannah, died in St Kitts aged 24. [St Michael's, Dumfries, gravestone]

LAWSON, WILSON, in Tortula in 1800. [NRS.CS26.915.35]

LAWTON, ALEXANDER, a Jacobite a prisoner transported to St Kitts in 1716. [SPAWI.1716.312][CTB.31.207]

LEALAND, WILLIAM, born 1687, from Bolton, Lancashire, bound from Liverpool for Antigua as an indentured servant in 1700. [LRO]

LEAUE, TEGO, from Corke, Ireland, aged 30, from emigrated via Plymouth aboard the Robert Bonaventure bound for St Kitts in February 1633. [TNA.157.18]

LE BAILLI DE SOUVRAY, ..., purchased St Croix from the Compagnie de St Christopher et Santa Cruz in 1651. [SPAWI.1734.388ii]

LE BARONE, ..., in St Kitts in 1672. [SPAWI.1672.903]

LE BOONE, JACQUE, in St Kitts in 1672. [SPAWI.1672.903]

THE PEOPLE OF THE LEEWARD ISLANDS, 1620 - 1860

LECKIE, HENRY, in St Thomas, married Anne Duncan, eldest daughter of Reverend John Duncan of New College, Edinburgh, at the Dutch Reformed Church parsonage of St Thomas on 25 June 1861, [AJ.5922]

LE CORNU, FRANCIS, a mariner aboard HMS Assistance died in the Leeward Islands, probate, 1693, PCC. [TNA]

LE CROC, ..., in St Kitts in 1672. [SPAWI.1672.903]

LEE, DANIEL, aged 25, bound aboard the Mathew of London, master Richard Goodladd, for St Kitts on 21 May 1635. [TNA.E157.20]

LEE, HENRY, aged 30, aboard the Paul of London, master Jo. Acklin, bound from Gravesend to St Kitts on 3 April 1635. [TNA.E157.20]

LEE, PHILIP, from the Isle of Wight, died 1688. [St John's, Fig Tree, Nevis, gravestone]

LEE, RICHARD, aged 18, bound aboard the Mathew of London, master Richard Goodladd, for St Kitts on 21 May 1635. [TNA.E157.20]

LEE, WALTER, aged 21, aboard the John of London, master James Waymoth, bound for St Kitts on 2 October 1635. [TNA.E157.20]

LEECKER, FREDERICK, in St Kitts, petitioned for denization in 1662. [SPAWI.1662.269]

LE GALL, JOHN, born 1794, Counsellor of St Vincent, died at English Harbour, Antigua, on 29 June 1851, buried in Falmouth, Antigua. [St Vincent mi]

LEIGH, GEORGE, in St Kitts, probate, 1766, PCC. [TNA]

LEITCH, JOHN, from Glasgow, was admitted as a burgher of St Eustatia on 8 August 1780. [TNA.CO318.8.83]

LE JAU, Reverend FRANCIS, a minister in Montserrat in 1705. [TCD]

LEONARD, GEORGE, a judge in Antigua and a councillor of the Virgin Islands, married Miss Martin a daughter of Henry Martin late President of the Virgin Islands, on 27 August 1791. [GM.61.872]

LEONARD, Mrs LEONORA, born 1771, daughter of Henry Martin former President of the Virgin Islands, and wife of George Leonard the President of the Virgin Islands, died on 18 January 1794. [GM.64.383]

LESLIE, Captain ANDREW, a mariner in London, then in Antigua, 1739. [NRS.CS16.1.68]

LESLIE, ANDREW, from Aberdeen, a Councillor and Colonel of Militia in Antigua, 17...

LESLIE, ANDREW, in Antigua in 1753. [NRS.CS96.644]

LESLIE, ANDREW, in Tortula in 1800. [NRS.CS26.915.35]

LESLIE, WILLIAM, a minister sent to Antigua in 1718. [EMA.40][Rawlinson ms.C393-394]

LESLIE, WILLIAM, in Antigua in 1760. [DA.Ogilvie pp.32]

LESLIE, WILLIAM, probate, 9 February 1772, Christiansted. [RAK.167.111]

LESLY, ANDREW, President of Antigua, died on 26 May 1780. [GM.50.298]

LESLEY, WILLIAM, a chaplain in the Leeward Islands in 1718. [Rawl. Ms.C.393.94]

THE PEOPLE OF THE LEEWARD ISLANDS, 1620 - 1860

LETTSON, PICKERING, born 1780, a lawyer, youngest son of Dr Lettson, died in Tortula on 28 October 1808. [GM.78.1127]

LETTSON, Mrs, widow of Pickering Lettson, died in Tortula on 24 January 1809. [GM.79.278]

LE VILLIER, ..., in St Kitts in 1672. [SPAWI.1672.903]

LEWIS, HUMPHREY, in Nevis, probate, 1697, PCC. [TNA]

LEWIS, JOHN, in Nevis, probate, 1701, PCC. [TNA]

LEWIS, Mrs, wife of J. Mason Lewis the Naval Commander in Antigua, died in London in 1814. [GM.84.418]

LEYS, JOHN, born 1791 in Aberdeen, emigrated to Canada in 1826, an engineer, died in St Croix on 8 April 1846. [AJ.5123]

LIDDELL, GEORGE, in Montserrat, probate, 1696, PCC. [TNA]

LIDDICOTT, JOHN, from St Cullom, aged 22, emigrated via Plymouth aboard the Robert Bonaventure bound for St Kitts in February 1633. [TNA.E157.18]

LILLIOT, MARTHA, aged 20, aboard the John of London, master James Waymoth, bound for St Kitts on 2 October 1635. [TNA.E157.20]

LINBERG, JACOB, in St Croix in 1768. [SSF]

LINDO, JAMES, born 1727, from Lancaster, master of the brig Swallow died 23 May 1758. [St George gravestone, Basse Terre, St Kitts]

LINDSAY, ALEXANDER, a factor for Archibald Hay in St Kitts in 1649. [NRS.GD34.8948]

LINDESAY, GERARD, in St Eustatia in 1785. [ASS.125/693]

LINDSAY, JOHN, from Ballymena, County Antrim, an indentured servant, bound from Liverpool aboard the Elizabeth and Ann, for Montserrat in 1700. [LRO]

LINDSAY, JOHN, a Jacobite, a prisoner transported to Antigua in 1716. [SPAWI.1716.310][CTB.31.204]

LINDSAY, JOHN, a skipper in Antigua, was admitted as a burgess of Old Aberdeen on 21 September 1742. [OABR]

LINDESAY, JOHAN, on the Dutch Leeward Islands, late Governor of St Eustatius, escaped to St Kitts in April 1729. [SPAWI.1729.684]

LINDSAY, JOHN, probate 11 November 1772, Christiansted. [RAK.122.390]

LINDESAY, LUDOVIC, a witness in St Eustatia in 1782. [ASS.124/136]

LINDSAY, MARGARITA, daughter of Joseph Lindsay and his wife Catrina Bennard, was baptised in St Eustatia on 2 January 1724, witnesses were John Lindsay jr and Margaret Lindsay. [ASS]

LINDESAY, MARGERITTA, born on St Eustatia, married Luca de Wint on St Thomas in 1740. [RAK.WIC.429]

LINDSAY, PAULINA, daughter of John Lindsay and his wife Elizabeth Simond, was baptised in St Eustatia on 15 November 1723. [ASS]

LINDSAY, RICHARD, probate 11 April 1781, Christiansted. [RAK.366.123]

LINDSAY, WILLIAM, in Antigua, will, 1763. [PWI]

LINDSAY, W., born 1755, from Antigua, died in Southampton on 19 February 1812. [GM.82.392]

LINDSAY, Miss, married Francis Forbes in Barbuda on 30 April 1764. [GM.34.250]

LINKLATTER, THOMAS, husband of Maria Willcocks, probate 1750, St Croix. [RAK]

LIPSCOMBE, CHRISTOPHER, born 1782, Bishop of Jamaica, eldest son of Reverend William Lipscomb in Walbury, Northallerton, died in St Thomas on 4 April 1843. [GM.ns20.201]

LIPSCOMBE, E F, born 1805, died at Cades Bay, Antigua, on 12 September 1853. [GM.ns40.649]

LITTLE, ALEXANDER, probate 10 June 1748, St Croix. [RAK.1747-1754, 150]

LITTLE, WILLIAM, born 1754, a servant from Surrey, via London aboard the Pemberton bound for St Kitts in 1774. [TNA.T47.9/11]

LITTLEJOHN, JAMES, son of Peter Littlejohn of the Mains of Hazlehead, Aberdeen, died in Guadaloupe in 1760. [APB.2.215]

LITTMAN, GEORGE, on Nevis in 1708. [TNA.CO152.157]

LIVINGSTON, WILLIAM, in Antigua in 1716. [FPA.270]

LIVINGSTONE, WILLIAM, in Antigua in 1757. [DA.Ogilvie pp.19]; a planter in Antigua, died 1774.

LIVINGSTONE, WILLIAM, probate 31 August 1770, Christiansted. [DAK.50]

LIZARS, ROBERT, Ensign of the 35th Regiment, died in Nevis on 25 November 1822. [DPCA.1070]

LLOYD, Captain JOHN, in Nevis, probate, 1696, PCC. [TNA]

LLOYD, JOSEPH, a merchant in Nevis, probate, 1690, PCC. [TNA]

LOBATTO, DEBORAH, was resettled in Nevis in 1712. [JCTP.1709-1715.386]

LOBATTO, SARAH, was resettled in Nevis in 1712. [JCTP.1709-1715.383]

LOCK, RICHARD, aged 20, aboard the Paul of London, master Jo. Acklin, bound from Gravesend to St Kitts on 3 April 1635. [TNA.E157.20]

LOCKHART, Mrs SARAH, wife of J. P. Lockhart, born 1776, died 19 June 1807. [St Anthony's mi, Montserrat]

LONG, WILLIAM, in St Thomas, Middle Island, St Kitts on 7 February 1678. [TNA.COl.42]

LOOBY, BAPTISTE, Justice of the Court of Common Pleas in the Virgin Islands in 1778. [JCTP.85.149]

LOREINE, ……., in St Kitts in 1672. [SPAWI.1672.903]

LORENZON, Inspector, in St Croix in 1802. [RDAG.I/2]

LOSACK, Admiral GEORGE, son of Richard Hawkshaw Losack in St Kitts, died in Milan, Italy, on 22 August 1829. [GM.99.465]

LOSACK, RICHARD HAWKSHAW, born 1730 in St Kitts, Lieutenant Governor of the Leeward Islands, died on 2 November 1813. [GM.83.622][EA.5206.13]

LOSACK, Miss, only daughter of Richard Losack in St Kitts, the Lieutenant Governor of the Leeward Islands, married John White of the Royal Navy, on 22 March 1796. [GM.66.253]

LOVE, ALLAN, from Greenock, a mariner in Montserrat, a sasine in 1778. [NRS.RS81.10]

LOVELL, LANGFORD, of Antigua, married Miss Heathcote, eldest daughter of Sir W Heathcote a Member of Parliament, on 28 April 1798. [GM.68.441]

LOW, JOHN, born 1684, from Lancashire, bound as an indentured servant from Liverpool to Antigua in 1700. [LRO]

LOWIS, ORIGINAL, aged 34, bound aboard the Mathew of London, master Richard Goodladd, for St Kitts on 21 May 1635. [TNA.E157.20]

LOWTHER, JOHN, a merchant from Lancaster, died in St Thomas on 5 July 1804. [GM.74.881]

LUCAS, CHARLES, from Antigua, died 5 August 1766. [GM.36.390]

LUCAS, THOMAS, in St Kitts, probate 1784, PCC. [TNA]

LUNDY, CHARLES, a Jacobite a prisoner transported to Antigua in 1716. [SPAWI.1716.310][CTB.31.204]

LUTHER, SUSANNA, born 1755, died 10 January 1810. [St Anthony's mi, Montserrat]

LYLE, JOHN, formerly a merchant in Nevis, die in Greenock, testament, 1791, Comm. Glasgow. [NRS]

LYNCH, AMBROSE BARTHOLEMEW, born 3 February 1703, a merchant in Antigua, died 2 September 1740. [St John's Cathedral, Antigua]

LYNCH, ARTHUR, in Plymouth, Montserrat, 1719. [TNA.CO152.13]

LYNCH, BARTHOLEMEW, a planter in Montserrat in 1712. [TNA.CO152.16]

LYNCH, JOHN, a planter in Montserrat in 1678. [TNA.CO1.22.17]

LYNCH, JOHN FRENCH, in St Kitts, probate 1788, PCC. [TNA]

LYNCH, NICHOLAS, born 1729, died 4 November 1769. [Bridgetown gravestone, Antigua]

LYNCH, PATRICK, in Plymouth, Montserrat, 1719. [TNA.CO152.13]

LYNCH, SARAH, wife of Dr Thomas Lynch, born around 1754, died 22 March 1774. [Bridgetown gravestone, St Philips, Antigua]

LYNE, SARAH POOLE, wife of Philip Lyne, from Antigua, died in London on 15 August 1825. [GM.95.188]

LYNG, ANN, in Nevis, probate, 1710, PCC. [TNA]

LYNG, WILLIAM, a merchant in Nevis, Commissioner for Prizes in Nevis, in 1704. [JCTP.XIX.214]; in Nevis, probate, 1705, PCC. [TNA]

LYON, DAVID, a Scottish mariner, married Rebecca Davids, widow of Jan Schoot, on 27 December 1736 in St Eustatia. [Afscriften huwelijksakten van St Eustatius van 1710-1750]

LYONS, HENRY, in Antigua, died on 6 January 1747. [GM.17.47]

LYON, WILLIAM, in St Kitts in 1776. [NLS.Acc.8793.37]

LYONS, versus Lyons, in Antigua, an appeal to the Privy Council Colonial in 1717. [Acts P.C.Col. 1727.379]

LYTON, JAMES, in Nevis, probate, 1719, PCC. [TNA]

LYTON, SARAH, in Nevis, a deposition, 1725. [TNA.CO186.1]

MCALLAN, WALTER, from Perthshire, was admitted as a burgher of St Eustatia on 9 August 1780. [TNA.CO318.8.83]

MCALPINE, GREGORY, in Antigua in 1754. [NRS.CS96.647]

THE PEOPLE OF THE LEEWARD ISLANDS, 1620 - 1860

MCARA, JEAN, eldest daughter of James McAra a merchant in Largs, married Thomas Walker a surgeon from Kinross, in St Thomas in 1813. [EA.5134.13]

MCARTHUR, Major JOHN, born 1648, settled at Figtree, St Thomas, Middle Island, St Kitts, Deputy Governor of St Kitts, father of Gillies, in St Kitts in 1696. [TNA. Association Oath Rolls]; in St Kitts in 1699, [SPAWI.1699.282/658][ActsPCCol], died 4 April 1704, buried in St Thomas. [DP.310]

MCARTHUR, JOHN, born in Argyll, died in St Croix in 1808. [EA.4700]

MCBEAN, AENEAS, in St Thomas, husband of Johanna Mackintosh, a sasine, 13 November 1798. [NRS.RS.Inverness.619]

MCBEAN, AENEAS, jr, of Tomatin, a merchant in Glasgow, died in St Thomas in 1810. [EA.4873.167]

MACBEAN, CAROLINE H H, only child of the late Aeneas MacBean of Tomatin, in St Thomas, married Lieutenant Colonel Robert Ross of the 4th Royal Irish Dragoon Guards, in Inverness on 7 April 1819. [GM.88.368][EA.5778.233]

MACBEAN, DONALD, a farm manager, died 24 August 1830, probate St Jan. [RAK.1826-1836, 63-71]

MCBEAN, ROBERT, in Tortula, married Margaret McIntosh, daughter of McIntosh of Dalmigavie, in Inverness on 13 December 1794. [SM.56.801]; late of Tortula, sasine, deed, 1798, 1802. [NRS.RS38.PR16.389; NRS.GD23.4.234]

MCBEAN, WILLIAM, in St Croix in 1790. [Caribbeana.5.265]

MCCALL, ..., brother of John McCall in Lurgan, Ireland, emigrated to Antigua before 1713. [TCD.750.1475]

MCCALLUM, DAVID, in Antigua in 1753. [NRS.CS96.644]

MCCALLUM, JOHN, a Jacobite, transported to Montserrat in 1716. [SPAWI.1716.313][CTB.31.205][CTP.CC43]

MCCANN, ARTHUR, probate March 1772, Christiansted. [RAK]

MCCANN, EDWARD, a Jacobite, transported to Montserrat in 1716. [SPAWI.1716.313][CTP.CC.43]

MCCAUL, JOHN, second son of Gilbert McCaul in Glasgow, a merchant in Antigua, died there on 17 April 1830. [S.1088]

MCCAUL, Mr, applied to be the British Consul in St Croix in 1819. [NRS.GD51.6.2030]

MCCAUL, JOHN GORDON, son of John McCaul a merchant in Glasgow, at Glasgow University in 1799 and at Oxford University in 1810 a merchant in St Croix in 1821, died in Cane Valley, St Croix on 16 March 1860. [NRS.CS17.1.40/571][Caribbeana.4.79]

MCCOM, BENJAMIN, in Antigua in 1753. [NRS.CS96.644]

MCCORMICK, JOHN, born 1794 in Scotland, a Presbyterian, a planter on Petersminde Estate, St Croix, in 1841. [1841 Census]

MCCOY, DANIEL, a Jacobite prisoner transported to Antigua in 1716. [SPAWI.1716.310][CTB.31.204]

MCCOY, DONALD, a Jacobite prisoner transported to Antigua in 1747. [P.3.30]

MCCOY, JOHN, a Jacobite prisoner transported to Montserrat in 1716. [SPAWI.1716.313][CTB.31.205][CTP.CC43]

MCCOY, PAUL, a Jacobite prisoner transported to Antigua in 1716. [SPAWI.1716.310][CTB.31.204]

MCCRACKEN, JOHN, a plasterer in Antigua, died 1800. [NRS.GD135.1693]

THE PEOPLE OF THE LEEWARD ISLANDS, 1620 - 1860

MCCULLOCH, ROBERT, a Jacobite prisoner transported to Montserrat in 1716. [SPAWI.1716.313][CTB.31.206][CTP.CC43]

MCDANELL, DANIEL, a Jacobite prisoner transported to Antigua in 1716. [SPAWI.1716.310]

MCDERMOT, ANDREW, probate 18 December 1771, Christiansted. [RAK.62.154]

MCDERMOTT, ANGUS, a Jacobite prisoner transported to Montserrat in 1716. [SPAWI.1716.313][CTB.31.206][CTP.CC43]

MCDERMOTT, JOHN, a Jacobite prisoner transported to Antigua in 1716. [SPAWI.1716.313][CTB.31.206]

MCDONALD, ANGUS, a Jacobite prisoner transported to Antigua in 1747. [P.3.46]

MCDONALD, ARCHIBALD, in St Kitts, a letter, 1809. [NRS.GD128.9.2]

MCDONALD, DENIS, a Jacobite prisoner transported to Montserrat in 1716. [SPAWI.1716.313][CTB.31.205][CTP.CC43]

MCDONALD, DONALD, a Jacobite prisoner transported to Antigua in 1716. [CTB.31.204]

MCDONALD, TERENCE, a Roman Catholic priest, died 10 November 1775, probate St Jan. [RAK. 1758-1775.222-225]

MCDONALD, WILLIAM, a Jacobite prisoner transported to Montserrat in 1716. [SPAWI.1716.313][CTB.31.206][CTP.CC43]

MACDONALD, ..., daughter of Lieutenant Colonel P J MacDonald of the 4th West Indian Regiment, was born in St Eustatia on 17 October 1862. [GM.ns.2.14.102]

MCDONALL, DENIS, a Jacobite prisoner transported to Montserrat in 1716. [SPAWI.1716.313][CTP.CC43]

MCDORTON, PHILIP, a Jacobite prisoner transported to Montserrat in 1716. [SPAWI.1716.313][CTB.31.206][CTP.CC43]

MCDOUGALL, ALLAN, a surgeon in St Kitts in December 1740. [CM.3262]

MCDOUGALL, DOUGALL, in St Kitts in 1776. [NLS.Acc.8793]

MCDOUGAL, DUNCAN, a merchant in St Kitts 1776 to 1778. [NLS.8793-8794]

MCDOUGALL, PATRICK, in St Kitts, later in Gallanecch, Argyll, 1780. [NRS.CS16.1.179]

MCDOUGALL, WILLIAM, in St Kitts, graduated MD from Edinburgh University in 1791. [EMG.23]

MCDOWELL, JAMES, a planter in St Kitts in 1777. [NLS.8795]

MCDOWELL, Colonel WILLIAM, a planter in St Kitts from 1729 to 1732. [NLS.8800]

MCDOWELL, Dr WILLIAM, probate, 8 July 1755, St Croix. [RAK]

MCEVOY, CHRISTOPHER, in St Croix in 1790. [Caribbeana.5.265]

MCEVOY, MICHAEL, in St Croix in 1790. [Caribbeana.5.265]

MCFARLANE, DANIEL, probate 21 January 1766, Fredericksted. [RAK]

MCFARLANE, DANIEL, a merchant in St Croix, co-owner of the Peggy in 1784. [Greenock Ship Register]; in St Croix in 1790. [Caribbeana.5.265]

MCFARLANE, DAVID, born 1737, 'fifty years in the West Indies', in Cane Valley, St Croix, died there on 8 January 1808. [SM.70.317] [NLS.8793.31] [Caribbeana.5.265]; his wife Margaret, died there on 4 September 1803. [EEC.14337]

MCFARLANE, GEORGE, in St Croix, graduated MD from Edinburgh University on 13 September 1803. [EMG.35][AJ.2906]

MCFARLANE, RODERICK, born 1810, late of St Kitts and New York, died in Tain on 10 September 1835. [AJ.4577]

MCFARLANE, WALTER, a merchant in St Croix, 1776-1778. [NLS.8793]

MCFARLANE, WALTER, died in Antigua on 26 September 1839. [SG.8.826]

MCGEE, REBECCA, died 18 December 1827, probate St Jan. [RAK.1826-1836.30-43]

MCGIBBON, DUNCAN, a Jacobite prisoner transported to Montserrat in 1716. [SPAWI.1716.313][CTB.31.206]

MCGILL, ROBERT, a merchant in Nevis, 1770-1780. [NLS.8793]

MCGILLIES, DANIEL, born 1687, a labourer from Arisaig, a Jacobite prisoner transported to Antigua in 1747. [P.3.90]

MCGILLIVRAY, DONALD, probate 28 February 1781, Christiansted. [RAK.297.82]

MCGILVARY, JOHN, a Jacobite prisoner transported to Antigua in 1716. [SPAWI.1716.310][CTB.31.204]

MCGREGOR of MCGREGOR, Sir JOHN ATHOLL, President of the Virgin Islands, died in Tortula on 11 May 1851; testament 1855. [NRS.SC70.1.88][EEC.22134][W.1231][FJ.964]

MCILROY, ARCHIBALD, probate 27 April 1768, Christiansted. [RAK.14.29]

MCINDOE, CHARLES, in St Croix in 1802. [RDAG.1/2]

MCINLIER, DUNCAN, a Jacobite transported to Montserrat in 1716. [SPAWI.1716.313]

MCINTOSH, ANGUS, a Jacobite transported to Montserrat in 1716. [SPAWI.1716.313][CTB.31.206]

MCINTOSH, ANN, a Jacobite prisoner transported to Antigua in 1747. [P.3.102]

MCINTOSH, JAMES, youngest son of Robert James McIntosh, died at Government House, St Kitts, on 20 August 1847. [AJ.5205]

MCINTOSH, JOHN, probate 30 April 1768, Christiansted. [RAK.50]

MCINTOSH, LACHLAN, a Jacobite prisoner transported to Antigua in 1716. [SPAWI.1716.310][CTB.31.204]

MCINTOSH, MALCOLM, a Jacobite prisoner transported to Montserrat in 1716. [SPAWI.1716.310][CTB.31.204]

MCINTOSH, ROBERT, from New York City, died in Tortula, probate April 1782, PCC. [TNA]

MCINTOSH, WILLIAM, a Jacobite prisoner transported to Antigua in 1716. [SPAWI.1716.310][CTB.31.204]

MCINTYRE, ANN, born 1727, from Argyll, a Jacobite banished to Antigua in 1747. [P.3.104]

MCINTYRE, DANIEL, a clerk or book-keeper to the firm of McNeil, Saddler and Claxton in St Kitts in 1760. [NRS.CS96.4370.30]

MCINTYRE, DENIS, a Jacobite prisoner transported to Montserrat in 1716. [SPAWI.1716.313][CTB.31.205]

MCINTYRE, JOHN, a Jacobite prisoner transported to Montserrat in 1716. [SPAWI.1716.313][CTB.31.205][CTP.CC43]

THE PEOPLE OF THE LEEWARD ISLANDS, 1620 - 1860

MCINTYRE, MARY, a Jacobite prisoner transported to Antigua in 1747. [P.3.106]

MACKAY, ALICE, wife of John Aitchison a merchant in the Virgin Islands, died in Tortula on 30 November 1797. [Cummertrees gravestone]

MACKAY, DANIEL, in St Croix, married Mrs John Muir, widow of John Muir in Demerara, in Morningside, Edinburgh, on 17 February 1825. [GM.95.273][BM.17.638]; born 1757, late of St Croix, died in Glebeside Row, Glasgow on 15 May 1839. [SG.8.768]

MACKAY, DONALD, second son of Murdo Mackay and his wife Jane Mackay in Strahnavaar, emigrated to Darien in 1699, settled in St Kitts in 1700. [BM.249][NRS.GD84.Sec.1/22/9b]

MACKAY, DONALD, in Antigua, letters, 1804-1831. [NRS.GD87.2.27]

MACKAY, FRANCIS, and Elizabeth Mackay, in St Croix in 1802. [RDAG.I/2]

MACKAY, Captain HUGH, of Borlay, in St Kitts by 1700. [NRS.GD21.1.1700; GD84.Sec.1/22/9b]

MACKAY, HUGH, a merchant in Antigua, eldest son of Lieutenant Colonel George Mackay of Bighouse and his wife Louisa Campbell, a deed, 26 June 1799. [NRS.RD3.308.5]; letters, 1797-1800. [NRS.GD87.2.25/27]; dead by 1818. [Book of Mackay, p.332]

MACKAY, JAMES, a mariner from Londonderry, died in Antigua, probate, 1693, PCC. [TNA]

MACKAY, JOHN, a minister sent to the Leeward Islands in 1739. [EMA.42]

MACKAY, ROBERT, seventh son of Donald Mackay of Bighouse and his wife Mary McInnes, died in Antigua on 29 September 1816. [GM.86.566][SM.56.62][DPCA.752]

MCKECHNIE, ALEXANDER, of Little Batturich, a merchant in Glasgow, later in St Kitts and in St Croix, a sasine, 6 January 1769. [NRS.RS10.Dunbarton.10.187]

MCKECHNIE, CLAUD, born 1819, MD, MRCSE, died 15 August 1853. [St Anthony's mi, Montserrat]

MCKENLY, WILLIAM, a minister sent to Nevis in 1773. [EMA.42]

MCKENNY, COLIN, a Jacobite prisoner transported to Antigua in 1716. [SPAWI.1716.310][CTB.31.204]

MACKENROT, ANTHONY, of Tortula, married Frances Bowe Gardiner, in London in 1811. [SM.73.878]

MCKENZIE, ALEXANDER, a Jacobite who was transported to Antigua aboard the Prince George in 1748. [TNA.T53.44]

MCKENZIE, ALEXANDER, died 24 April 1762, probate 1767 Christiansted also Fredericksted. [RAK.1760-1775, 9-10]

MACKENZIE, ANDREW LAING, born 1839, son of John MacKenzie a miller and his wife Janet Laing, died on 15 January 1847, buried in Antigua. [Greenock gravestone]

MCKENZIE, COLIN, probate 8 January 1777, Christiansted. [RAK.305.102]

MCKENZIE, HECTOR, a Jacobite who was transported to Antigua aboard the Prince George in 1748. [TNA.T53.44]

MCKENZIE, JOHN, formerly a merchant in St Kitts, died in Glasgow on 19 October 1797. [GM.67.984]

THE PEOPLE OF THE LEEWARD ISLANDS, 1620 - 1860

MCKENZIE, THOMAS, a Jacobite prisoner transported to St Kitts in 1716. [SPAWI.1716.312][CTB.31.217]

MCKEY, PETER, probate 24 March 1773, Christiansted. [RAK.180.178]

MCKIE, JOHN, born 1798, son of Peter McKie and his wife Margaret Rodie in Whithorn, Galloway, died in Antigua on 14 November 1821. [Whithorn gravestone]

MCKINLAY, FINLAY, aboard the Joanna bound for Antigua in 1790. [NRS.E504.15.56]

MCKINLAY, FRASER, master of the Mary of Antigua bound from Greenock to Newfoundland in 1789. [NRS.E504.15.52]

MCKINLAY, ROBERT, a merchant in Antigua, co-owner of the Mercury of Greenock in 1792. [NRS.CE60.11.3/59]

MCKINLAY, WILLIAM, of St Kitts, graduated MA from Aberdeen University on 31 March 1772. [AUL]

MCKINNEY, ALEXANDER, a merchant in Nevis and St Kitts in 1661, agent for George McCartney a merchant in Belfast. [PRONI.MCI19.1]

MCKINNON, CHARLES WILLIAM, in Antigua in 1757. [DA.Ogilvy pp.24]

MCKINNON, Dr DANIEL, born 1658, settled in Antigua, married Elizabeth Thomas, parents of Samuel, [St John's Town Library, Antigua, ms]; in Antigua in 1696. [TNA. Association Oath Rolls]; admitted as a burgess of Glasgow in 1717, [GBR]; died 1720, probate 20 March 1720, Antigua.

MACKINNON, SAMUEL, son of Dr Daniel Mackinnon, married Susanna Cunningham in St Kitts 1725. [HS.7.6/34]

MCKINNON, WILLIAM, born 1699, son of Daniel McKinnon, second son of Lachlan McKinnon of McKinnon, late of Antigua, died on 8 October 1769. [Bath Abbey gravestone]

MCKINNON, Lieutenant Colonel, son of William McKinnon in Antigua, married Miss Call, daughter of Sir John Call, in London on 3 October 1804. [SM.66.806]

MACKINTOSH, ALEXANDER, probate 11 April 1767, Fredericksted. [RAK]

MACKINTOSH, JAMES, infant son of Robert James Mackintosh, died at Government House, St Kitts, on 29 August 1847. [GM.ns28.558]

MCKITTRICK, JAMES, in Antigua in 1753. [NRS.CS96.645]

MCLAREN, ALEXANDER, a Jacobite prisoner transported to Antigua in 1716. [SPAWI.1716.310]

MCLAREN, ALEXANDER, in St Kitts, testament, 1868. [NRS.SC70.1.140/13]

MCLAREN, DANIEL, a Jacobite prisoner transported to Antigua in 1716. [SPAWI.1716.310][CTB.31.204]

MCLAREN, JOHN, a Jacobite prisoner transported to Antigua in 1716. [SPAWI.1716.310][CTB.31.204]

MCLAREN, JOHN, probate 1777, Christiansted. [RAK.268.264]

MCLAREN, WALTER, a Jacobite prisoner transported to St Kitts in 1716. [SPAWI.1716.312][CTB.31.207]

MCLARTY, MALCOLM, born 1845, son of Malcolm McLarty and his wife Helen Gow Thomson, died in St Croix on 10 February 1863. [Port Glasgow gravestone]

THE PEOPLE OF THE LEEWARD ISLANDS, 1620 - 1860

MCLAUGHLAND, ALLAN, probate 7 May 1777, Christiansted. [RAK.291.52]

MCLAUGHLAND, CHARLES, probate 8 April 1772, Christiansted. [RAK.97.307]

MCLEA, FINLAY, in Antigua in 1760. [DA. Ogilvie pp.33]

MCLEAN, DANIEL, a Jacobite prisoner transported to Montserrat in 1716. [SPAWI.1716.313][CTB.31.205][CTP.CC43]

MCLEAN, JOHN, died 24 April 1762, probate Christiansted. [RAK.1760-1775.10]

MCLEAN, PETER, a Jacobite prisoner transported to Antigua in 1716. [SPAWI.1716.310][CTB.31.204]

MCLEAN, Captain, Governor of Crab Island in the Leewards, 1698. [DSP.78]

MCLEAR, ALEXANDER, a Jacobite prisoner transported to Montserrat in 1716. [SPAWI.1716.313][CTB.31.205][CTP.CC43]

MCLEARINS, ALEXANDER, a Jacobite prisoner transported to Antigua in 1716. [SPAWI.1716.310][CTB.31.204]

MCLENNAN, MICHAEL, probate 20 June 1761, Christiansted. [RAK.308]

MCLEOD, NORMAN, died in St Thomas on 23 May 1805. [SM.67.805][AJ.3015]

MCLINTOCK, LAWRENCE, probate 16 December 1772, Christiansted. [RAK.160.107]

MCMAHON, Mrs ELIZABETH DALRYMPLE, born 1761, from St Kitts, died in London on 8 September 1845. [GM.ns.24.434]

MCMICHAEL, ROBERT, probate 31 October 1768, Fredericksted. [RAK]

MCNABB, ALEXANDER, a Jacobite prisoner transported to Montserrat in 1716. [SPAWI.1716.313][CTB.31.206][CTP.CC43]

MCNABB, JOHN, a Jacobite prisoner transported to Montserrat in 1716. [SPAWI.1716.313][CTB.31.206][CTP.CC43]

MACNAMARA, Miss, eldest daughter of John Macnamara, married Lord Cranstoun in St Kitts on 25 August 1807. [GM.77.886][SM.69.956]; their daughter was born there on 15 August 1808. [GM.78.1125]; and a son was born in Cranstoun House there on 15 August 1809. [GM.79.789][SM.71.799]; Lord James Edmond Cranstoun died in St Kitts on 5 September 1818. [GM.88.470]

MACNAMARA, Mrs, widow of J MacNamara in St Kitts, and mother of Lady Cranstoun, died on 21 June 1818. [GM.88.643]

MCNAMAROE, DANIEL, in the parish of Sandy Point, St Kitts on 7 February 1678. [TNA.COI.42]

MCNEAL, HECTOR, born in Rosebank, Roslin, on 22 October 1746, later in St Kitts, Guadaloupe, Grenada, and Jamaica. [NRS.NRAS.0052]

MCNEIL and CLAXTON, merchants in St Kitts, 1756; 1758-1781. [NRS.CS16.1.98; CS96.4370; CS237.T4.1]

MCNEIL, HECTOR, in Antigua in 1749, father of John McNeil. [NRS.PS3.11.161]; testament, 1749, Comm. Glasgow. [NRS]

MCNEILL, HUGH, a merchant in Antigua, later in Ballantrae, Ayrshire, testament, 7 March 1752, Comm. Glasgow. [NRS]

MCNEILL, HUGH, in St Kitts, 1766. [NRS.CS16.1.125]

THE PEOPLE OF THE LEEWARD ISLANDS, 1620 - 1860

MCNEILL, NEILL, a merchant in Bristol, later in St Kitts and St Croix, 1760s. [NRS.CS16.1.115/117/120]; sometime a merchant in Bristol then in St Kitts, brother of Malcolm McNeill of Ardlally, Islay, in 1768. [NRS.CS27.907][NRS.CC12.2.2]; a merchant in St Kitts, a deed, 1799. [NRS.RD4.267.1096]; in St Kitts, later in Ardtally, Islay, Argyll, testament, 4 February 1777, Comm. The Isles. [NRS]

MCNEILL, SAMUEL, in St Kitts, 1766. [NRS.CS16.1.125]

MCNEILL, ..., probate, 20 July 1765, Fredericksted. [RAK]

MCNISH, JOHN, a surgeon in Antigua later in Glasgow, 1782. [NRS.CS17.1.1]

MCNISH, ROBERT, died in Antigua on 5 February 1827. [S.862.242]

MCNORMER, DUNCAN, a Jacobite prisoner transported to Montserrat in 1716. [SPAWI.1716.313][CTB.31.206][CTP.CC43]

MCPHERSON, ALEXANDER, a Jacobite transported to Montserrat in 1716. [SPAWI.1716.313][CTB.31.206]

MCPHERSON, DANIEL, a Jacobite prisoner transported to Antigua in 1716. [SPAWI.1716.310][CTB.31.204]

MCPHERSON, DANIEL, probate, 10 June 1748, St Croix. [RAK.1747-1754.135]

MCPHERSON, DONALD, a Jacobite prisoner transported to St Kitts in 1716. [SPAWI.1716.312][CTB.31.207]

MCQUEEN, DANIEL, a Jacobite transported to Antigua in 1716. [SPAWI.1716.310][CTB.31.204]

MCTAIR, WILLIAM, in St Kitts, 1776. [NLS.Acc.8793.28]

MCVEY, GEORGE, merchant in St Kitts, 1766. [NRS.CS16.1.125]

MCVEY, GEORGE, born 1744, died in Antigua on 23 March 1773. Brother of Stewart McVey in Tobago. [St John's Cathedral, Antigua]

MCVEY, STEWART, merchant in St Kitts, 1766. [NRS.CS16.1.125]

MADAN, JANE, in St Kitts, probate 1791, PCC. [TNA]

MADAN, MARTIN, in Nevis, probate, 1704, PCC. [TNA]

MADAN, Reverend MARTIN, in St Kitts, probate 1790, PCC. [TNA]

MADDOCK, SAMUEL, died in Nevis on 3 September 1755. [GM.25.428]

MAGENIS, CHARLES, a merchant in St Croix, 1770. [RDAG.I.50]

MAHONY, GEORGE, in St Kitts, probate, 1799, PCC. [TNA]

MALLEY, AUGUSTINE, in St Croix in 1770. [RDAG.I.50]

MANDERSTON, ANDREW, died in Antigua in January 1770. [St Paul's Cathedral]

MANNING, AUGUSTUS, in St Kitts, probate, 1798, PCC. [TNA]

MANNING, JOHN, born 1673, died 16 March 1725, husband of Joanah born 1683, died 19 May 1722, parents of William, Christian, Ann, Mary Ann, Samuel, and Rebecca. [Trinity gravestone, Palmetto Point, St Kitts.]

MANNING, Miss, only daughter of the late Richard Manning in Antigua, married Henry Pearson, a merchant in London, in Antigua in June 1787. [GM.57.933]

MANNING, WILLIAM, in St Croix, probate, 1793, PCC. [TNA]

MARBURY, MICHAEL. in St Kitts, probate, 1641, PCC. [TNA]

THE PEOPLE OF THE LEEWARD ISLANDS, 1620 - 1860

MARCHANT, NATHANIEL, from Antigua, died in Sidmouth, Devon, on 19 February 1804. [GM.74.191]

MARDENBOROUGH, PETER, on Saba, petitioned the Dutch West India Company in Amsterdam in 1772. [DNA.Inv.1151]

MARDENBOROUGH, THOMAS, on Saba, petitioned the Dutch West India Company in Amsterdam in 1772. [DNA.Inv.1151]

MARK, ALEXANDER, in St Croix in 1768. [SSF]

MARKHAM, B P, in St Kitts in 1765. [PCCol.1765.658]

MARKHAM, WILLIAM, born 1754, an attorney-at-law, from London aboard the Mathew bound for St Kitts in 1774. [TNA.T47.9/11]

MARKOE, ABRAHAM, in Spanish Town plantation, St Croix, ca.1755; in 1768. [SSF]; later in Philadelphia, founder of the Philadelphia Light Horse Troop, fought at Brandywine.

MARSH, WILLIAM, aged 26, bound aboard the Mathew of London, master Richard Goodladd, for St Kitts on 21 May 1635. [TNA.E157.20]

MARSHALL, ANDREW, a horse-thief, was transported from Glasgow to Antigua in 1752. [AJ.260]

MARSHALL, JOHN, from St John's, Antigua, died in Perth, testament 30 March 1785, Comm. Glasgow. [NRS] [testament refers to his brother Andrew Marshall in St John's, Antigua.]; services of heirs, 1786. [NRS]

MARSHALL, ROBERT, a bigamist, was transported from Glasgow to Antigua in 1752. [AJ.260]

MARSHALL, THOMAS, master of the Glasgow of St Kitts, trading between Scotland and St Kitts in 1742. [NRS.E504.15.1]

MARSHALL, Captain THOMAS, probate 20 December 1780, Christiansted. [RAK.459.94]

MARTIN, FRANCIS, born 1734, a gentleman returning to St Kitts aboard the Pemberton via Whitehaven in 1774. [TNA.T47.9/11]

MARTIN, GEORGE, in Tortula in 1821. [NRS.CS17.1.40/8]

MARTYN, PATRICK, in the parish of Sandy Point, St Kitts on 7 February 1678. [TNA.COI.42]

MARTIN, ROBERT, in Antigua in 1757. [DA.Ogilvie pp.14]

MARTIN, ROBERT, born 1751, a gentleman, via London aboard the William and Elizabeth bound for Antigua in 1774. [TNA.T47.9/11]

MARTIN, SAMUEL, died in Antigua on 25 December 1701. [St John's Cathedral, Antigua]

MARTIN, SIMON, from St Ives, a husbandman aged 18, who emigrated via Plymouth aboard the Margaret bound for St Kitts in 1634. [TNA.E157.18]

MARTIN, S., was murdered by his slaves in Antigua, 1702. [PCCol.1702.71]

MARTIN, THOMAS, aged 20, from Cardinham, a husbandman who emigrated via Plymouth aboard the Margaret bound for St Kitts in 1634. [TNA.E157.18]

MARTIN, THOMAS, a merchant in Antigua, was admitted as a burgess of St Andrews in 1739. [StABR]

MARTIN, Miss, daughter of Henry Martin late President of the Leeward Islands, married George Leonard, a judge in Antigua and a Councillor of the Virgin Islands on 27 August 1791. [GM.61.872]

THE PEOPLE OF THE LEEWARD ISLANDS, 1620 - 1860

MARTIN, Mrs, wife of Samuel Martin in Antigua, from Egham, died in the West Indies in 1810. [GM.80.491]

MASON, JOHN, born 1767, died in St Kitts on 23 September 1821. [GM.91.571]

MASSEY, ELIZABETH, a widow from Northampton, died in Antigua, probate 1686, PCC. [TNA]

MASTERMAN, LUCY, daughter of John Masterman, married George Cumming Miller, Captain of the 54th Regiment of Foot, brother of Sir William Miller of Glenlee, Kirkcudbrightshire, in Antigua on 18 June 1850. [AJ.5349]

MASSEY, GEORGE, born 1731, died 14 August 1779, husband of Ann, born 1717, died 9 February 1796. [St John's gravestone, Antigua]

MASSY, RICHARD, a yeoman, an indentured servant bound from Bristol to Nevis in 1660. [BRO]

MASTERS, ELIZABETH, from Bath, bound from Bristol to St Kitts in 1660. [BRO]

MATALA, Sergeant DENNIS in Halfwaytree Division, St Kitts on 7 February 1678. [TNA.COl.42]

MATTHEWS, CHARLES, in Antigua, will, 1751. [Glamorgan Record Office: d/df/f21-25b]

MATHEW, EDWARD F R, born 1833, youngest son of Reverend E W Mathew in Pentlowhall, Essex, died in Basseterre, St Kitts, on 27 October 1858. [GM.ns,2.6.100]

MATHEW, GEORGE, from Ludswan, a husbandman aged 23, who emigrated via Plymouth aboard the _Margaret_ bound for St Kitts in 1634. [TNA.E157.18]

THE PEOPLE OF THE LEEWARD ISLANDS, 1620 - 1860

MATTHEW, Sir WILLIAM, Governor of the Leeward Islands. [JCTP:19.5.1704]; Lieutenant General William Mathew, Councillor of Antigua on 26 September 1721, [PCCol.1721, App.ii.821]; died in Antigua on 30 September 1752. [GM.22.478] [SM.14.510]

MATHEW, WILLIAM ISAAC, master mason, died 15 November 1739 in Antigua. [Fort James gravestone]

MAULE, JAMES, a minister, died in Antigua before 1697. [NRS.S/H]

MAURY, JOHN, a yeoman, an indentured servant bound from Bristol to St Kitts in 1660. [BRO]

MAW, Sergeant WILLIAM, in St Thomas, Middle Island, St Kitts on 7 February 1678. [TNA.COI.42]

MAWFREY, EDWARD, aged 15, bound aboard the Mathew of London, master Richard Goodladd, for St Kitts on 21 May 1635. [TNA.E157.20]

MAXWELL, Colonel CHARLES WILLIAM, Governor of St Kitts and the Virgin Islands, married Miss Douglas, daughter of Colonel Douglas of Greencroft, in Lockerby House, Dumfries-shire, on 5 April 1821. [GM.91.372]; she died in St Kitts on 9 January 1823. [GM.93.473]

MAXWELL, EDWARD, probate 2 November 1774, Christiansted. [RAK.233.228]

MAXWELL, WILLIAM, in Antigua in 1753, [NRS.CS96.644]

MAY, WILLIAM, born 1602, a seaman from Maymard in Somerset, bound from Dartmouth to St Kitts in 1634. [TNA]

MAYNARD, WILLIAM, a gentleman, from Portsmouth aboard the Dorsetshire bound for St Kitts in 1775, to settle in Nevis. [TNA.T47.9/11]

THE PEOPLE OF THE LEEWARD ISLANDS, 1620 - 1860

MEAD, WILLIAM, a planter in Nevis, a complaint in 1702. [PCCol.1702.50]

MEERS, ELLENOR, born 1755, died 16 December 1769. [St Anthony's mi, Montserrat]

MEKINS, EDWARD, aged 18, aboard the John of London, master James Waymoth, bound for St Kitts on 2 October 1635. [TNA.E157.20]

MELDRUM, GEORGE, a Jacobite prisoner transported to Antigua in 1716. [SPAWI.1716.310][CTB.31.204]

MELVILLE, JANE, second daughter of the late Thomas Melville in St Vincent, married George Herbert Cox of the 53rd Regiment, in Twickenham, London, on 17 May 1848. [GM.ns.30.88]

MELVIN, FRANCIS, probate 31 October 1767, Fredericksted. [RAK.12]

MENDEZ, RACHEL, with three children, on Nevis in 1678. [TNA.CO1]

MENZIES, NINIAN, a merchant from Glasgow, formerly in Richmond, Virginia, died in St Eustatia on 18 February 1781. [SM.43.223]; testament, 1799, Comm. Edinburgh. [NRS]

MERAC, JOHN, youngest son of L. Merac a merchant in London, died in St Kitts in January 1803. [GM.73.283]

MERAE, JOHN, an Anglican minister in St Kitts in 1672. [FPA.279]

MERCHANT, HENRIETTA, daughter of Nathaniel Merchant in Antigua, married Robert Liston of Damhead, in St Andrew's Episcopal Church in Glasgow on 27 February 1796. [Scottish Antiquary.X.23]

MERRIFIELD, EDWARD, aged 19, aboard the Paul of London, master Jo. Acklin, bound from Gravesend to St Kitts on 3 April 1635. [TNA.E157.20]

MESSENGER, RICHARD, from Creekard in Wiltshire, an indentured servant aboard the Elisabeth and Ann master William Benn, bound from Liverpool to Montserrat in March 1700. [LRO]

METCALF, OSWELL, aged 22, aboard the John of London, master James Waymoth, bound for St Kitts on 2 October 1635. [TNA.E157.20]

MEUNIER, FRANCIS, a Huguenot in the French sector of St Kitts was forced to abandon his plantation, father of Mary the widow of Peter Maillard, and Arouet wife of …… Guychard, a petition in 1714. [SPAWI.1714.74/327]

MEURE, ………, a Huguenot in St Kitts in 1716. [JCTP.1716.197]

MEYER, HENRY, a merchant planter in Antigua, who was denisized in 1675. [SPAWI.1675.376]

MEYERS, MARTINUS, Commander of St Martins in 1711.

MILDON, WILLIAM, in Nevis, probate, 1669/1676, PCC. [TNA]

MILLER, Dr WILLIAM, in Antigua, was admitted as a burgess and guilds-brother of Ayr on 17 October 1767. [ABR]; he was dead by 1818. [NRS.RS54.GR1113/272]

MILLIKEN, WILLIAM, in St Kitts in 1757. [NRS.GD237.12.47]

MILLINGTON, ROWLAND, aged 24, bound aboard the Mathew of London, master Richard Goodladd, for St Kitts on 21 May 1635. [TNA.E157.20]

MILLS, FRANCES, in St Kitts, probate 1774, PCC. [TNA]

MILLS, GEORGE RICE, born 1824, died in Nevis on 9 December 1853. [GM.ns.41.329]

THE PEOPLE OF THE LEEWARD ISLANDS, 1620 - 1860

MILLS, JOHN, in St Kitts, probate 1769, PCC. [TNA]

MILLS, JOHN COLHOUN, former President of Nevis, died at sea on 15 July 1828. [GM.98.286]

MILLS, M., in Nevis, 1701. [RSM]

MILLS, PAIXFIELD, born 1818, Chief Justice of Nevis, died there on 1 January 1854. [GM.ns.41.329]

MILLS, PETER MATHEW, in St Kitts, probate 1792, PCC. [TNA]

MILLS, THOMAS, in St Kitts, probate 1768, PCC. [TNA]

MILLS, THOMAS M., in Nevis, probate, 1774, PCC. [TNA]

MILLS, WILLIAM, in St Kitts, probate 1779, PCC. [TNA]

MILNE, ALEXANDER, son of Peter Milne in Old Meldrum, died in St Croix in 1810. [EA.4900]

MILNE, ANDREW, a Jacobite prisoner transported to Antigua in 1747. [P.3.196]

MILWARD, THOMAS, aged 18, bound aboard the Mathew of London, master Richard Goodladd, for St Kitts on 21 May 1635. [TNA.E157.20]

MINOR, THOMAS, in Nevis, probate, 1712, PCC. [TNA]

MINOR, WILLIAM, in Nevis, probate, 1696, PCC. [TNA]

MITCHELL, ALEXANDER, a merchant in Antigua in 1778. [NRS.CS16.1.173/159]

MITCHELL, HENRY, in Nevis, probate, 1681, PCC. [TNA]

MITCHELL, HUGH, sr., a planter, died on 3 February 1758, husband of Maria Matthews, probate, St Jan. [RAK.1758-1775.1A]

MITCHELL, JOHN, probate 1 February 1767, Christiansted. [RAK]

MITCHELL, ROBERT, probate 30 January 1782, Christiansted. [RAK.331.174]

MITCHELL, WALTER, a Jacobite who was transported to Antigua aboard the Prince George in 1748. [TNA.T53.44]

MITCHELL, WILLIAM, died 12 February 1802, probate St Jan. [RAK.1797-1807.23]

MITCHELL, WILLIAM, born 1763 in East Seaton, Arbroath, settled in St Croix in 1784, died at Buss End, St Croix, on 16 March 1834. [AJ.4514][NRS.S/H]

MINOR, WILLIAM, in Nevis, probate, 1696, PCC. [TNA]

MOODY, GEORGE, a Jacobite prisoner transported to Montserrat in 1716. [SPAWI.1716.313][CTB.31.205][CTP.CC43]

MOIR, Dr ALEXANDER, born in Mortlich, Banffshire, Bursar of King's College, Aberdeen, died in St Croix in 1766. [SM.28.615] [AJ: 8.12.1766]

MOIR, HENRY, a Jacobite who was transported to Antigua aboard the Prince George in 1748. [TNA.T53.44]

MOIR, ROBERT, a Jacobite who was transported to Antigua aboard the Prince George in 1748. [TNA.T53.44]

MOLINEUX, CATHERINE, in St Kitts, probate 1794, PCC. [TNA]

MOLINEUX, ……., in Montserrat in 1724. [SPAWI.1724.400]

MOLINEAUX, …., Speaker of the General Assembly of Montserrat, died on 2 October 1761. [GM.21.538]

MOLINEAUX, CRISP, of Thundersley Hall, Essex, late Sheriff of Norfolk, died in St Kitts on 4 December 1792. [GM.62.1220]; in St Kitts, probate 1793, PCC. [TNA]

THE PEOPLE OF THE LEEWARD ISLANDS, 1620 - 1860

MONCRIEFF, ROBERT, a minister who was sent to Antigua in 1749. [EMA.46][FPA.283]

MONOD, GASPAR JOEL, chaplain to the Governor of Guadaloupe in 1759. [FPA.317]

MONTANACQ, JOHANN ARNOLD, a Dutch Reformed Church minister, husband of Elisabeth Barner on St Thomas in 1753. [RAK.WIC.429]

MONTGOMERIE, Dr GAVIN, born 1727 in Renfrewshire, died on 30 August 1772 in Antigua. [Vernon's Estate, gravestone]

MONTGOMERIE, HUGH, in St Kitts, probate, 1700, PCC. [TNA]

MONTGOMERY, JOHN, a merchant in Tortula, later in Port Glasgow, 1795. [NRS.AC7.67]

MONTGOMERY, ROBERT, a merchant in St Croix, 1809, 1822, records, 1809-1829. [NRS.CS239.S49/9; CS17.1.41/643; CS96.4488]

MONTGOMERY, WILLIAM, in Antigua in 1753. [NRS.CSS96.644]

MOODY, GEORGE, a Jacobite banished to Jamaica, landed on Montserrat in 1716. [SPAWI.1716.313][CTB.31.205]

MOORE, ADRIANA, daughter of William Moore in St Eustatia, married Robert Semple from Demerara, in Glasgow on 30 September 1817. [BM.2.126]

MOORE, ELIZABETH, from St Eustatia, married James McInroy from Demerara, in Broomloan on 25 December 1797. [EEC.4201]

MOORE, THOMAS, born 1710, died in Antigua on 22 July 1754. [St John's Cathedral, Antigua]

MOORE, WILLIAM, born 1726, died after 1788, from Dumfries, a merchant in St Eustatia, an Episcopalian church-warden there, married Patricia Lilley, parents of Thomas and William. [SG]

MOREFLAT, ..., in St Kitts in 1672. [SPAWI.1672.903]b

MORETON, JONATHAN B., merchant in St Croix in 1802. [RDAG.I/2]

MORGAN, JOHN, aboard the barque Dove at Barbados bound for Nevis on 29 October 1679. [TNA]

MORRIS, EDWARD, born 1613, a locker from Exeter, bound from Dartmouth to St Kitts in 1634. [TNA]

MORRIS, MARY MELBOROUGH, wife of George Horne from Edinburgh, died in Basseterre, St Kitts, on 12 May 1869. [S.8060]

MORRIS, THOMAS, a Councillor of Antigua, 26 September, 1721. [PCCol.App.ii.821]

MORRIS, VALENTINE, a privateer in Antigua in 1702, [CTB.XIX.213]; was appointed a Councillor of Antigua on 26 September 1721. [PCCol.1721.App.ii.821]

MORRISON, AGNES, born 1823, daughter of John Morrison, the Assistant Clerk of Session, wife of Donald Mackenzie Morrison a merchant in Antigua, died in St John's, Antigua, on 18 May 1853. [EEC.22447]; they married on 8 April 1851 in St John's, Antigua. [EEC.22118]

MORRISON, JAMES, a Jacobite prisoner transported to Antigua in 1716. [SPAWI.1716.310][CTB.31.204]

MORRISON, Reverend JOHN, to Nevis in 1699, probate 1704, PCC. [TNA][EMA46][DP335]

MORRISON, JOHN, in Antigua in 1753. [NRS.CS96.644

MORISON, JOHN, a merchant in Tortula, son of James Morison of Dunbrae, a deed, 18 September 1803. [NRS.RD3.303.743]

THE PEOPLE OF THE LEEWARD ISLANDS, 1620 - 1860

MOROSEY, TIMOTHY, in Nevis, probate, 1697, PCC. [TNA]

MORSON, ARTHUR, born 1776, son of William Morson, a merchant in Antigua, died in Brompton on 19 May 1793. [GM.63.485]

MORSON, RICHARD WILLOCK, second son of Walter Skerret Morson in Montserrat, died in Antigua on 17 September 1823. [BM.15.131]

MORSON, WALTER SKERRET, MD, in Montserrat, married Jane Jameson, second daughter of Robert Jameson a Writer to the Signet, in Edinburgh on 25 October 1822. [S.302.348]

MORTIMER, GEORGE, a Jacobite prisoner transported to Montserrat in 1716. [SPAWI.1716.313][CTB.31.206][CTP.CC43]

MORTIMER, WILLIAM, a planter in Antigua, last will and testament, 1 January 1818, Comm. Moray. [NRS]

MORTON, JOHN, in Nevis, probate, 1770, PCC. [TNA]

MORTON, ROWLAND, aged 17, bound aboard the Mathew of London, master Richard Goodladd, for St Kitts on 21 May 1635. [TNA.E157.20]

MORTON, WALTER, son of Hugh Morton in Leith, died in St Croix on 5 July 1797. [EEC.416]

MOUCHET, ..., in St Kitts in 1673. [SPAWI.1673.1048]

MOUNTAIN, JO., aboard the Paul of London, master Jo. Acklin, bound from Gravesend to St Kitts on 3 April 1635. [TNA.E157.20]

MOYSES, MATHEW, aged 17, , aboard the Paul of London, master Jo. Acklin, bound from Gravesend to St Kitts on 3 April 1635. [TNA.E157.20]

MUIR, ANDREW, in St Croix, later in Glasgow, testament, 14 December 1814, Comm. Glasgow. [NRS]

MUIR, Dr JOHN, in Antigua in 1757. [DA.Ogilvie pp.24]

MUIR, JOHN, from Antigua, graduated MD from Glasgow University in 1790. [RGG.457]; was admitted as a burgess and guilds-brother of Ayr on 2 October 1790. [ABR]; to Antigua in 1791. [NRS.NRAS.3572.2.135]

MUIR, JOHN, a merchant in Antigua in 1790. [NRS.CS16.1.173/412]

MULLENEUX, JO., aged 24, aboard the John of London, master James Waymoth, bound for St Kitts on 2 October 1635. [TNA.E157.20]

MULLER, J. L., in St Croix in 1802. [RDAG.I/2]

MUNDAY, MARY, bound from Bristol to Nevis in 1660. [BRO]

MUNRO, GEORGE, in Antigua in 1753. [NRS.CS96.644]

MUNRO, JOHN, in St Kitts, probate 1766, PCC. [TNA]

MUNRO, WILLIAM, a surgeon in Antigua, a sasine in 1830. [NRS.RS.Argyll.1551]

MUNRO, ..., son of W. Munro, was born in St Kitts on 20 June 1869. [S.8107]

MURE, HELEN, wife of ....Hunter a merchant in Antigua in 1779. [NRS.CS16.1.175]

MURE, MARGARET, wife of Dr William Bowie a physician in Antigua in 1779. [NRS.CS16.1.175]

MURFEY, JOHN, in St Thomas, Middle Island, St Kitts on 7 February 1678. [TNA.COI.42]

MURPHY, CORNELIUS, in the parish of St John Capistar, St Kitts, on 28 January 1678. [TNA.COI.42]

MURPHY, DAVID in St Thomas, Middle Island, St Kitts on 7 February 1678. [TNA.COl.42]

MURPHY, DERMOND, in the parish of Sandy Point, St Kitts on 7 February 1678. [TNA.COl.42]

MURPHY, PATRICK, in the parish of St John Capistar, St Kitts, on 28 January 1678. [TNA.COl.42]

MURPHY, TEIGE, in the parish of Sandy Point, St Kitts on 7 February 1678. [TNA.COl.42]

MURPHY, WILLIAM, in the parish of Sandy Point, St Kitts on 7 February 1678. [TNA.COl.42]

MURRAY, ANDREW, a merchant in Antigua, 8 January 1709, [St John's Town Library ms, Antigua], was admitted as a burgess of Glasgow on 9 October 1717. [GBR]

MURRAY, GEORGE, son of William Murray a merchant in New Street, Canongate, died in Antigua in September 1798. [SM.61.72][AJ.2665]

MURRAY, HENRY, a Jacobite prisoner transported to Antigua in 1716. [SPAWI.1716.310][CTB.31.204][TNA.CO5.190]

MURRAY, JAMES, probate 31 August 1767, Fredericksted. [RAK.12]

MURRAY, JOHN S., in St Eustatia in 1784. [ASS.inv.125/571]

MURRAY, JOHN, in St Kitts, son of William Murray a merchant in Aberdeen, services of heirs, 1792. [NRS]

MURRAY, PATRICK, a Jacobite prisoner transported to St Kitts in 1716. [SPAWI.1716.312][CTB.31.207]

MURRAY, WILLIAM, a Jacobite prisoner transported to St Kitts in 1716. [SPAWI.1716.312][CTB.31.207]

MURRIN, ELIZABETH, aged 21, aboard the John of London, master James Waymoth, bound for St Kitts on 2 October 1635. [TNA.E157.20]

MUSGRAVE, Mrs ELIZA, born 1791, wife of William Musgrave, died in Antigua on 12 February 1815. [Upper Walronds gravestone, St Philips]

MUSGRAVE, WILLIAM, eldest son of Anthony Musgrave MD in Antigua, died in Edinburgh on 26 November 1840. [GM.ns.15.221]

MUSQUETA, EPHRAIM, a planter, was resettled in Nevis in 1712. [JCTP.1712.386]

MUSSON, JOHN T, born 1812, son of G S Musson in Antigua, died in London on 25 April 1847. [GM.ns.27.672]

MUTER, JOHN, of the Customs Service in St Lucia, second son of Reverend Dr Robert Muter in Kirkcudbright, died in Jamaica in February 1815, testament, 1816, Comm. Edinburgh. [NRS]

MYLES, ROBERT, from Perth, died in Antigua on 6 December 1803. [EA.4082.03][EEC.14220][AJ.2875]

NAESER, F.G., in St Croix in 1802. [RDAG.I/2]

NAIRNE, PETER, born 1761, third son of Reverend John Nairne and his wife Elizabeth Gordon in Anstruther, Fife, a merchant in Basseterre, St Kitts, died in 1786, testament, 16 November 1786, Comm. St Andrews. [NRS]

NAPIER, JAMES, died 28 July 1758, husband of [1] Rebecca, [2] Mary, probate, 1 June 1761, Christiansted. [RAK. 1755-1761]

THE PEOPLE OF THE LEEWARD ISLANDS, 1620 - 1860

NAPIER, Mrs MARY, wife of [1] John Napier, [2] Alexander Brabner, probate Christiansted, [RAK. 1755-1761]

NASS, JOHN, on Saba, petitioned the Dutch West India Company in Amsterdam in 1772. [DNA.Inv.1151]

NASS, THOMAS, on Saba, petitioned the Dutch West India Company in Amsterdam in 1772. [DNA.Inv.1151]

NAUCARRO, ELLIN, aged 20, from Penryn, emigrated via Plymouth aboard the Robert Bonaventure bound for St Kitts in February 1633. [TNA.E157.18]

NEALL, JOHN, a merchant in St Croix in 1770. [RDAG.I.50]

NEILD, WILLIAM CAMDEN, born 1777, eldest son of James Neild in London, a Councillor of Antigua, died in Falmouth on 19 October 1810. [GM.80.1810]

NELME, RICHARD, aged 20, bound aboard the Mathew of London, master Richard Goodladd, for St Kitts on 21 May 1635. [TNA.E157.20]

NESBIT, WALTER, was appointed a councillor of Nevis. [JCTP: 20.2.1759]

NEISBIT, Dr., from Nevis, died in Salisbury on 5 October 1781. [GM.51.491]

NESMITH, Captain ROBERT, at Halfway Tree, St Kitts, in 1667. [TNA.CO1.42/193]; an Assemblyman in St Kitts in 1677. [SPAWI.1678.741]

NETBY, ANTHONY, aged 20, bound aboard the Mathew of London, master Richard Goodladd, for St Kitts on 21 May 1635. [TNA.E157.20]

NETHERWAY, Colonel JOHN, Governor of Nevis, probate, 1692, PCC. [TNA]

THE PEOPLE OF THE LEEWARD ISLANDS, 1620 - 1860

NETHEWAY, JONATHAN, in Nevis, probate, 1701, PCC. [TNA]

NEW, SAMUEL, in Nevis, probate, 1763, PCC. [TNA]

NEWALL, JOHN, from Bristol, died in Antigua in November 1808. [GM.79.277]

NEWDON, JOHN, from St Tue, a husbandman aged 28, who emigrated via Plymouth aboard the Margaret bound for St Kitts in 1634. [TNA.E157.18]

NEWMAN, HANIBAL, a yeoman, an indentured servant bound from Bristol to Nevis in 1660. [BRO]

NEWTON, SAMUEL, in St Croix in 1768. [SSF]

NEWTON, WILLIAM, in St Kitts, probate, 1796, PCC. [TNA]

NIBBS, JEREMIAH, born 1727, died in Antigua on 27 May 1746. [St John's Cathedral, Antigua]

NICOL, ALEXANDER, from Mains of Melgund in Angus, an indentured servant bound for Antigua in 1784. [DA.H3330]

NICHOLLS, ARNOLD, a yeoman, an indentured servant bound from Bristol to St Kitts in 1660. [BRO]

NICHOLLS, WILLIAM, an indentured servant bound from Bristol to St Kitts in 1660. [BRO]

NICHOLSON, JOHN, a Jacobite prisoner transported to Antigua in 1716. [SPAWI.1716.313][CTB.31.204]

NICHOLSON, JOHN, from Kelso, Roxburghshire, a carpenter in Tortula, a deed, 1775. [NRS.RD2.236/1.499]

NICHOLSON, W T, M.D., died in Nevis on 2 September 1848. [GM.ns.30.558]

NIELSEN, GREGORY HOEG, in St Croix in 1768. [SSF]

THE PEOPLE OF THE LEEWARD ISLANDS, 1620 - 1860

NINIAN, ALEXANDER, a merchant in Tortula in 1800. [GA.T-ARD.13.1],

NISBET, DAVID, a merchant in St Kitts in 1776. [NLS.ms8793.4]

NISBET, JAMES, in Nevis in 1776. [NLS.Acc.8796.4/32]

NISBET, MARY EMILIA, daughter of Walter Nisbet in Nevis, married James Lockhart of Castlehill, in Edinburgh on 11 July 1773. [EMR]

NISBET, REDE, a merchant in Nevis before 1789, sought ordination in the Church of England. [FPA.287]

NISBET, ROBERT, from Lanarkshire, a merchant in Nevis, later in St Kitts, testament, 1743, Comm. Edinburgh. [NRS]

NISBET, WALTER, a merchant in Nevis, testament, 1743, Comm. Edinburgh. [NRS]

NISBET, WALTER, a planter in Nevis in 1777. [NLS.ms8793]; probate 16 February 1799, PCC. [TNA]

NISBET, Mrs, widow of W Nisbet in Nevis, died in Bath on 2 December 1819. [EA.5847.375]

NORRIS, J., M.D., from St Croix, died in London on 21 December 1815. [GM.85.643]

NORRIS, Reverend T., a former military chaplain in the Leeward Islands, died in London on 6 October 1816. [GM.86.467]

NOTT, THOMAS, aged 18, aboard the Paul of London, master Jo. Acklin, bound from Gravesend to St Kitts on 3 April 1635. [TNA.E157.20]

O'BYRNE, Mrs, born 1716, wife of Patrick O'Byrne, gave birth to twins in St Croix in February 1770. [SM.32.342]

OCHTERLONY, DAVID, in Antigua in 1757. [DA.Ogilvie pp.21]

OESTERMAN, THOMAS, in Antigua in 1709. [SPAWI.1709.443]

OFFLENT, JOHN, aged 20, bound aboard the Mathew of London, master Richard Goodladd, for St Kitts on 21 May 1635. [TNA.E157.20]

O'GARA, G., in Plymouth, Montserrat, 1719. [TNA.CO152.13]

OGERON, ………, Governor of Tortuga in 1677. [SPAWI.1677.383]

OGILVY, ADAM, youngest son of Sir John Ogilvy, died in Antigua on 29 July 1799. [GM.69.900][SM.61.724][AJ.2703]

OGILVY, HENRY, a Jacobite prisoner transported to St Kitts in 1716. [SPAWI.1716.312][CTB.31.207]

OGILVIE, JAMES, in St Croix in 1765. [NRS.AC.Decreets.1; 19 July 1765]; a merchant in St Croix, 1770. [RDAG.I.50]

OGILVIE, JOHN, born 1753, son of William Ogilvie and his wife Helen Baird in Banff, died in Antigua on 30 August 1770. [Banff gravestone]

OGILVIE, JOHN, in Antigua in 1761. [DA.Ogilvie ms.63]

OGILVIE, THOMAS, in Antigua in 1802, a letter. [NRS.GD205.box11/7][NRS.NRAS.Inverquharity ms.31/7]

OKEY, ADELINE, only child of C H Okey in Antigua, married Sir William Snagg, the Chief Justice of Antigua and Montserrat, in Salisbury on 29 June 1865. [GM.ns.2.19.235]

OLDER, RICHARD, aged 24, aboard the Paul of London, master Jo. Acklin, bound from Gravesend to St Kitts on 3 April 1635. [TNA.E157.20]

OLIPHANT, CHARLES, a Jacobite transported aboard the Prince George bound for Antigua in 1748. [TNA.T53.44]

THE PEOPLE OF THE LEEWARD ISLANDS, 1620 - 1860

OLIPHANT, LAWRENCE, a Jacobite prisoner transported to St Kitts in 1716. [SPAWI.1716.312][CTB.31.207]

OLIVER, RICHARD, born 1664 in Bristol, a planter in Antigua, Speaker of the House of Assembly there in 1704, a Member of the Council there in 1708, Colonel of the Militia of Antigua in 1715, died on 29 May 1716. [St John's mi, Antigua]

OLIVER, RICHARD, born 7 January 1734, died 16 April 1780. [St John's mi, Antigua]

OLIVIE, ..., a planter in Basse Terre, St Kitts before 1704. [SPAWI.1704.221]

O'MALLEY, THOMAS, a British Army physician from 1801-1826, graduated MD at St Andrews University in 1816, Health Officer on St Kitts. [StAUR]

ONETH, HULINNE, born 1600, a husbandman from St Stevens in Cornwall, bound from Dartmouth to St Kitts in 1634. [TNA]

ORR, ANDREW, from East Lothian, was admitted as a burgher of St Eustatia on 8 August 1781. [TNA.CO318.8.83]

ORR, JAMES, probate 30 November 1774, Christiansted. [RAK.195.24]

ORR, SAMUEL, a minister sent to the Leeward Islands in 1710, by 1726 he was minister of St Philip's, Antigua. [EMA.48][FPA.276]

OSBORN, ABIGAIL, daughter of Kean and Margaret Osborn, died on 9 December 1770. [Vernon's Estate gravestone, Antigua]

OSBORNE, ANN, in Antigua, married J S Tracey, Secretary to Rear Admiral Sir A. Cochrane, in Antigua in 1807. [SM.69.316]

OSBORN, GRACE PARSON, born 1776, eldest daughter of Humphrey Osborn in St Kitts, died in Southampton on 5 January 1853. [GM.ns.39.221]

OSBORNE, JANE, married Captain McCulloch of the Royal Navy, in Antigua on 30 September 1810. [EA.4898.367]

OSBORN, ROBERT WEIR, in St Croix in 1790. [Caribbeana.5.265]

OSWALD, JOSEPH, a Jacobite prisoner transported to Antigua in 1716. [SPAWI.1716.310][CTB.31.204]

OTTLEY, DREURY, born 1740, from St Kitts, died in London on 2 April 1822. [GM.92.379][DPCA.1028]

OTTLEY, Mrs ELIZABETH, born 1735, wife of Richard Otley, daughter of Ashton Warner the Attorney General and his wife Elizabeth, mother of Drewry, Elizabeth, Mary Trant, and Elizabeth, died in Antigua on 28 August 1766. [St John's Cathedral]

OTTLEY, GEORGE WEATHERILL, former Councillor of Antigua, died in Southampton on 16 July 1856. [GM.ns.2.1.283]

OTTLEY, JAMES PARSON, in St Kitts, probate 1779, PCC. [TNA]

OTTLEY, MATILDA ELWIN, fourth daughter of George Weatherill Ottley, of Parry's, Antigua, married George Fenton Fletcher Boughey, a Captain of the 59th Regiment, third son of the late Sir J. F. Boughey, in Antigua on 16 December 1842. [GM.ns.19.311]

OTTLEY, RICHARD, in St Kitts, probate 1775, PCC. [TNA]

OTTLEY, WILLIAM, in St Kitts, probate 1775, PCC. [TNA]

OTTLEY, W., from St Kitts, died in Cambridge on 28 September 1815. [GM.85.379]

OVERY, ………, in St Kitts in 1672. [SPAWI.1672.903]

OWEN, ANNE, from Worcester, an indentured servant bound from Bristol to St Kitts in 1660. [BRO]

OWEN, THOMAS, from Exeter, bound from Bristol to Nevis in 1660. [BRO]

OYSTERMAN, JOHN, a planter in Nevis in 1712. [JCTP.P224]

PADMORE, J., born 1758, a gentleman via London aboard the Pemberton bound for St Kitts in 1774. [TNA.T47.9/11]

PAINE, ROBERT, from Marrozun, a husbandman aged 29, who emigrated via Plymouth aboard the Margaret bound for St Kitts in 1634. [TNA.E157.18]

PALMER, JO., aged 19, bound aboard the Mathew of London, master Richard Goodladd, for St Kitts on 21 May 1635. [TNA.E157.20]

PALMER, NATHAN, from Carmarthen, bound from Bristol to Nevis in 1660. [BRO]

PAPINE, GABRIEL, a Huguenot who was granted land in St Kitts in 1696. [PCCol.1716.275; 1738.417][SPAWI.1715.585iii]

PAPLE, JO., aged 21, bound aboard the Mathew of London, master Richard Goodladd, for St Kitts on 21 May 1635. [TNA.E157.20]

PAPON, PETER, in St Kitts, probate 1783, PCC. [TNA]

PAPPS, HENRY SPENCER, born 1800 in Antigua, eldest son of Henry Papps a solicitor in Hamilton, Canada West, died in London on 9 March 1867. [GM.ns.3.3.548]

PARKE, DANIEL, former Governor of Antigua, deceased by 1733. [PCCol.1733.290]

THE PEOPLE OF THE LEEWARD ISLANDS, 1620 - 1860

PARK, GEORGE, born 3 November 1777 in Dunottar, Kincardineshire, son of William Park and his wife Rebecca Middleton, died in Guadaloupe in 1807. [Fetteresso gravestone]

PARKE, THOMAS DUNBAR, and his wife Lucy, in Antigua, a petition, 20 December 1733. [PCCol.1733.290]

PARKER, SAMUEL, aged 19, aboard the John of London, master James Waymoth, bound for St Kitts on 2 October 1635. [TNA.E157.20]

PARKER, WILLIAM, aged 17, bound aboard the Mathew of London, master Richard Goodladd, for St Kitts on 21 May 1635. [TNA.E157.20]

PARRIS, FANNY HENRIETTA, born 1785 in Cardiff, wife of Richard Neave Parris, died 19 March 1817 in Nevis. [St John's, Fig Tree, Nevis, gravestone][GM.87.646]

PARRIS, JAMES NEW, born 1767, a Councillor of Nevis, and Lieutenant Colonel of the Nevis Militia, died in Maidstone on 19 February 1846. [GM.ns.25.443]

PARSON, EDWARD, in St Kitts, probate 1780, PCC. [TNA]

PARSON, Reverend JAMES, born 1747, brother of John Parson in Botesdale, died in St Croix on 10 August 1811. [GM.81.657]

PARSON, WILLIAM WOODLEY, in St Kitts, probate 1770, PCC. [TNA]

PATERSON, JOHN, from Glasgow aboard the Susanna bound for Antigua in 1757. [NRS.CS96.653]

PATERSON, JOHN, a merchant in St Kitts in 1800. [NRS.CS18.714.25]

THE PEOPLE OF THE LEEWARD ISLANDS, 1620 - 1860

PATERSON, WILLIAM, son of Reverend Henry Paterson in Gateside, Dumfries-shire, died in Antigua on 18 July 1843. [EEC.20650]

PATNELLIE, ANN, only daughter of George Patnellie a merchant in Tortula, married John Stobo a surgeon, in Edinburgh in 1809. [SM.72.77]

PATTINSON, WILLIAM, in St Kitts, probate 1779, PCC. [TNA]

PATTISON, EBENEZER, died of yellow fever at St John's, Antigua, in 1817. [S.1.42]

PATULLO, THOMAS, paymaster of the 93rd Regiment of Foot, died in Antigua on 18 April 1827. [AJ.4143]

PAYNE, EDWARD, a tailor, bound from Bristol to Nevis in 1660. [BRO]

PAYNE, JO., aged 18, bound aboard the Mathew of London, master Richard Goodladd, for St Kitts on 21 May 1635. [TNA.E157.20]

PAYNE, LUCRETIA, in St Kitts, probate 1794, PCC. [TNA]

PAYNE, RALPH, was appointed Chief Justice of St Kitts in 1759. [JCTP:14.11.1759]; he died in 1763. [GM.32.97]

PEACHEY, JOHN, in St Kitts, probate 1781, PCC. [TNA]

PEARCE, ROBERT, an estate owner in Antigua and in St Kitts, married Miss Pycraft on 28 January 1745. [GM.15.108]

PEARNE, HENRY, a minor, son of the late Colonel Pearne a planter in Antigua, 1708. [PCCol.1708.190]

PEARNE, ROBERT, in Reed's Island, Antigua, died 1717. [PCCol.1766.730]

PEARSON, MICHAEL, emigrated from Leith to Darien in 1698, settled on Crab Island on 7 October 1698. [DSP.80]

PECHELLS, ..., a Huguenot in St Kitts in 1716. [JCTP.1716.197]

PESHALL, SAMUEL, died in Antigua on 18 November 1753. [St John's Cathedral, Antigua]

PESHALL, SANDERS, died in Antigua on 10 September 1754. [St John's Cathedral, Antigua]

PECKFORD, SAMUEL, an indentured servant, bound from Bristol to Barbados and Nevis in 1679. [BRO]

PEDDIE, ROBERT, MD, died in Antigua on 16 November 1841. [EEC.20307]

PEDERSEN, OLE, a timber merchant in St Croix in 1802. [RDAG.I/2]

PEDLER, FRANCIS, from St Breage, a husbandman aged 28, who emigrated via Plymouth aboard the Margaret bound for St Kitts in 1634. [TNA.E157.18]

PEDLER, ROBERT, from St Breage, a husbandman aged 22, who emigrated via Plymouth aboard the Margaret bound for St Kitts in 1634. [TNA.E157.18]

PELAWNE, MAURICE, in St Thomas, Middle Island, St Kitts on 7 February 1678. [TNA.COI.42]

PELE, Mrs S., eldest daughter of the late John Heaver, died in Antigua in November 1816. [GM.86.626]

PEMBERTON, Reverend JOSEPH HERBERT, born 10 September 1787, Rector of St George's, Nevis, died 19 September 1870. [St George's gravestone, Nevis]

PEMBERTON, Mrs MARGARET, widow of William Pemberton in Nevis, probate 3 March 1789.

PEMBERTON, ROBERT, sr, of parish of St George, Nevis, probate 28 October 1784, Nevis.

PEMBERTON, THOMAS SEATON, and Adriana Daniell, eldest daughter of James Daniell, President of Nevis, were married in St James, Windward, Nevis, on 2 May 1833.

PEMBERTON, THOMAS, from St Kitts, married Jane Blanshard, youngest daughter of the late John Blanshard of the Honourable East India Company Service, in Broadstairs on 12 August 1846. [GM.ns.26.420]

PEMBERTON, WILLIAM, in Nevis, probate 20 September 1784, Nevis.

PENCHEON, CATHERINE MARY, died 11 February 1873. [St Anthony's mi, Montserrat]

PENHEIRO, ISAAC, a planter on Nevis, 1708, resettled on Nevis in 1712. [TNA.CO152.157; JCTP.1712.386]

PENISTON, GEORGE, born 1772, died 23 January 1820. [St George gravestone, Basse Terre, St Kitts]

PENN, FRANCIS, aged 22, bound aboard the Mathew of London, master Richard Goodladd, for St Kitts on 21 May 1635. [TNA.E157.20]

PENNINGTON, JOHN, aged 40, from Symon Ward, emigrated via Plymouth aboard the Robert Bonaventure bound for St Kitts in February 1633. [TNA.E157.18]

PENNY, Reverend JOHN, born 1805, garrison chaplain at Sandy Point, St Kitts, died there in September 1840. [GM.ns.14.670]

PEPLOW, THOMAS, born 1661, an estate owner in St Kitts, died on 19 April 1752. [GM.22.192]

PERKES, HENRY, died on Nevis, probate, 1658, PCC. [TNA]

THE PEOPLE OF THE LEEWARD ISLANDS, 1620 - 1860

PERRY, MICHAEL. in Nevis, probate, 1690, PCC. [TNA]

PETER, ..., in St Kitts in 1672. [SPAWI.1672.903]

PETER, GEORGE F. CAREW, born 3 August 1821, son of W. Peter, MP, died 1 June 1865. [Antiguan Archives]

PETERSON, GEORGE, on Saba, petitioned the Dutch West India Company in Amsterdam in 1772. [DNA.Inv.1151]

PETERSON, JAMES, on Saba, petitioned the Dutch West India Company in Amsterdam in 1772. [DNA.Inv.1151]

PETERSON, PETER, on Saba, petitioned the Dutch West India Company in Amsterdam in 1772. [DNA.Inv.1151]

PETERSON, RICHARD, on Saba, petitioned the Dutch West India Company in Amsterdam in 1772. [DNA.Inv.1151]

PETERSEN, THOMAS, in St Croix in 1802. [RDAG.I/2]

PETRIE, ALEXANDER, in Antigua, nephew of Alexander Petrie a merchant in Elgin, Moray, 1777. [NRS.CS16.1.171]; in 1778 [NRS.CS16.1.173/357]

PERROTT, A., second son of the late G Perrott in Cracombe, Worcestershire, died in St Kitts in 1811. [G.81.292]

PEW, JOHN, late in Antigua, later in Leith, probate, 1800, PCC. [TNA]

PHILP, JOHN, born 1684, son of James Philp of Almerieclose, Arbroath, and his wife Jean Corbet, a Jacobite in 1715, fled to Holland, joined the New Dutch West India Company, a Militia Captain in St Martins, Governor there in 1728, husband of Rachel Hartmann, parents of John and Susan, died in December 1746. [NRS.RS35.15.37][Gosling, 132-139]

PHIPPS, CONSTANTINE, in St Kitts, probate 1769, PCC. [TNA]

THE PEOPLE OF THE LEEWARD ISLANDS, 1620 - 1860

PHIPPS, JAMES, in St Kitts, probate, 1786, PCC. [TNA]

PICKE, ANDREW, aged 34, from Great Dalby, emigrated via Plymouth aboard the Robert Bonaventure bound for St Kitts in February 1633. [TNA.E157.18]

PICK, HENRY, a yeoman, bound from Bristol to Nevis in 1660. [BRO]

PICKERING, JOHN, former Governor of Tortula, a Quaker, died in 1768. [GM.38.302]

PICKERING, THOMAS, from Great Budworth in Cheshire, an indentured servant aboard the Elisabeth and Ann master William Benn, bound from Liverpool to Montserrat in March 1700. [LRO]

PICKWOOD, ROBERT WILLIAMS, born 1778, son of Robert Pickwood in Vintry, died in St Kitts on 8 February 1834. [GM.104.670]

PIERRO, ..., a planter in Fig Tree Quarter, St Kitts, before 1717. [JCTP.1717.261]

PIETERSZOON, ABRAHAM HEYLOGER, Vice Commander of St Martin from 1746.

PINHEIRO, ISAAC, an alien, was granted denization on 2 February 1695. [S.P.Dom. Warrant Book, 40.16]; a planter on Nevis in 1708, [TNA.CO152-157]; resettled on Nevis in 1712. [JCTP.109-1715.383]; a merchant in Charlestown, Nevis, father of Moses, Sarah, Rebekah, and Judith.

PINHEIRO, Mrs ESTHER, widow of Isaac Pinheiro in Nevis, a merchant and ship-owner, trading between Nevis and Boston, 1716-1722, 1728 -. [TNA.CO.187/1/2]

PINNEY, AZARIAH, in Nevis, probate, 1720, PCC. [TNA]

THE PEOPLE OF THE LEEWARD ISLANDS, 1620 - 1860

PINNEY, HESTER, in Nevis, probate, 1740, PCC. [TNA]

PINNEY, JOHN, born 3 May 1686, son of Azariah Pinney, married in 1708 to Maria daughter of William Helme, died 11 December 1720. [St John's, Fig Tree, Nevis, gravestone]

PINNEY, JOHN FREDERICK, in Nevis, probate, 1762, PCC. [TNA]

PINNEY, MARY, in Nevis, probate, 1735, PCC. [TNA]

PINNEY, RICHARD, born 1739, a planter, bound from Portsmouth aboard the London Packet bound for Nevis in 1774. [TNA.T47.9/11]

PIRIE, ANDREW, born 1797 in Aberdeen, a merchant, died in St John's, Antigua, on 22 June 1871. [AJ.6447]

PITT, JAMES CHARLES, born 1760, son of the Earl of Chatham, Commander of HMS Hornet, died at English Harbour on 13 November 1780. [St Paul's gravestone, Antigua]

PLOTT, JOHN, a carpenter from Harrow-on-the-Hill, Middlesex, an indentured servant bound from Bristol to Nevis in 1660. [BRO]

PLUNKETT, Captain, a planter and ship-owner in Guadaloupe 1652. [HMC.36: Ormonde NS.1.163]

POGSON, Captain JOHN, from Horncastle, Lincolnshire, died 29 May 1686, husband of Hester …., died 9 October 1696, grandsons Freeman Pogson died 24 July 1696, and John Pogson died 20 June 1720. [Middle Island gravestone, St Kitts]

POGSON, JOHN, in St Kitts, probate 1784, PCC. [TNA]

POLLARD, THOMAS, aged 23, from Paranenth, emigrated via Plymouth aboard the Robert Bonaventure bound for St Kitts in February 1633. [TNA.E157.18]

THE PEOPLE OF THE LEEWARD ISLANDS, 1620 - 1860

PONTEGRAVE, ..., in St Kitts in 1672. [SPAWI.1672.903]

POOLE, Miss, daughter of James Poole the Governor of St Kitts, married John Prowse in Norton Fitzwarren, Somerset, on 14 August 1777. [GM.48.439]

POOR, RICHARD, at English Harbour, Antigua, will, 1798. [PWI]

POORE, Archdeacon, born 1816, died in St Kitts on 28 August 1861. [GM.ns.2.11.570]

PORTER, CHARLES RAIN, from Antigua, married Miss Rowland at Parham Hill on 11 February 1762. [GM.32.93]

PORTER, JOHN, in St Kitts, probate, 1687, PCC. [TNA]

PORTER, W. B. H., of the Post Office in Tortula, a letter, 1852. [BM.Add.ms35805/439]

PORTHE, ..., Customs Inspector of St Croix in 1750s, in 1768. [SSF]

POTTER, WILLIAM, master of the New Triton, died in July 1750. [St Phillips, Antigua]

POWELL, THOMAS, aged 21, bound aboard the Mathew of London, master Richard Goodladd, for St Kitts on 21 May 1635. [TNA.E157.20]

POWELL, THOMAS, aged 24, bound aboard the Mathew of London, master Richard Goodladd, for St Kitts on 21 May 1635. [TNA.E157.20]

POWNALL, Sir GEORGE, born 1755, Provost Marshal General of the Leeward Islands, died in Brighton on 17 October 1834. [GM.104.556]

POYETT, ..., in St Kitts in 1673. [SPAWI.1673.1048]

PRAETORIUS, J., a merchant in Christianstaed, St Croix, in 1789. [RDAG]

PRANT, DOMINIC JAMES, born 1775, died in Montserrat on 10 December 1803. [GM.74.182]

PRESTON, RICHARD, aged 21, aboard the Paul of London, master Jo. Acklin, bound from Gravesend to St Kitts on 3 April 1635. [TNA.E157.20]

PREUIT, JAMES GEORGE, in St Kitts, executor to Edward Wood's testament, 1825.

PRICE, Mrs ANNA, born 1818, wife of Thomas Price, son of S. R. Price in Cornwall, died in Tortula on 13 July 1857. [GM.ns.2.3.347]

PRICHARD, MARGARET, aged 17, bound aboard the Mathew of London, master Richard Goodladd, for St Kitts on 21 May 1635. [TNA.E157.20]

PRIHN, PAUL, a slave merchant in St Croix in 1770. [RDAG.I.3/50]

PRINGLE, ANN YOUNG, daughter of the late Walter Pringle in St Kitts, married John Dalrymple, son of Sir James Dalrymple of Newhailes, in Edinburgh on 26 June 1774. [EMR]

PRINGLE, MARGARET, daughter of Walter Pringle late of St Kitts, died in Edinburgh on 17 March 1772. [AJ.1263]

PRINGLE, WALTER, a merchant in St Kitts, died in 1760, father of Thomas, Eleanora, Rebecca, Ann, and Margaret, testament, 1776, Comm. Edinburgh. [NRS]

PRINGLE, Mrs WALTER, died in St Kitts on 19 August 1766. [SM.28.558]

PRINGLE, WILLIAM, a surgeon, late from Antigua, now in Kelso, Roxburghshire, a sasine, 18 February 1754. [NRS.RS27.143/203]

THE PEOPLE OF THE LEEWARD ISLANDS, 1620 - 1860

PRICHARD, THOMAS, a yeoman, an indentured servant bound from Bristol to Nevis in 1660. [BRO]

PROBYN, THOMAS, Governor of St Kitts, died on 10 January 1819. [GM.88.182]

PROCTOR, JOSEPH, a Jacobite prisoner transported to Antigua in 1716. [SPAWI.1716.310][CTB.31.204]

PULLEN, Mrs, born 1666, died in Antigua, in 1766. [FDJ.4126]

PURCELL, NICHOLAS, born 1751, a planter, via London aboard the Turnbull bound for Tortola in 1774. [TNA.T47.9/11]

PUREFOY, SAMUEL, from St Ives, a husbandman aged 13, a husbandman who emigrated via Plymouth aboard the Margaret bound for St Kitts in 1634. [TNA.E157.18]

PYLE, WILLIAM, in St John, Antigua, owner of the sloop Linnet, a petition, 1780. [PCCol.1780.478]

PYMON, ..., Governor of St Martin in 1736. [SPAWI.1737.20ii]

QUEELY, DOROTHY, a widow in St Kitts, testament, 1777, Comm. Edinburgh. [NRS]

QUELCH, Captain JAMES SPENCER, born 1779, died in Basseterre, St Kitts, on 28 July 1856. [GM.ns.2.1.520]

QUICK, ELIZABETH, born 1616, from Barnstable in Devon, bound from Dartmouth to St Kitts in 1634. [TNA]

QUINCEY, SAMUEL, in Antigua, letters, 1777-1781, [University of London:ms AL.321]; a barrister, died on passage from Tortula aboard the Sally bound for England on 9 August 1789. [GM.59.861]

RACER, GEORGE FRIDERICUS, a Dutch Reformed Church minister in St Croix in 1744. [RAK.WIC.429]

RADFORD, HENRY, aged 20, aboard the John of London, master James Waymoth, bound for St Kitts on 2 October 1635. [TNA.E157.20]

RAECX, EVERARD, Commander of St Eustatia in 1728. [SPAWI.1729.684]

RAIT, JAMES, born 1653, son of Reverend John Rait and his wife Elizabeth Beattie in Inverkeilor, Angus, died in Nevis in 1675. [Inverkeilor gravestone][F.3.439]

RAMSAY, ALEXANDER, probate, 28 July 1779, Christiansted. [RAK.259.273]

RAMSAY, ANDREW, a Jacobite prisoner transported to St Kitts in 1716. [SPAWI.1716.312][CTB.31.209]

RAMSAY, GEORGE, a wheelwright and farmer from Strathbogie, a Jacobite who was transported aboard the Prince George bound for Antigua in 1748, [TNA.T53.44][P.3.260]

RAMSAY, GEORGE, in Antigua in 1760. [DA.Ogilvie MS.46]; son of James Ramsay of Tullymurdoch, in Antigua later in St Vincent, testament, 1775, Comm. Edinburgh. [NRS]

RAMSAY, GEORGE, probate, 16 September 1765, Christiansted. [RAK]

RAMSAY, GILBERT, born in 1650s, educated at King's College, Aberdeen, in 1673, ordained by the Bishop of Galloway in 1686, to Antigua in 1686, minister at St Paul's, Antigua, until 1692, minister of Christ Church in Barbados from 1692 until 1727, died in Bath, England, on 5 May 1728, probate, 1720, PCC. [TNA]; Bath Abbey mi, [NRS.RD3.143.507][Caribbeana.3.268]

THE PEOPLE OF THE LEEWARD ISLANDS, 1620 - 1860

RAMSAY, JAMES, a minister sent to the West Indies in 1761, by 1770 he was rector of St John's Capisterre, St Kitts. [EMA.51][FPA.285]

RAMSAY, JOHN, in Antigua, a deed, 2 July 1806. [NRS.GD83.989]

RAMSAY, WILLIAM, a Jacobite prisoner transported to St Kitts in 1716. [SPAWI.1716.312][CTB.31.209]

RAMSAY, Lieutenant General, Governor of Antigua, died on 1 November 1819. [EA.5862.71]

RANNIE, JAMES, from Demerara, died in St Kitts on 14 May 1779. [SM.41.455]

RANO, JANE ELIZABETH, born 1804 in Basse Terre, died 1866. [St George gravestone, Basse Terre, St Kitts]

RASVELT, WIGBOLDUS, a Dutch Church Reformed minister in St Thomas in 1728. [RAK.WIC.430][NWIC.588.646]

RATCLIFFE, THOMAS WILKINSON, born 1791, from Castle Coakley, Sr Croix, died in London on 21 December 1854. [GM.ns.43.221]

RATSEY, EDWARD, in St Kitts, probate 1774, PCC. [TNA]

RATTRAY, JOHN, a widower from Scotland, settled in St Martins, married Catherina Simons, widow of Lucas Raapzaat, born in Saba but a resident of St Eustatia, there on 21 June 1734. ['Afscriften huwelijkakten van St Eustatius van 1710 -1750']

RAVENSHAW, WILLIAM, at Prince's Quarter, St Croix, 17... [RDAG]

RAWLINS, HENRY, in St Kitts, probate 1782, PCC. [TNA]

RAWLINS, JO., aged 18, bound aboard the Mathew of London, master Richard Goodladd, for St Kitts on 21 May 1635. [TNA.E157.20]

RAWLINS, Miss, born 1750, from Portsmouth, England, aboard St the <u>Weatherall</u> bound for St Kitts in May 1775, 'returning home'. [TNA.T47.9/11]

RAWLINS, Miss ANNA, born 1757, from Portsmouth, England, aboard the <u>Weatherall</u> bound for St Kitts in May 1775, 'returning home'. [TNA.T47.9/11]

RAWLINS, ANNA TAYLOR, daughter of the late Stedman Rawlins in St Kitts, married Captain Rwlins of the 30th Regiment, in Eltham, Kent, on 22 August 1803. [GM.73.788]

RAWLINS, JOSEPH, in St Kitts, probate, 1797, PCC. [TNA]

RAWLINS, STEDMAN, in St Kitts, probate, 1796, PCC. [TNA]

RAWLINS, WILLIAM WHARTON, died in St Kitts on 9 December 1840. [GM.ns.15.558]

RAWLINGS, Miss, daughter of Stidman Rawlings, married Captain Anthony Young, in St Kitts on 21 June 1787. [GM.57.738]

RAYMOND, ……, a planter at Pensez y Bien, and a property owner in Basse Terre, St Kitts before 1717. [JCTP.1717.261]

READ, MARMADUKE, aged 25, bound aboard the <u>Mathew of London</u>, master Richard Goodladd, for St Kitts on 21 May 1635. [TNA.E157.20]

READ, NATHANIEL, a militiaman in Montserrat in 1654. [Remonstrances ……., London, 1654]

REASON, RALPH, aged 23, aboard the <u>Paul of London</u>, master Jo. Acklin, bound from Gravesend to St Kitts on 3 April 1635. [TNA.E157.20]

REDHEAD, ELLEN, daughter of the late George Redhead in Antigua, formerly a Captain of the 3rd Guards Regiment, married Lieutenant James Athill of the Royal Navy, in London on 13 March 1850. [GM.ns.33.657]

REDHEAD, GEORGE, born 1737, from Antigua, died in London on 5 December 1801. [GM.71.1155]

REDWOOD, LEDEATT, eldest son of George Washington Ledeatt t in Antigua, married Elizabeth Jane Braithwaite, eldest daughter of Miles Braithwaite in Barbados, in London on 13 January 1846. [GM.ns.25.308]

REED, ELIZABETH, born 1615, a spinster from Exeter, bound from Dartmouth to St Kitts in 1634. [TNA]

REED, GEORGE, youngest son of George Reed of Hallcross House, Fisherrow, Musselburgh, died in St Kitts on 12 September 1860. [S.1663]

REES, Colonel BARTHOLEMEW, on Nevis ca.1720 [HS.7.6/33]

REEVE, THOMAS, aged 24, bound aboard the Mathew of London, master Richard Goodladd, for St Kitts on 21 May 1635. [TNA.E157.20]

REID, ALEXANDER, a Jacobite prisoner transported to Antigua in 1716. [SPAWI.1716.310][CTB.31.204]

REID, DAVID, a journeyman wright in Glasgow, indentured for 4 years' service with William Brown and Company in St Kitts in 1767. [GA.0623.T-MJ.427.23]

REID, GEORGE, was appointed Customs searcher and waiter in Guadaloupe in 1810. [NRS.GD51.6.1730]

REID, GILES, in St Croix in 1790. [Caribbeana.5.265]

REID, JAMES, in Antigua, was admitted as a burgess of Glasgow in 1727. [GBR]

REID, MARK HORNE, youngest son of Robert Reid a surgeon in Antigua, matriculated at Glasgow University in 1802, graduated MD in 1803. [MAGU.202]

REID, PATRICK, in Waulkmill, Tarland, Aberdeenshire, later in Antigua, 1763. [NRS.CS17.1.2]

REID, ROBERT SAMUEL, born in Antigua, eldest son of Robert Reid a surgeon, matriculated at Glasgow University in 1791, a surgeon who died in Antigua on 16 September 1804. [SM.67.74][MAGU.165][AJ.2968]

REID, THOMAS, from Ayrshire, was admitted as a burgher of St Eustatia on 8 August 1780. [TNA.CO318.8.83]

REID, Dr WILLIAM, born 1746 in Banff, 'studied physics and surgery under Dr Sanders a physician in Banff', settled in Antigua in 1765, died in St John's, Antigua, on 14 November 1773. [SM.36.111]

REINOLDS, JO., aged 20, bound aboard the *Mathew of London*, master Richard Goodladd, for St Kitts on 21 May 1635. [TNA.E157.20]

REINOLDS, THOMAS, aged 18, bound aboard the *Mathew of London*, master Richard Goodladd, for St Kitts on 21 May 1635. [TNA.E157.20]

REMEE, ..., in St Kitts in 1672. [SPAWI.1672.903]

RENOULT, ELIZABETH, a Huguenot planter in St Kitts before 1688; 1714; estates restored in 175. [JCTP.1712][PCCol.1715.1225] [SPAWI.1690.1212; 1714.631; 1715.375]

RENOULT, Mrs, from France, with her four daughters in St Kitts in 1714, 1717. [JCTP.1717.208][SPAWI.1714.631/662]; in St Kitts in 1729. [SPAWI.1730.58]

RENSBY, RICHARD, aged 28, from St Stephen's, emigrated via Plymouth aboard the Robert Bonaventure bound for St Kitts in February 1633. [TNA.E157.18]

REYNOLDS, JOHN, aged 23, aboard the Paul of London, master Jo. Acklin, bound from Gravesend to St Kitts on 3 April 1635. [TNA.E157.20]

REYSURE, ABRAHAM, on Nevis in 1678. [TNA.CO1]

RHODES, JOHN, a plantation overseer in St Kitts 1723. [HS.7.6/34]

RICHMOND, ROBERT, a surgeon, son of Matthew Richmond a nurseryman in Edinburgh, died in St Croix on 22 May 1805. [SM.67.885]

RICHARDS, WILLIAM, bound from Bristol to St Kitts in 1660. [BRO]

RICHARDSON, ALEXANDER, rector of the Anglican church in St Eustatius in 1771. [ASS]

RICHARDSON, GEORGE, in Nevis, probate, 1723, PCC. [TNA]

RICHARDSON, ROBERT, aged 20, aboard the Paul of London, master Jo. Acklin, bound from Gravesend to St Kitts on 3 April 1635. [TNA.E157.20]

RICHARDSON, WILLIAM, aged 24, aboard the John of London, master James Waymoth, bound for St Kitts on 2 October 1635. [TNA.E157.20]

RICHARDSON, WILLIAM, a planter, died 9 May 1747, husband of Susanna Hasel, probate, St Croix. [RAK.1741-1748. 307]

RICHARDSON, WILLIAM, late in St Vincent, married Elizabeth Gardiner, daughter of David Gardiner of Kirktonhill, there on 7 October 1789. [GM.59.954]

RICHARDSON, Mr, a gentleman from Kent, from Portsmouth aboard the Ann bound for St Kitts in 1774. [TNA.T47.9/11]

RICHES, GEORGE, born 1751, a clerk from Yarmouth, from Yarmouth on board the Effingham bound for St Kitts in 1775. [TNA.T47.9/11]

RICHES, JOHN, born 1752, a clerk from Yarmouth, from Yarmouth on board the Antonetta bound for St Kitts in 1775. [TNA.T47.9/11]

RICHMOND, ROBERT, a surgeon, son of Matthew Richmond a nurseryman in Edinburgh, died in St Croix on 22 May 1805. [SM.67.885]

RIDDELL, JAMES, a merchant in Guadaloupe, 1782. [NRS.CS17.1.1/197]

RIDDIE, RICHARD, born 1750, a gentleman, from London aboard the Generous Planter bound for St Kitts in 1775. [TNA.T47.9/11]

RIDGEWAY, JAMES, born 1677, from Prestbury, Cheshire, an indentured servant from Liverpool bound for St Kitts in 1699. [LRO]

RIDLEY, ALEXANDER, a Jacobite prisoner transported to Antigua in 1716. [SPAWI.1716.310][CTB.31.204]

RIDLEY, JOHN, a Jacobite prisoner transported to Antigua in 1716. [SPAWI.1716.310][CTB.31.204]

RIGAUD, Reverend S Jordan, Bishop of Antigua, son of the late Stephen Peter Rigaud, died in Antigua on 16 May 1859. [GM.ns2.9.84]

THE PEOPLE OF THE LEEWARD ISLANDS, 1620 - 1860

RINK, WILLEM HENDRIK, Vice Commander of St Martin from 1790 to 1807.

RISHFORD, GEORGE, aged 24, aboard the Paul of London, master Jo. Acklin, bound from Gravesend to St Kitts on 3 April 1635. [TNA.E157.20]

RITCHIE, JOSEPH, a Jacobite prisoner transported to Antigua in 1716. [SPAWI.1716.310][CTB.31.204]

RITCHIE, ROBERT, from Fife, was admitted as a burgher of St Eustatia on 21 November 1780. [TNA.CO318.8.84V]

RIVERS, SHADLOCK, born in St Kitts, fifth son of Shadlock Rivers a merchant, matriculated at Glasgow University in 1794. [MAGU.177]

ROBERDEAU, ISAAC, married Mary Cunningham in St Kitts in 1723, later settled in Philadelphia. [HS.7.6/34]

ROBERTSON, ALEXANDER, a Jacobite prisoner transported to Antigua in 1716. [SPAWI.1716.310]

ROBERTSON, DANIEL, a Jacobite prisoner transported to Antigua in 1716. [SPAWI.1716.310][CTB.31.204]

ROBERTSON, DUNCAN, a Jacobite prisoner transported to Antigua in 1716. [SPAWI.1716.310][CTB.31.204]

ROBERTSON, DUNCAN, a Jacobite prisoner transported to Montserrat in 1716. [SPAWI.1716.313][CTB.31.205][CTP.CC43]

ROBERTSON, FRANCIS, a Jacobite prisoner transported to Antigua in 1716. [SPAWI.1716.310]

ROBERTSON, JAMES, a Jacobite prisoner transported to Antigua in 1716. [SPAWI.1716.310]

THE PEOPLE OF THE LEEWARD ISLANDS, 1620 - 1860

ROBERTSON, JAMES, a Jacobite prisoner transported to Montserrat in 1716. [SPAWI.1716.313][CTB.31.205][CTP.CC43]

ROBERTSON, JOHN, a Jacobite prisoner transported to Antigua in 1716. [SPAWI.1716.310]

ROBERTSON, JOHN, a Jacobite prisoner transported to Montserrat in 1716. [SPAWI.1716.313][CTB.31.205][CTP.CC43]

ROBERTSON, JAMES, born 1750, Chief Justice of the Virgin Islands, died in Tortula on 23 November 1818. [GM.88.87]

ROBERTSON, Dr JOHN, died in Antigua in 1797. [GM.67.804]

ROBERTSON, MARGARET, in Antigua in 1753. [NRS.CS96.645]

ROBERTSON, Reverend ROBERT, born 18 March 1682 in Edinburgh, Rector of St Paul's, Charles Town, Nevis, 1707, 1726, 1727, died 6 April 1739. [St Paul's gravestone][FPA.275] [SPAWI.1727.771xi]

ROBERTSON, WILLIAM, died at Windy Hill, Tortula, on 26 January 1807. [GM.77.376]

ROBINSON, DANIEL, a servant of Robert Cunningham in St Kitts, 1734. [HS.7.6/34]

ROBINSON, JOHN, a Jacobite prisoner transported to St Kitts in 1716. [SPAWI.1716.312][CTB.31.207]

ROBINSON, JOSEPH, probate, 1750, St Croix. [RAK]

ROBINSON, Captain THOMAS, died in Antigua on 8 December 1751. [Vernon's Estate gravestone, Antigua]

ROBINSON, WILLIAM, aged 26, bound aboard the Mathew of London, master Richard Goodladd, for St Kitts on 21 May 1635. [TNA.E157.20]

ROBINSON, ..., son of William Robinson the President of Montserrat, was born in Government House, Montserrat, on 12 August 1864. [GM.ns2.17.643]

ROBISON, WILLIAM, a servant of William Salmon in Antigua, was admitted as a burgess and guilds-brother of Ayr on 5 February 1757. [ABR]

ROCHE, PATRICK, an estate owner in Montserrat, died in 1763. [GM.33.518][FDJ.3805]

RODIN, ELINOR, from Falmouth, Cornwall, bound from Bristol to Nevis in 1660. [BRO]

ROE, JOHN, a gentleman in Antigua, will, 1717. [PWI]

ROEBUCK, CHARLES AUGUSTUS, born 1845, son of the late Jarvis Roebuck in St Croix, died in London on 3 September 1859. [GM.ns2.7.434]

ROGERS, JOHN, in St Thomas, Middle Island, St Kitts on 7 February 1678. [TNA.COl.42]

ROGERSON, Mr, a planter, from Portsmouth aboard the Ann bound for St Kitts in 1774. [TNA.T47.9/11]

ROLLAND, ROBERT, a merchant burgess of Ayr who died in St Kitts in 1646, testaments 1648-1649, Comm. Glasgow. [NRS]

ROME, THOMAS, a merchant in Antigua, son of Thomas Rome of Clouden, a sasine, deeds, in 1714, 1715, 1719. [NRS.GD78.208; GD135.1615; RS23.105.448; RD2.104.657/665/739/991; RD4.117.321]

ROMNEY, Lady PRISCILLA, in St Kitts, probate 1771, PCC. [TNA]

ROOBY, MARTIN, aged 23, from Guindiron, emigrated via Plymouth aboard the Robert Bonaventure bound for St Kitts in February 1633. [TNA.E157.18]

ROOPE, TURNER, Assistant Commissary General in St Croix in 1802. [RDAG.I/2]

ROPER, HANNA, aged 23, aboard the Paul of London, master Jo. Acklin, bound from Gravesend to St Kitts on 3 April 1635. [TNA.E157.20]

ROSE, CATHERINE, daughter of John Rose of Holme, and wife of Captain George Eiston of the 35th Regiment, died in Guadaloupe on 29 May 1794. [SM.56.588]

ROSE, CHARLES, son of John Rose and his wife Mary Grant in Wester Alves, Moray, a schoolmaster in Christ Church, Barbados, from 1728 to 1732, then a minister in St Peter's, Parham, Antigua, Depute Judge of the Admiralty Court there, graduated Doctor of Laws at King's College, Aberdeen, on 28 January 1748. [Fasti Aberdonensis, Aberdeen, 1854, fo.447]; in Antigua in 1753. [NRS.CS96.644][EMA.53][FPA.192/234/279/283]

ROSENS, DANIEL, in Nevis in 1678. [SPAWI.1678.849][PCCol.1678.1237]

ROSETER, THOMAS, of Washboro, aged 20, a husbandman who emigrated via Plymouth aboard the Margaret bound for St Kitts in 1634. [TNA.E157.18]

ROSS, CHARLES, a merchant in Antigua, son of Walter Ross, services of heirs, 1789, [NRS]; a merchant in Antigua in 1794. [ECA.Moses.172.6745]

ROSS, DANIEL, a merchant in Nevis, 1778. [NRS.CS16.1.174.434]; probate, 1790, PCC. [TNA]

ROSS, ELIZABETH GARRETT, only child of John Crosbie in Antigua, wife of Reverend James Way in Adwell, Oxford, died 16 May, 1810. [GM.80.594]

ROSS, HUGH, a Jacobite banished to Antigua in 1716. [SPAWI.1716.310][CTB.31.204]

ROSS, HUGH, in Montserrat, 1766. [NRS.CS16.1.125]

ROSS, JANE, born 1753, via London aboard the Harlequin bound for Nevis in 1774. [TNA.T47.9/11]

ROSS, Captain JOHN, in Antigua in 1758. [DA.Ogilvie pp.28]

ROSS, JOHN, a storekeeper in Antigua, 1784. [NRS.AC7.61]

ROSS, JOHN, second son of Zachery Ross of Hawk, a gentleman in St Thomas, matriculated at Glasgow University in 1804, graduated MD in 1811. [MAGU.209]

ROSS, JOHN, in Antigua, later in Aberdeen, testament, 12 September 1816, Comm. Aberdeen. [NRS]

ROSS, MALCOLM, in St Eustatius in 1778. [ASS.inv.125/141]

ROTHWELL, ELIZABETH, a single woman, an indentured servant bound from Bristol to Nevis in 1660. [BRO]

ROWBOTHAM, CHARLES, son of Mr Rowbotham of the Bristol Theatre, died in Antigua on 17 October 1810. [GM.80.659]

ROWBOTHAM, JOHN, son of Mr Rowbotham of the Bristol Theatre, died in Antigua on 10 November 1810. [GM.80.659]

ROWLAND, RICHARD, a planter in St Kitts, died on 27 June 1761. [GM.21.334]; husband of Elizabeth.... [she died in 1744], parents of Rebecca and Margaret. [St George monumental inscription, Basse Terre, St Kitts]

ROWLAND, Miss, at Perham Hill, married Charles Ram Porter in Antigua on 11 February 1762. [GM.32.93]

ROYNON, CHARLES, in Nevis, probate, 1708, PCC. [TNA]

RUAN, FRANCES, youngest daughter of the late William Ruan, MD, married James Caw jr. of St Thomas, in St Croix on 14 September 1859. [GM.ns2.7.529]

RUAN, MARY BEACH, third daughter of W H Ruan MD in St Croix, married John Morrison jr from Glasgow, in Southampton on 18 April 1859. [GM.ns.2.6.537][CM.21707]

RUAN, WILLIAM, a planter, died 29 July 1835, probate, St Jan. [RAK.1826-1836, 236-252]

RUAN, WILLIAM, MD, eldest son of William Ruan a merchant in St Croix, matriculated at Glasgow University in 1810, graduated MD from Edinburgh University in 1818, married Christian Dumbreck, second daughter of William Dumbreck of South Coates, Edinburgh, at Hannah's Rest Estate, St Croix, on 16 February 1823. [BM.15.492]; their daughter was born on 28 November 1824. [F.152]; he died in St Croix on 29 November 1857. [MAGU.249][EMG.57][FH.152]

RUMSAY, ROBERT MURRAY, the Colonial Secretary of St Kitts, married Louisa Frances Wharton, third daughter of the late William Wharton a Councillor of St Kitts, on 12 December 1844. [GM.ns23.311]

RUOSLEY, JAMES, born 1613, a husbandman from London, bound from Dartmouth to St Kitts in 1634. [TNA]

RUSH, WILLIAM, aged 20, bound aboard the Mathew of London, master Richard Goodladd, for St Kitts on 21 May 1635. [TNA.E157.20]

RUSSELL, JAMES, in Nevis, probate, 1674, PCC. [TNA]; born 1600, Governor of Nevis from 1665 to 1671, died in England on 15 November 1674. [St James mi, Bristol]

RUSSELL, Sir JAMES, in Nevis, probate, 1688, PCC. [TNA]

RUSSELL, Major LOCKHART, in Antigua, a sasine, 3 October 1783, [NRS.RS.Elgin.71]; a deed, 3 October 1787. [NRS.RD3.247.403]

RUTHERFORD, JAMES, a former tenant in Longnewton, Roxburghshire, died in St Kitts on 28 November 1818. [EA.5748.71]

RUTHERFORD, JOHN, a surgeon in Antigua, in 1744, son of Thomas Rutherford a merchant in Edinburgh. [NRS.CS16.1.75]

RUTHERFORD, THOMAS, jr., a merchant from Sheffield, eldest son of Andrew Rutherford a merchant in Jedburgh, Roxburghshire, died in Christianstad, St Croix, on 22 November 1808. [SM.71.398][EA.4750]

RYAN, JOHN, from Montserrat, graduated from Leiden University in the Netherlands on 11 December 1769. [UL]

SABIN, THOMAS, born 1759, a mercantile clerk from Oxford, via London aboard the Generous Friend bound for Antigua in 1774. [TNA.T47.9/11]

SADDLER, JAMES, a merchant in St Kitts, in Bristol in 1782, [NRS.CS17.1.1/37]; a deed, 1797, [NRS.RD2.270.347];1781. [NRS.CS16.1.183]; son of William Saddler in St Kitts, reference in deed, 1798. [NRS.RD4.268.167]

SADDLER, WILLIAM, in St Kitts, probate 1766, PCC. [TNA]

SADDLER, WILLIAM, of Nicolatown, St Kitts, a merchant in St Kitts, 1765. [NRS.CS16.1.120]; a deed, deceased by 1797, [NRS.RD2.270.347]; reference to in a deed of 1799. [NRS.RD4.267.1096]; services of heirs, 1781. [NRS]

SAGRAN, ..., a French agent in St Eustatia in 1737. [SPAWI.1737.318]

SAINT ALBAN, ..., a French subject in St Eustatia in 1688. [PCCol.1733.259]

SAINT DENNY, ..., in St Kitts in 1672. [SPAWI.1672.903]

SAINT LAURENCE, ..., Governor of Guadaloupe in 1671. [SPAWI.1671.508]

SAINT LEON, ..., the Governor of Guadaloupe in 1674. [SPAWI.1674.1333]

SAINT MARKE, ..., in St Kits in 1672. [SPAWI.1672.903]

SAINT SANRESIS, Chevalier, in St Kitts in 1678. [SPAWI.1678.741ix]

SALINAVE, ELIZABETH, a Huguenot in St Kitts in 1690, 1714, 1715. [SPAWI.1690.1212; 1714.619/628/630xi/xiv/662; 1715.147i]

SALINAVE, ..., a planter in St Kitts before 1712. [JCTP.1716.180]

SALKELD, JAMES, a Jacobite prisoner transported to Antigua in 1716. [SPAWI.1716.310][CTB.31.204]

SALMON, WILLIAM, aged 25, bound aboard the Mathew of London, master Richard Goodladd, for St Kitts on 21 May 1635. [TNA.E157.20]

SALMON, WILLIAM, in Antigua in 1757. [DA.Ogilvie.pp.23]; was admitted as a burgess and guilds-brother of Ayr on 5 February 1757. [ABR]

THE PEOPLE OF THE LEEWARD ISLANDS, 1620 - 1860

SALOMONSZOON, JOHANNES, Commander of St Eustatia in 1690s

SALVETAT, PETER, a planter in St Kitts in 1723. [SPAWI.1723.532]

SAM, GREGORY, aged 15, from Chidleigh, emigrated via Plymouth aboard the Robert Bonaventure bound for St Kitts in February 1633. [TNA.E157.18]

SAMSON, THOMAS, son of Thomas Samson, 1777-1856, died in St Croix. [Kilmarnock, Laigh, gravestone]

SANDERS, FRANCIS, jr., born 1691, died 18 July 1742, husband of Sarah Sanders. [St George gravestone, Nevis]

SANDERS, HENRIETTA, wife of John Sanders, died 29 December 1746. [St John's, Fig Tree, Nevis, gravestone]

SANDERS, JOHN, from Marozion, a husbandman aged 18, who emigrated via Plymouth aboard the Margaret bound for St Kitts in 1634. [TNA.E157.18]

SANDERSON, JOSEPH, master of the Thomas Martin of Antigua trading between Scotland and New Brunswick in 1814. [NRS.E504.15.105]

SANDERSON, WILLIAM HENRY, born in St Kitts on 4 August 1788, an officer of the Royal Navy. [St George, Basse Terre, St Kitts, mi]

SANDLEY, ROBERT, aged 20, bound aboard the Mathew of London, master Richard Goodladd, for St Kitts on 21 May 1635. [TNA.E157.20]

SANGSTER, JOEL, a merchant in St John's, Antigua, a witness, 24 March 1797. [NRS.RD2.271.419]

SANGSTER, WILLIAM, born 1755, a clerk book-keeper from London, via London aboard the Friendship bound for Montserrat in 1774. [TNA.T47.9/11]

SAUNDERS, EMMA, born 1831, daughter of Richard Saunders the Customs Collector of Montserrat, died 23 February 1846. [St Anthony's mi, Montserrat]

SAUNDERS, HENRY, born 1826, son of Richard Saunders the Customs Collector of Montserrat, died 16 July 1852. [St Anthony's mi, Montserrat]

SAUNDERS, ROBERT, a shipbuilder, late of Antigua, 21 October 1796. [NRS.SC20.36.17]

SAUNDERS, WALTER, a carpenter, bound from Bristol to Nevis in 1660. [BRO]

SAVAGE, GEORGE, in Antigua in 1753. [NRS.CS96.645]

SAVAGE, Mrs, widow of George Savage, died in Antigua on 1 May 1806. [GM.76.583]

SAVAGE, WILLIAM, in St Kitts, probate, 1763, PCC. [TNA]

SAYER, SAMUEL, born 1740, died 11 December 1803, husband of Jane, born 1740, died 26 February 1779, parents of Samuel Sayer who died 21 February 1779. [St John's Cathedral gravestone, Antigua]

SCARSBRICK, WILLIAM, aged 23, aboard the *Paul of London*, master Jo. Acklin, bound from Gravesend to St Kitts on 3 April 1635. [TNA.E157.20]

SCARVILLE, DANIEL, born 1638, a master shipwright at H.M. Dockyard in Antigua for 14 years, died 9 October 1701. [St John's Cathedral, Antigua]

SCHAFFER, W., judge and recorder in Fredericksted, St Croix in 1770. [RDAG.I.50]

SCHAW, JAMES, in Montserrat, 1754. [JCTP:21.6.1759]

THE PEOPLE OF THE LEEWARD ISLANDS, 1620 - 1860

SCHEURMAN or MARROW, ISABEL, in Montserrat, 1699. [SPAWI.1699;132/683]

SCHEURMAN, PETER, a tailor in Antigua, 1709. [SPAWI.1709:459]

SCHIMMELMANN, HEINRICH ERNST, born 1743, planter of La Grange and The Princess estates in St Croix, Governor General of St Croix, died 1793.

SCHOLLAR, Mrs ANN, born 1755, wife of Thomas Schollar at English Harbour, Antigua, died 20 January 1780. [St Mary's gravestone, Antigua]

SCHONING, Comptroller, in St Croix in 1770. [RDAG]

SCHORER, LUCAS, Commander of the Dutch garrison at Fort Orange, St Eustatia, in 1689.

SCHOTT, JOHN P., born 1743, a gentleman, via London aboard the Pemberton bound for St Kitts in 1774. [TNA.T47.9/11]

SCOTLAND, JOHN, a merchant in Antigua, a deed, 24 April 1773. [NRS.RD3.232.432]

SCOTLAND, Lieutenant THOMAS, of the Royal Navy, son of Thomas Scotland in Antigua, died there in December 1812. [GM.83.284][EA.5132.13]

SCOTLAND, Mrs, wife of Thomas Scotland in Antigua, died at Hextable House, Kent, on 23 August 1815. [GM.85.281]

SCOTT, ALEXANDER, born on 22 July 1746 in Auchtergaven, Perthshire, a merchant, planter, and magistrate in Antigua, died 13 January 1787. [St John's gravestone, Antigua]

SCOTT, CHRISTIANA, born 1748, sister of Alexander Scott above, wife of David Ross, died 27 December 1781. [St John's gravestone, Antigua]

SCOTT, COLIN PATRICK, second son of Reverend John Scott in Muthill, died in Antigua in July 1794. [SM.56.588][EA.3209.214]

SCOTT, DAVID, a merchant in Antigua a deed, 1779. [NRS.RD4.226.1004]

SCOTT, ELISABETH, probate, 18 March 1778, Christiansted. [RAK.357.249]

SCOTT, GEORGE, probate, 4 June 1777, Christiansted. [RAK.96.249]

SCOTT, JAMES, probate 1 May 1776, Christiansted. [RAK.254.268]

SCOTT, JOHN, a gentleman in Nevis, probate, 1654, PCC. [TNA]

SCOTT, JOHN, a Jacobite prisoner transported to Montserrat in 1716. [SPAWI.1716.313][CTB.31.206][CTP.CC43]

SCOTT, JOHN, son of Gavin Scott a farmer in Auchinglen, Lanarkshire, died in St Martin's on 24 March 1807. [SM.69.477]

SCOTT, Captain ROBERT, probate 12 August 1772, Christiansted. [RAK.144.33]

SCOTT, WALTER, a Jacobite prisoner transported to Antigua in 1716. [SPAWI.1716.310][CTB.31.204]

SCOTT, WILLIAM, a minister sent to the West Indies in 1764, a minister on Nevis in 1770. [EMA.54][FPA.286]

SCOTT, WILLIAM HENRY, a merchant in St Eustatia, son of Alexander Scott a merchant in Edinburgh, died in Antigua on 12 May 1789. [GM.XII.601.212]

SCOTT, Mrs, born 1745, bound via Portsmouth aboard the William and Elizabeth bound for Antigua in 1774. [TNA.T47.9/11]

THE PEOPLE OF THE LEEWARD ISLANDS, 1620 - 1860

SCOTT, Mrs, widow of David Scott in Antigua, married Major General Richardson, in Bath on 9 November 1808. [GM.78.1039]

SCOTT, Mrs, widow of Dr William Scott in St Thomas, died in Paris on 26 December 1840. [EEC.20154]

SCOTT, ..., daughter of Mr Scott, was baptised in the Anglican church in St Eustatia on 8 October 1773. [ASS]

SCOTT, ..., son of Archibald Scott, was born in Antigua on 22 December 1859. [W.21.2161]

SCROPE, EDMUND, in Nevis, probate, 1695, PCC. [TNA]

SEARLE, DANIEL, Governor of Barbados and the Leeward Islands in 1650s. [PCCol]

SEATON, DANIEL, a Jacobite prisoner transported to Antigua in 1716. [SPAWI.1716.310][CTB.31.204]

SEATON, HENRY, in St Kitts in 1776. [NLS.Acc.8793.21]

SEATON, THOMAS, a Jacobite banished to Antigua in 1716. [SPAWI.1716.310][CTB.31.204]

SECKER, THOMAS, born 1760, a mercantile clerk from London, via London aboard the Generous Friend bound for Antigua in 1774. [TNA.T47.9/11]

SEDDEN, NICHOLAS, aged 20, aboard the Paul of London, master Jo. Acklin, bound from Gravesend to St Kitts on 3 April 1635. [TNA.E157.20]

SEDGWICK, ELVIRA CRICHTON, eldest daughter of Samuel Sedgwick, M.D. in Antigua, married Richard Nugent, M.D., from Dublin on 29 February 1848. [GM.ns29.538]

SEDGWICK, HENRY, in Nevis, probate, 1685, PCC. [TNA]

THE PEOPLE OF THE LEEWARD ISLANDS, 1620 - 1860

SELBIE, THOMAS, a Jacobite prisoner transported to Antigua in 1716. [SPAWI.1716.310][CTB.31.204]

SELKRIG, ROBERT, a planter in Nevis, a deed, 1788. [NRS.RD4.245.703]

SELWYN, HENRY CHARLES, Lieutenant Governor of Montserrat, died in Gloucester in 1807. [GM.77.684]

SEMPILL, JOHN, in St Croix in 1790. [Caribbeana.5.265]

SEMPLE M J, Councillor of Montserrat, married Miss Walsh Porter, in 1810. [EA.4885.255]

SEMPLE, JOHN, son of Robert Semple in Greenhead, Glasgow, died in St Thomas in 1818. [S.69.18]

SENTENCE, HENRY, aged 20, aboard the Paul of London, master Jo. Acklin, bound from Gravesend to St Kitts on 3 April 1635. [TNA.E157.20]

SENYOR, ISAAC, on Nevis in 1678. [TNA.CO1]

SEVAT, BELTHAZAR, in Nevis, probate, 1650, PCC. [TNA]

SEVERIN, JOHN, a planter in St Kitts from 1686. [SPAWI.1690.1124/1125/1177/1178]

SHARPE, CHARLES, born 1737, a planter in St Kitts, from Portsmouth aboard the Charles Shayse bound for St Kitts in 1774. [TNA.T47.9/11]

SHARP, GILES, son of Henry Sharp in St Kitts, was apprenticed in Edinburgh in 1764. [REA]

SHARPE, HENRY, was appointed a councillor of Nevis. [JCTP: 20.2.1759]

SHARP, JOHN, was educated at King's College, Aberdeen, a minister sent to Virginia in 1699, and by 1701 was in the Leeward Islands. [EMA.54][KCA.99][F.Ab.442]

SHARP, THOMAS, born 1745, a planter, from Plymouth aboard the Albion bound for St Vincent in 1775. [TNA.T47.9/11]

SHARROCH, DAVID, a Jacobite prisoner transported to Antigua in 1747. [P.3.308]

SHAW, AENEAS, in Nevis, probate 1782, PCC. [TNA]

SHAW, DERMOND in St Thomas, Middle Island, St Kitts on 7 February 1678. [TNA.COI.42]

SHAW, Dr JAMES, in Montserrat, was admitted as a burgess of Edinburgh in 1748. [EBR]

SHAW, JAMES, late of Montserrat, a sasine, 8 April 1775; was granted the lands of Preston on 6 August 1777. [NRS.RGS.117.241; RS27.219.33]

SHAW, JOHN, a Jacobite prisoner transported to Antigua in 1716. [SPAWI.1716.310][CTB.31.204]

SHEEN, WALTER, in Tortula, testament, 9 June 183, Comm. Edinburgh. [NRS]

SHELTON, RICHARD, a yeoman, an indentured servant bound from Bristol to Nevis in 1660. [BRO]

SHERIFF, JAMES WATSON, born in Antigua, President of Nevis, died there on 9 March 1866. [GM.ns3.1.754],

SHERIFF, JOHN, in Antigua in 1757. [DA.Ogilvie pp.19]

SHERIFF, JOHN, in St Thomas, eldest son of Matthew Sheriff tacksman of Captainhead, a deed, 7 November 1783. [NRS.RD4.234.764]

SHERIFF, JOYCE CLANDIA, only daughter of James Watson Sheriff the Attorney General of Antigua, died in London on 24 August 1853. [GM.ns40.428]

SHERIFF, ROBERT, eldest son of Robert Sheriff a merchant in Glasgow and London, was educated at Glasgow Univerity in 1819, a merchant in New York, died on Diamond Estate, St Croix, on 18 August 1847. [ANY.2.183]

SHERLOCK, JO., aged 20, aboard the John of London, master James Waymoth, bound for St Kitts on 2 October 1635. [TNA.E157.20]

SHIELDS, JOHN, a Jacobite prisoner transported to Antigua in 1716. [SPAWI.1716.310][CTB.31.204]

SHIELL, HENRY M., born 1827, died 1 February 1869, husband of Rostta, born 1834, died 30 September 1886. [St Anthony's mi, Montserrat]

SHIELS, JAMES, probate 1776, Christiansted. [RAK.318.133]

SHIPHERD, JOHN, in Nevis, probate, 1770, PCC. [TNA]

SHIPLEY, MORDAUNT JAMES, born 1781, second son of the Dean of St Asaph, died at Russell's Rest, Nevis, on 27 November 1806. [GM.77.179]

SHIRLEY, Sir THOMAS, of Oathall, Sussex, former Governor of Antigua and St Kitts, died in Bath on 21 February 1800. [GM.70.286]

THE PEOPLE OF THE LEEWARD ISLANDS, 1620 - 1860

SHIFFEFF, ROBERT, of New York, died in St Croix on 18 August 1847, papers, 1849, [NRS.CS313.13]; testament, 1859. [NRS.SC70.1.101]

SHIVAZ, GEORGE, late in Antigua, then in Glasgow, died at Sweethope, Borthwick, in April 1795, testament, 22 April 1796, Comm. Glasgow. [NRS]

SHORDICHE, JOHN CLEVELAND, second son of Paul Rycaut Shordiche, died in Antigua on 6 November 1864. [GM.ns2.18.116]

SHORDICHE, PAUL RYCAUT, son of Paul Rycaut Shordiche, died in Antigua on 13 July 1865. [GM.ns2.19.392]

SHORTE, JOANE, born 1614, from Exeter, bound from Dartmouth to St Kitts in 1634. [TNA]

SHORTER, DUNCAN, a Jacobite prisoner transported to Montserrat in 1716. [SPAWI.1716.313][CTB.31.205][CTP.CC43]

SIM, JOHN, born 1744, late in Antigua, died 29 November 1807, husband of Mary Stephens, 1755-1847. [Banff gravestone]

SIMMONS, CHARLES, on Saba, petitioned the Dutch West India Company in Amsterdam in 1772. [DNA.Inv.1151]

SIMMONS, JAMES, on Saba, petitioned the Dutch West India Company in Amsterdam in 1772. [DNA.Inv.1151]

SIMMONS, JOHN, on Saba, petitioned the Dutch West India Company in Amsterdam in 1772. [DNA.Inv.1151]

SIMMONS, JOSHUA, on Saba, petitioned the Dutch West India Company in Amsterdam in 1772. [DNA.Inv.1151]

SIMMONS, PETER, on Saba, petitioned the Dutch West India Company in Amsterdam in 1772. [DNA.Inv.1151]

SIMMONS, THOMAS, on Saba, petitioned the Dutch West India Company in Amsterdam in 1772. [DNA.Inv.1151]

SIMPSON, DUNCAN, probate 31 March 1773, Fredericksted. [RAK]

SIMPSON, JAMES, in Antigua in 1757. [DA.Ogilvie pp.15]

SIMPSON, WALTER, a merchant in Antigua in 1760, executor of Walter Pringle's testament, above.

SINCLAIR, GILBERT, was baptised in St Eustatia in 1768. [ASS]

SKEEN, MARY, died on 28 September 1819, probate St Jan. [RAK.1807-1828]

SKERRETT, EDWARD, in Plymouth, Montserrat, in 1719. [TNA.CO152.13]

SKERRETT, NICHOLAS, in Plymouth, Montserrat, in 1719. [TNA.CO152.13]

SKERRETT, ROBERT, a planter in Montserrat in 1712. [TNA.CO152.16]; in Plymouth, Montserrat, in 1719. [TNA.CO152.13]

SKERRETT, TITON, in Plymouth, Montserrat, in 1719. [TNA.CO152.13]

SKOSE, RICHARD, born 1597, a seaman from Newton Abbot, bound from Dartmouth to St Kitts in 1634. [TNA]

SLATER WILLIAM, husband Harriet Hopkins Brazier who died 11 July 1821, mother of Harriet who died 19 December 1824. [St John's, Fig Tree, Nevis, gravestone]

SLAUGHTER, PETER, a yeoman, an indentured servant bound from Bristol to Nevis in 1660. [BRO]

SLAVELIE, RICHARD, aged 40, from Stonehouse, emigrated via Plymouth aboard the Robert Bonaventure bound for St Kitts in February 1633. [TNA.E157.18]

THE PEOPLE OF THE LEEWARD ISLANDS, 1620 - 1860

SLEMAN, THOMAS, from St Hillary, a husbandman aged 18, who emigrated via Plymouth aboard the Margaret bound for St Kitts in 1634. [TNA.E157.18]

SLOWCUNA, JOHN, born 1759, a clerk from Kent, via London aboard the Elenor bound for Antigua in 1775. [TNA.T47.9/11]

SMALES, HENRY, in St Kitts, probate, 1694, PCC. [TNA]

SMALLMAN, EDWARD, aged 21, aboard the Paul of London, master Jo. Acklin, bound from Gravesend to St Kitts on 3 April 1635. [TNA.E157.20]

SMARGIN, ABRAHAM, a planter who was resettled on Nevis in 1712. [JCTP.1712.386]

SMART, ADAM, in Antigua in 1758. [NRS.GD219.289.9]

SMEATHMAN, Reverend CHARLES, from Melbourne, Australia, eldest son of the late Major Smeathman, died in St Kitts on 17 June 1855. [GM.ns54.439]

SMITH, ALEXANDER, a Jacobite prisoner transported to Montserrat in 1716. [SPAWI.1716.313][CTB.31.206]

SMITH, DANIEL, in Nevis, probate, 1647, PCC. [TNA]

SMITH, DANIEL, in St Kitts, 1731. [RSM]; Councillor of Nevis, a petition, 9 February 1737. [PCCol.1737.395]

SMITH, DANIEL, a Jacobite prisoner transported to Montserrat in 1716. [SPAWI.1716.313][CTB.31.205][CTP.CC43]

SMITH, ENGLISH, in Nevis, probate, 1664, PCC. [TNA]

SMITH, GEORGE, aged 17, bound aboard the Mathew of London, master Richard Goodladd, for St Kitts on 21 May 1635. [TNA.E157.20]

SMITH, JAMES, born 1698 in Arbroath, died in Antigua in 1745. [Arbroath Abbey gravestone]

SMITH, JO., aged 22, bound aboard the Mathew of London, master Richard Goodladd, for St Kitts on 21 May 1635. [TNA.E157.20]

SMITH, JOHN, from Stockland, Somerset, bound from Bristol to Nevis in 1660. [BRO]

SMITH, JOHN, in Nevis, probate, 1705, PCC. [TNA]

SMITH, JOHN, a Scottish mariner, married Johanna Davidts., a widow from St Martin's, in St Eustatia on 9 November 1745. ['Afscriften huwelijksakten van St Eustatius van 1710-1750']

SMITH, LEWIS LUDOVICK, from Forres, Moray, then in Antigua, later in St Kitts in 1821. [NRS.CS17.1.40/252]

SMITH, MICHAEL, in Nevis, probate, 1675, PCC. [TNA]

SMITH, PETER, 'a Dutchman' in St Thomas in 1699. [SPAWI.1699.616]

SMITH, RICHARD, aged 22, aboard the John of London, master James Waymoth, bound for St Kitts on 2 October 1635. [TNA.E157.20]

SMITH, ROGER, a robber, transported from Glasgow to Antigua in 1752. [AJ.260]

SMITH, SAMUEL, born 1725, died 23 November 1758. [St John's Cathedral, Antigua]

SMITH, WILLIAM, a planter in St Kitts until French conquest in April 1665, later in Ireland, a petition in 1674. [PCCol.1674.1000]

THE PEOPLE OF THE LEEWARD ISLANDS, 1620 - 1860

SMITH, WILLIAM, was educated at Cambridge University, an Anglican minister of St John's Figtree, near Charlestown, Nevis, from 1719 to 1724, later rector of St James, Nevis, in 1730s.

SMITH, WILLLIAM, a merchant in Christiansted, St Croix, a deed witness on 13 April 1821. [NRS.RD5.204.550]

SMYTH, BENJAMIN, born 1789, former Naval Officer General of Antigua, died in Westbury, Buckinghamshire, on 27 December 1840. [GM.ns15.330]

SNAGG, Mrs ANN, wife of Sir William Snagg the Chief Justice, died in Antigua on 16 February 1861. [GM.ns2.10.470]

SNAGG, Sir WILLIAM, the Chief Justice of Antigua and Montserrat, married Adeline Okey, only child of C H Okey in Antigua, in Salisbury on 29 June 1865. [GM.ns.2.19.235]

SOANES, FRANCIS, son of Richard Soanes and his wife Jane, died in Antigua on 9 January 1701. [St John's Cathedral, Antigua]

SOANES, JOHN, died in Antigua on 10 April 1741. [St John's Cathedral, Antigua]

SOANES, JOHN, died in Antigua on 3 January 1753, son of Richard Soanes and his wife Anne. [St Paul's, Antigua]

SOBODKER, JOHANNES, on Hogensborg Plantation, St Croix, around 1755; in 1768. [SSF]

SOLOMAN, NICOLAUS, in St Croix in 1768; in 1768. [SSF]

SOULEGRE, PETER, a planter in St Kitts, 1712, 1714, 1717, 1719, 1723, 1729, co-owner of the frigate <u>St Christopher</u> before the Admiralty Court of the Leeward Islands on 3 January 1719; a Councillor of St Kitts in 1724, in London by 1737. [JCTP.1717.260' 1729.16/21/103/366][SPAWI. 1714.678ii; 1723.531/722; 1729.632/633/1035; 1737.55iii] [PCCol.1719.1316]

SOULEGRE, Miss, daughter of Colonel Soulegre, married Stephen Theodore Janssen, in Antigua on 13 December 1750. [GM.20.570]

SPEERE, ELIZABETH, aged 20, bound aboard the Mathew of London, master Richard Goodladd, for St Kitts on 21 May 1635. [TNA.E157.20]

SPENCE, PHILIP, born 1760, a mercantile clerk from Kent, via London aboard the Generous Friend bound for Antigua in 1774. [TNA.T47.9/11]

SPENCE, WILLIAM, born 1680, from Cambridge, an indentured servant, bound from Liverpool aboard the Elizabeth and Ann, bound for Montserrat in 1700. [PA.193]

SPENCER, JAMES, born 1741, a carpenter in London, from there aboard the Margaret and Rebecca bound for Antigua in 1775. [TNA.T47.9/11]

SPENDERGRASS, THOMAS, aged 24, aboard the Paul of London, master Jo. Acklin, bound from Gravesend to St Kitts on 3 April 1635. [TNA.E157.20]

SPIER, ANDREW, of Marshyland, Beith, died in St Croix in 1852. [S.7.4.1852]

SPINK, JOHN, born 1821, son of John Spink and his wife Barbara Carey, died in St Thomas on 17 August 1850. [Arbroath Abbey gravestone]

SPINK, MARGARET, from Scotland, settled in St Eustatia, married [1] Theophilius Lengton from Saba, in St Eustatia in 1730, [2] Nathaniel Clee, from London, in St Eustatia in 1733. ['Afscriften huwelijksakten van St Eustatius van 1710-1750']

SPOONER, CHARLES, in St Kitts, probate 1790, PCC. [TNA]

SPOONER, JOHN, of St Mary Cayon, St Kitts, married Hannah... in 1722, parents of Susanna, baptised 1722, and Hungerford baptised 1726. [CAR.I.3]

SPOONER, JOHN, Chief Justice of St Kitts 1725. [HS.7.6/34]

SPOONER, JOHN, in St Kitts, probate 1786, PCC. [TNA]

SPURING, RICHARD, sr., born 1767, died in Antigua in June 1804. [GM.74.784]

SPURR, ROBERT, aged 24, aboard the Paul of London, master Jo. Acklin, bound from Gravesend to St Kitts on 3 April 1635. [TNA.E157.20]

SQUIRE, S J, an attorney from Plymouth, died in Tortula on 9 January 1804. [GM.74.374]

STACKS, GEORGE, born 1751, a clerk from London, via Bristol bound for Nevis in 1774. [TNA.T47.9/11]

STANLEY, JOHN, in St Kitts, probate, 1799, PCC. [TNA]

STAPLE, RICHARD, from London, died in St Kitts in 1728, probate, PCC. [TNA]

STAPLETON, ANNA, in St Kitts, probate, 1799, PCC. [TNA]

STAPLETON, EDMUND, brother of Sir William Stapleton in Yorkshire, died 18 August 1680. [St John's, Fig Tree, Nevis, gravestone]

STAPLETON, PIERCE, aged 22, bound aboard the Mathew of London, master Richard Goodladd, for St Kitts on 21 May 1635. [TNA.E157.20]

STATE, WILLIAM, in the parish of Sandy Point, St Kitts on 7 February 1678. [TNA.COI.42]

STEDMAN, ANN SARAH, second daughter of William Stedman MD, in St Croix, married Joseph Bushby, in St Croix on 23 July 1823. [BM.14.623][DPC.1106]

STEDMAN, Mrs ELIZABETH, wife of William Stedman MD, died in St Croix on 20 September 1843. [GM.ns20.670]

STEDMAN, LUCRETIA GORDON, eldest daughter of William Stedman MD in St Croix, died in Portobello near Edinburgh on 1 March 1841. [GM.ns15.669][EEC.20189]

STEEDMAN, WILLIAM, MD, born 13 June 1764 in Thurso, Caithness, second son of Thomas Steedman and his wife Anne Murray in Anderstown, educated at Glasgow University in 1782, a physician in St Croix, married Elisabeth Gordon, daughter of Dr George Gordon in St Kitts, in Glasgow on 2 February 1795, [SM.57.132]; a Knight of the Order of Dannebrog, died in St Croix on 7 April 1844.
[GM.ns21.670][Caribbeana.4.17][MAGU.132][SG.1312]

STEELE, WILLIAM, in St Thomas, Middle Island, St Kitts, in 1667. [TNA.CO1.42.193]

STEENBERGEN, Miss, from St Kitts, married Sir Thomas Durrant in Scottow, Norfolk, on 5 October 1799. [GM.69.900]

STENHOUSE, WILLIAM, a Lieutenant of HMS Jason died at St John's harbour, Antigua, on 13 June 1805. [CM.13094]

STEPHEN, FRANCES YOUNG, eldest daughter of William Stephen in St Kitts, married Robert Claxton a barrister on 26 October 1816. [GM.86.622]

STEPHENS, JOHN, a tailor from Bristol, an indentured servant bound from Bristol to St Kitts in 1660. [BRO]

STEPHENS, PHILLIPA, born 1606, a spinster from Ashberton in Devon, bound from Dartmouth to St Kitts in 1634. [TNA]

THE PEOPLE OF THE LEEWARD ISLANDS, 1620 - 1860

STEVENS, JUDITH, born 1615, a spinster from Exeter, bound from Dartmouth to St Kitts in 1634. [TNA]

STEVENSON, ELEANOR, a widow, died in Antigua in May 1750. [Windward Estate mi, Antigua]

STEVENSON, HUGH, in Antigua, was admitted as a burgess and guilds-brother of Ayr on 4 June 1783. [ABR]

STEVENSON, ROBERT, son of Allan Stevenson a store-keeper in St Kitts, was apprenticed in Edinburgh in 1796. [REA]

STEWART, CHARLES, a Jacobite prisoner transported to Antigua in 1716. [SPAWI.1716.310][CTB.31.204]

STEWART, CHARLES, a robber, was transported from Glasgow to Antigua in 1752. [AJ.260]

STEWART, DANIEL, a Jacobite prisoner transported to Antigua in 1716. [SPAWI.1716.310][CTB.31.204]

STEWART, DUNCAN, a Jacobite prisoner transported to Montserrat in 1716. [SPAWI.1716.313][CTB.31.205][CTP.CC43]

STEWART, HUGH, from St Croix, died in Glasgow on 26 October 1826. [AJ.4115]

STEWART, JOHN, a Jacobite prisoner transported to Antigua in 1716. [SPAWI.1716.310]

STEWART, JOHN, a Jacobite prisoner transported to Montserrat in 1716. [SPAWI.1716.313][CTB.31.205][CTP.CC43]

STEWART, JOHN, a Jacobite prisoner transported to Antigua in 1747. [P.3.346]

STEWART, WALTER, a Jacobite prisoner transported to St Kitts in 1716. [SPAWI.1716.312][CTB.31.209]

STEWART, WILLIAM, a Jacobite transported to Antigua in 1715. [SPAWI.1716.310][CTB.31.204]

STOBO, ALEXANDER, a surgeon, married Henrietta, daughter of Robert Isaacs and niece of W. R. Isaacs, the President of the Virgin Islands, in Tortula on 18 June 1833. [SG.174]

STOBO, JOHN, from Tortula, graduated MD from Marischal College, Aberdeen, on 3 May 1816. [AUL]; a member of HM Council of the Virgin Islands, died in Tortula on 3 February 1830. [S.14.1065]

STOE, WILLIAM, aged 18, bound aboard the Mathew of London, master Richard Goodladd, for St Kitts on 21 May 1635. [TNA.E157.20]

STODDART, GEORGE ALEXANDER, from St Kitts, died in New York on 31 August 1796. [GM.67.252][EEC.12294]

STOKES, JAMES, in St Kitts, probate 1783, PCC. [TNA]

STORMONTH, JAMES, of Pitscandly, died in St Kitts, testament, 1761, Comm. Edinburgh. [NRS]

STOTHART, Captain MATHEW, born 1779, died in St Croix on 28 May 1817. [GM.87.183]

STOTT, FRANCIS, aged 32, aboard the Paul of London, master Jo. Acklin, bound from Gravesend to St Kitts on 3 April 1635. [TNA.E157.20]

STRACHAN, ADAM, a schoolmaster who was sent to the Leeward Islands in 1700. [EMA.57]

STRATHER, WILLIAM CARLISLE, only son of E. Strather in Nevis, married Charlotte Anne Seymour Ormby, youngest daughter of the late Lieutenant General Ormby, on 2 May 1837. [GM.ns.8.528]

THE PEOPLE OF THE LEEWARD ISLANDS, 1620 - 1860

STREATER, JOHN, in Nevis, probate, 1694, PCC. [TNA]

STREATER, SARAH, in Nevis, probate, 1694, PCC. [TNA]

STRENNAH, ALEXANDER, in Nevis, probate, 1700, PCC. [TNA]

STRITCH, LUCK, in Christiansted, St Croix, in 1770. [RDAG]

STROCK, JAMES, a Jacobite prisoner transported to Antigua in 1716. [SPAWI.1716.310][CTB.31.204]

STRODE, NATHANIEL, in St Croix, probate, 1796, PCC. [TNA]

STRODE, Miss, daughter of Nathaniel Strode in St Croix, died in Bristol on 25 December 1813. [GM.84.96]

STURDY, JO, aged 26, bound aboard the Mathew of London, master Richard Goodladd, for St Kitts on 21 May 1635. [TNA.E157.20]

SULLIVAN, CORNELIUS, in the parish of Sandy Point, St Kitts on 7 February 1678. [TNA.COI.42]

SULLIVAN, DANIEL in St Thomas, Middle Island, St Kitts on 7 February 1678. [TNA.COI.42]

SULLIVAN, DERMOT, a planter in Montserrat in 1678. [TNA.CO1.22.17]

SULLIVAN, JOHN, in St Croix in 1768. [SSF]

SULLIVAN, MURTOW, in St Thomas, Middle Island, St Kitts on 7 February 1678. [TNA.COI.42]

SULLIVAN, Sergeant TEAGE in Halfwaytree Division, St Kitts on 7 February 1678. [TNA.COI.42]

SUTHERLAND, JOHN, a Jacobite prisoner transported to Antigua in 1716. [SPAWI.1716.310][CTB.31.204]

SUTTON, MARY, daughter of John Sutton, late of St Croix, services of heirs, 1756. [NRS]

SVARTE. JACOB, a Dutch Reformed Church minister in St Thomas in 1731. [RAK.WIC.431]

SWALES, GEORGE, aged 19, bound aboard the Mathew of London, master Richard Goodladd, for St Kitts on 21 May 1635. [TNA.E157.20]

SWANSON, THOMAS, born 1765, settled in St Kitts, died in Edinburgh on 7 July 1820. [Greyfriars gravestone, Edinburgh]

SWANSTON, CAROLINE, in St Kitts, a sasine, 10 April 1833. [NRS.RS.Edinburgh.42.34]

SWANSTON, ELIZA, youngest daughter of Dr Swanston in St Kitts, married John Swanston from Banden, Ireland, in Edinburgh on 13 December 1824. [S.516.817]

SWANSTON, HELEN, second daughter of James Swanston of Marshall Meadows, Berwickshire, died in St Kitts on 16 February 1869. [S.7999]

SWANSTON, SHERLAND, born 1730, a merchant from London, bound from Portsmouth aboard the London Packet bound for Nevis in 1774. [TNA.T47.9/11]

SWANSTON, WILLIAM, born 1765, a surgeon and physician in St Kitts in 1800, son of John Swanston tenant of Seggiedean, [NRS.CS26.910.30]; appointed John Swanston in Haddington as his attorney, a deed, 23 April 1796, [NRS.RD3.276-293]; a deed, 10 November 1801. [NRS.RD3.291.782]; a surgeon in St Kitts, son of John Swanston in Haddington, a sasine, 12 October 1802, [NRS.RS.Shetland.452]; a sasine, 5 June 1818, [NRS.RS.Edinburgh.13.99]; died in Edinburgh on 7 July 1854, [Greyfriars gravestone, Edinburgh]

SWINEY, MICHAEL, in St Thomas, Middle Island, St Kitts on 7 February 1678. [TNA.COl.42]

SWINTON, JOHN, a cooper, arrived in Boston on 18 June 1712 aboard the Mary, a sloop, from Nevis. [PA.137]

SWORD, JOHN, a Jacobite prisoner transported to St Kitts in 1716. [CTB.31.207]

SYDSERF, WALTER, in Antigua in 1750s, sasines, [NRS.RS.Edinburgh.141/188; 144/1-5; 150/188]; died on 13 March 1760. [GM.30.154]

SYMES, JOHN, was appointed a councillor of Montserrat. [JCTP: 27.2.1759]

SYMONDES, RICHARD, from Wantage, a husbandman aged 28, who emigrated via Plymouth aboard the Margaret bound for St Kitts in 1634. [TNA.E157.18]

SYMONDS, JAMES, in Nevis, probate, 1762, PCC. [TNA]

SYMONDS, Mrs MARY, wife of James Symonds, born 1692, died 10 September 1751. John Butler, her brother, died 20 May 1717. [St George gravestone, Nevis]

SYMONDS, ROBERT, in the parish of Sandy Point, St Kitts on 7 February 1678. [TNA.COl.42]

SYMMONS, RICHARD, born 1739 in Bristol, Customs Collector of Montserrat, died 31 December 1820. [St Anthony's mi, Montserrat]

SYMON, STEPHEN, aged 18, from Plimpton, emigrated via Plymouth aboard the Robert Bonaventure bound for St Kitts in February 1633. [TNA.E157.18]

TABERY, ………, in St Kitts in 1672. [SPAWI.1672.903]

TADDE, ALEXANDER, aged 38, bound aboard the Mathew of London, master Richard Goodladd, for St Kitts on 21 May 1635. [TNA.E157.20]

TAILOUR, GEORGE, MD of Glasgow University, in St Kitts, was admitted to the Royal College of Physicians of Edinburgh on 5 February 1771. [NRS.NRAS.726]

TAILOUR, JOHN, from St Kitts, graduated MD at Edinburgh University in 1776. [EUL][EMG.13]

TAIT, THOMAS, a Jacobite prisoner transported to Antigua in 1716. [SPAWI.1716.310][CTB.31.204]

TANGERLO, PETER, in St Croix in 1768. [SSF]

TAYLOR, ALEXANDER, probate 1 November 1780, Christiansted. [RAK.89.278]

TAYLOR, ARCHIBALD, from Fife, was admitted as a burgher of St Eustatia on 7 August 1780. [TNA.CO318.8.83]

TAYLOR, CHARLES, a mariner from Bristol, died in Nevis, probate, 1691, PCC. [TNA]

TAYLOR, FLETCHER ROBERT, born 14 October 1809 in Tortola, died in St Kitts on 12 February 1841. [St George gravestone, Basse Terre, St Kitts]

TAYLOR, GEORGE, a physician in St Kitts, executor of Dorothy Queely's testament 1777.

TAYLOR, JAMES, a Jacobite prisoner transported to Antigua in 1716. [SPAWI.1716.310][CTB.31.204]

TAYLOR, JAMES R., son of James Taylor in Milton Cottage, Bishopbriggs, later manager of the Barcaldine Estate in Argyll, died in Antigua on 14 June 1853. [EEC.22463][S.27.7.1853]

THE PEOPLE OF THE LEEWARD ISLANDS, 1620 - 1860

TAYLOR, JANE, in St Croix, 1770. [RDAG.I.50]

TAYLOR, JOHN, a shoemaker, bound from Bristol to Nevis in 1660. [BRO]

TAYLOR, JOHN, a merchant in Nevis in 1777. [NLS.ms.8793.4]; his wife Grace born 1747, died 9 September 1776, their three children – Ann born 1769, died 12 February 1774, Sophia, born 1770, died 14 February 1774, and Lewis, born 7 September 1776, died 9 September 1776. [St John's Cathedral gravestone, Antigua]

TAYLOR, JOHN, a goldsmith in Greenock, later in St Eustatia, died in March 1786, testament, 1784, Comm. Edinburgh. [NRS]

TAYLOR, JOHN DUNCOMBE, from Antigua, a Captain of the 46th Regiment, married Miss Van Der Horst, second daughter of Elias Van Der Horst, the United States Consul, on 5 May 1798. [GM.68.533]

TAYLOR, JOHN DUNCOMBE, born in Antigua, from Clifton, Gloucestershire, died at Sion Hill, Antigua, on 28 February 1835. [GM.105.558]

TAYLOR, JOSHUA, from Aughton, Lancashire, an indentured servant from Liverpool bound for St Kitts in 1699. [LRO]

TAYLOR, MARGARET, daughter of the late N. Taylor in Antigua, married Reverend John Halton of St Peter's in Chester, in 1822. [GM.92.88]

TAYTON, MARY, born 1757, a spinster, from London aboard the Generous Planter bound for St Kitts in 1775. [TNA.T47.9/11]

TELFER, ALEXANDER, a watchmaker in Antigua, services of heirs, 1806. [NRS]

TELLIER, ……., in St Kitts in 1672. [SPAWI.1672.903]

TEMS, GEORGE, aged 20, bound aboard the Mathew of London, master Richard Goodladd, for St Kitts on 21 May 1635. [TNA.E157.20]

TENNANT, JOHN, a merchant in St Kitts, 1765. [NRS.AC7.51]

TERRILL, THOMAS, aged 18, bound aboard the Mathew of London, master Richard Goodladd, for St Kitts on 21 May 1635. [TNA.E157.20]

THALBITZER, CARL H., agent in St Croix for the Danish Guinea Company in 1755.

THAUVATT, Captain ANDREW., a Huguenot who was granted land in St Kitts in 1696, and in 1698. [PCCol.1716.197/275; 1738.417] [SPAWI.1715.585; 1716.432; 1731.505]

THEGHANE, DANIELL, in the parish of Sandy Point, St Kitts on 7 February 1678. [TNA.COI.42]

THEGHANE, DENNIS, in the parish of Sandy Point, St Kitts on 7 February 1678. [TNA.COI.42]

THEGHAN, TEAGE, in the parish of Sandy Point, St Kitts on 7 February 1678. [TNA.COI.42]

THIBOU, DANIEL, printer of the Royal Danish American Gazette, St Croix, 1770-1793.

THIBOU, ESTHER, from Antigua, married George Blount in London on 2 January 1753. [GM.23.51]

THIBOU, ISAAC, in Antigua, 1739, [PCCol.1739.484];1783. [NRS.CS17.1.2]

THIBOU, JACOB, a planter and merchant in Antigua in 1708/1718/1728. [SPAWI.1709.150.XI.484xxvi; 1718.413] [PCCol.1729.177]

THE PEOPLE OF THE LEEWARD ISLANDS, 1620 - 1860

THIBOU. WALTER, in Antigua, 1772. [NRS.CS17.1.151]

THOGAN, TIMOTHY, in St Thomas, Middle Island, St Kitts on 7 February 1678. [TNA.COl.42]

THOM, GEORGE, born 1828, died in St Kitts on 18 November 1850. [AJ.5370]

THOMAS, DAVIE, aged 40, bound aboard the Mathew of London, master Richard Goodladd, for St Kitts on 21 May 1635. [TNA.E157.20]

THOMAS, GEORGE, Governor of the Leeward Islands, letters, [JCTP:26.4.1758; 24.1.1760]

THOMAS, HENRY, aged 15, from Luxulian, emigrated via Plymouth aboard the Robert Bonaventure bound for St Kitts in February 1633. [TNA.E157.18]

THOMAS, JOHN, aged 26, from St Tiffey, emigrated via Plymouth aboard the Robert Bonaventure bound for St Kitts in February 1633. [TNA.E157.18]

THOMAS, JO, aged 14, bound aboard the Mathew of London, master Richard Goodladd, for St Kitts on 21 May 1635. [TNA.E157.20]

THOMAS, MARY, an indentured servant bound from Bristol to St Kitts in 1660. [BRO]

THOMAS, RICHARD, aged 40, bound aboard the Mathew of London, master Richard Goodladd, for St Kitts on 21 May 1635. [TNA.E157.20]

THOMAS, RICHARD MORRIS, former President of the Virgin Islands, died in Heddington on 10 September 1843. [GM.ns20.444]

THOMAS, ROGER, aged 22, bound aboard the Mathew of London, master Richard Goodladd, for St Kitts on 21 May 1635. [TNA.E157.20]

THOMAS, WILLIAM, a yeoman, bound from Bristol to Nevis in 1660. [BRO]

THOMAS, WILLIAM, in Antigua, a letter dated 9 May 1702. [PCCol.1702.71]

THOMAS, WILLIAM, born 1728, died in Antigua on 30 August 1762. [Bridgetown gravestone, Antigua]

THOMASON, JAMES B., son of Thomas Thomason, HM Consul in Tortula, married Maria Burke, in St Croix on 15 October 1791. [GM.61.1157]

THOMSON, ALEXANDER, from Inverness-shire, probably settled in St Kitts, married Margarith Flawn from St Eustatia, there on 11 March 1749. [Afscriften huwelijksakten van St Eustatia 1710-1750]

THOMSON, ANNE, in St Croix, probate, 1796, PCC. [TNA]

THOMSON, ARCHIBALD, a merchant in Nevis in 1778. [NLS.ms.8793]

THOMSON, CHRISTOPHER, aged 21, aboard the John of London, master James Waymoth, bound for St Kitts on 2 October 1635. [TNA.E157.20]

THOMSON, C., the Attorney General of St Kitts, married Maria Byrne, only daughter of N. Byrne, in London on 10 January 1832. [GM.102.78]; he died in Liverpool on 19 March 1848. [GM.ns29.562]

THOMSON, EDWARD, aged 18, bound aboard the Mathew of London, master Richard Goodladd, for St Kitts on 21 May 1635. [TNA.E157.20]

THOMSON, JO., aged 19, aboard the John of London, master James Waymoth, bound for St Kitts on 2 October 1635. [TNA.E157.20]

THOMSON, JO., aged 25, bound aboard the Mathew of London, master Richard Goodladd, for St Kitts on 21 May 1635. [TNA.E157.20]

THOMPSON, JOHN, a plantation manager in St Kitts 1734. [HS.7.6/35]

THOMSON, JOHN, in Antigua, letters, 1802-1806. [NRS.SC39.107.12]

THOMPSON, MARY, a widow in Montserrat, 1754. [JCTP:21.6.1759]

THOMSON, Mrs MARY or MARION, widow of William Thomson in St Kitts, died 20 April 1818, testament, 1819, Comm. Edinburgh. [NRS]

THOMSON, PATRICK, a shoemaker in Dundee, a Jacobite prisoner transported to Antigua in 1747. [P.3.272]

THOMSON, RALPH, in St Thomas, Middle Island, St Kitts on 7 February 1678. [TNA.COl.42]

THOMSON, ROBERT, in St Kitts, probate 1776, PCC. [TNA]

THOMSON, ROBERT, born 1738, former Governor of the Leeward Islands, also President of St Kitts, died in London on 2 March 1816. [GM.86.372]

THOMSON, ROBERT, in Nevis in 1776. [NLS.Acc.8793]

THOMPSON, ROBERT, in St Croix in 1790, [Caribbeana.5.265]

THOMPSON, SAMUEL, a merchant in Christianstaed, St Croix, in 1789, [RDAG]; in St Croix in 1790, [Caribbeana.5.265]; a planter on St Croix, will, 1795. [PWI]; probate, 1794, PCC. [TNA]

THOMPSON, WILLIAM, from London, an indentured servant aboard the Elisabeth and Ann master William Benn, bound from Liverpool to Montserrat in March 1700. [LRO]

THOMSON, WILLIAM, a Jacobite banished to Antigua in 1716. [CTB.31.204][SPAWI.1716.310]

THOMPSON, WILLIAM, probate 14 January 1762, Christiansted. [RAK]

THOMSON, WILLIAM, a planter in St Kitts in 1776. [NLS.Acc.8793/42]; married Mary Clark, a daughter of Gilbert Clark a writer in Canongate, in Edinburgh on 5 February 1779, [EMR]; deceased, late in St Kitts, husband of Mary Thomson in Edinburgh, in 1821. [NRS.CS17.1.40/173]

THOMSON, WILLIAM, in St Kitts, probate 1788, PCC. [TNA]

THORBURN, WILLIAM, a Jacobite prisoner transported to Antigua in 1716. [SPAWI.1716.310][CTB.31.204]

THORNTON, DANIEL, from St Kitts, died 21 July 1777. [GM.48.335]

THORNTON, Major JOHN, in Nevis, probate, 1716, PCC. [TNA]

THORNTON, JOHN, died 29 August 1752, probate, 19 November 1760, Christiansted, also St Croix. [RAK.1747-1782.182]

THRONN, Lieutenant, in St Croix in 1768. [SSF]

THURSTON, JAMES ROBINSON, in St Kitts, graduated MD at King's College, Aberdeen, on 22 February 1800. [KCA.144]

THE PEOPLE OF THE LEEWARD ISLANDS, 1620 - 1860

TILEY, ALEXANDER, bound from Bristol to Nevis in 1660. [BRO]

TOBIN, JAMES WEBB, son of James Tobin in Bristol, died in Nevis on 30 October 1814. [GM.84.675]

TOBEY, RICHARD, in the parish of St John Capistar, St Kitts, on 28 January 1678. [TNA.COI.42]

TODD, Reverend GEORGE HENRY, born 1813, minister in Montserrat, died 26 October 1869. [St Anthony's mi, Montserrat]

TODD, JAMES, in St Croix in 1790. [Caribbeana.5.265]

TODD, JOHN, a Jacobite prisoner transported to Antigua in 1716. [SPAWI.1716.310][CTB.31.204]

TOMLINSON, MATHEW, aged 31, bound aboard the Mathew of London, master Richard Goodladd, for St Kitts on 21 May 1635. [TNA.E157.20]

TOMLINSON, JOHN, the Deputy Governor of Antigua, died 20 September 1753. [GM.23.445][SM.40.686]

TORRANCE. ANNABELLA DOUGLAS, born in Kilmarnock on 2 March 1821, wife of Reverend W. O. Allan, died in St Thomas on 29 June 1862. [St Thomas gravestone]

TOVEY, MARGARET, in Nevis, probate, 1725, PCC. [TNA]

TOVEY, RICHARD, a brewer, an indentured servant, bound from Bristol to Nevis in 1660. [BRO]

TOWER, ALEXANDER, born 15 July 1801, son of George Tower, a merchant in Aberdeen, and his wife Euphemia Sutherland, was educated at King's College, Aberdeen, 1815-1819, a planter in St

Croix, married Eliza, third daughter of Edward Dewhurst of Bog of Allen, in St Croix on 22 April 1835, later in Torquay. [KCA.2.423][NRS.S/H][AJ.4561]

TOWER, ANN, born 1792, eldest daughter of John Tower in St Croix, died in Ferryhill, Aberdeen, on 5 April 1814. [AJ.3457]

TOWER, ANN, from Edinburgh, daughter of John Tower in Aberdeen, died in St Croix on 8 January 1843. [EEC.20574][AJ.4964][NRS.Est.Def.c2078]

TOWER, JAMES, in St Croix in 1776. [NLS.Acc.8793/30]

TOWER, JAMES, son of John Tower in Aberdeen, educated at Marischal College, Aberdeen, from 1774 to 1778, graduated MD in 1804, late of St Thomas, died in Logie, Crimond, on 8 May 1818. [St Nicholas gravestone, Aberdeen][MCA.II.347][KCA.2.395]

TOWERS, JOHN MARTIN, born 1764, son of Robert and Sarah Towers, died 25 August 1765 in Antigua. [St John Cathedral]

TOWERS, JOHN, a merchant in St Croix, witness to a deed, 21 December 1784. [NRS.RD3.244.530]; died in Aberdeen on 3 April 1799. [St Nicholas gravestone, Aberdeen]

TOWER, ROBERT, born 1738, died in Antigua on 25 October 1769. [St John's Cathedral]

TOWER, SARAH, born 1766, daughter of Robert and Sarah Tower, died 20 March 1785, wife of John Kelsick. [St John's Cathedral]

TOWLE, WILLIAM HENRY, born 1835, a surgeon from Nuneaton, died 28 June 160. [GM.ns2.9.323]

TOWN, ANNE, daughter of the late George Town in Aberdeen, died in St Croix on 8 January 1843. [GM.ns19.556]

THE PEOPLE OF THE LEEWARD ISLANDS, 1620 - 1860

TOWNSEND, RICHARD, aged 19, aboard the John of London, master James Waymoth, bound for St Kitts on 2 October 1635. [TNA.E157.20]

TOWSON, ROBERT, in St Croix, probate, 1788, PCC. [TNA]

TRANT, JAMES, of Montserrat, married Miss Barrett, only daughter of the late Wisdom Barrett of Jamaica, in London in 1798. [GM.68.1147]

TRAVERS, JOHN, in St Kitts, probate, 1681, PCC. [TNA]

TREMILL, WILLIAM, a carpenter and a planter in Antigua, father of John Tremill, 1678

TRENEEGHAU, ROBERT, aged 34, from Helston, emigrated via Plymouth aboard the Robert Bonaventure bound for St Kitts in February 1633. [TNA.E157.18]

TRENNUEERE, EDWARD, aged 18, from Helston, emigrated via Plymouth aboard the Robert Bonaventure bound for St Kitts in February 1633. [TNA.E157.18]

TREVE, SARAVEL, aged 20, bound aboard the Mathew of London, master Richard Goodladd, for St Kitts on 21 May 1635. [TNA.E157.20]

TREWIN, JANE, aged 26, from Plimpton, emigrated via Plymouth aboard the Robert Bonaventure bound for St Kitts in February 1633. [TNA.E157.18]

TRISTED, THOMAS, in Martinique, probate, 1799. [TNA]

TRISTRANT, SIMON, from St Thomas to South Carolina in 1701. [SPAWI.1701.180]

TROTTER, JOHN, in Antigua in 1760. [DA.Ogilvie pp.30]

TROUGHTON, ..., died in Antigua in 1704. [St John's Cathedral, Antigua]

TRUE, ANTONY, aged 18, bound aboard the Mathew of London, master Richard Goodladd, for St Kitts on 21 May 1635. [TNA.E157.20]

TRUMBALL, MICHAEL, a Jacobite prisoner transported to Montserrat in 1716. [SPAWI.1716.313][CTB.31.205][CTP.CC43]

TUCKER, WILLIAM, from Milford, an indentured servant bound from Bristol to Nevis in 1660. [BRO]

TUCKER, ..., in Fredericksted, St Croix, in 1770. [RDAG.I.50]

TUCKER and SMITH, in West End, St Croix, 177-. [RDAG]

TUCKET, WILLIAM, born 1737, a planter, bound from Portsmouth aboard the London Packet bound for Nevis in 1774. [TNA.T47.9/11]

TUDHOPE, JEAN, widow of William Tudhope a surgeon in Antigua, 1794. [ECA.Moses.172/6745]

TUDWAY, CLEMENT, a merchant in London and Antigua, probate, 1689, PCC. [TNA]

TUITT, DIANA A.S., born 1835, died 3 May 1875. [St Anthony's mi, Montserrat]

TUITE, ANN, in St Croix, probate, 1777, PCC. [TNA]

TUITE, NICHOLAS, was born in Montserrat in 1705

TUITE, NICHOLAS, in St Croix, probate 1772, PCC. [TNA]

TULLIDEPH, WALTER, a surgeon in Antigua, 1735, 1760, [BM.Sloane.3984/36; 4049/3][DA.Ogilvie pp 48]; 1755. [NRS.AC7.47.598/602]; was admitted as a burgess of Edinburgh on 30 September 1757, [EBR]; of Tullideph Hall in Angus, died in Antigua on 16 March 1772. [SM.34.276]; papers, 1751-1771. [NRS.GD205.28.232]; a letter book, [NRS.GD205.53.8]

TULLIDEPH, WILLIAM, son of the minister of Dunbarney, was apprenticed to a surgeon in Edinburgh in 1718, emigrated to Antigua in 1726, a physician there, married Mary Burroughs there in 1736.

TURNBULL, PETER, a planter in Montserrat, husband of Margaret Lyle, later in Greenock by 1791, his will was subscribed on 22 June 1809, and confirmed in Renfrew on 20 February 1816. [NRS.SC53.56.1/57]

TURNBULL, THOMAS, a planter in Antigua, testament, 20 March 1817, Comm. Edinburgh. [NRS]

TURNER, MATHEW, aged 46, aboard the Paul of London, master Jo. Acklin, bound from Gravesend to St Kitts on 3 April 1635. [TNA.E157.20]

TURNER, THOMAS, aged 25, bound aboard the Mathew of London, master Richard Goodladd, for St Kitts on 21 May 1635. [TNA.E157.20]

TURNEY, GEORGE, in Antigua, probate, 1687, PCC. [TNA]

TYLER, PHILIP, in Nevis, probate, 1687, PCC. [TNA]

TYNDALL, Dr, from Plymouth, died in St Thomas on 24 January 1851. [GM.ns35.574]

TYRE, JOHN, a merchant in Tortula in 1800. [GA.T-ARD.13/1]

TYRELL, TIM, in Nevis, 1722. [RSM]

TYSON, MARY ANNE, eldest daughter of George Tyson in St Kitts, married J G Pigeunit, in Boxwell, Gloucestershire, in December 1829. [GM.99.558]

TYSON, PETER THOMAS, Speaker of the Assembly of St Kitts, died on 25 March 1767. [GM.37.192]

TYSON, Mrs SARAH, born 1692, wife of Thomas Tyson, mother of Seaborn, William, Thomas, Fraysso, John, Sarah [1], Sarah [2], and Mary. [St George gravestone, Basse Terre, St Kitts.]

UNDERWOOD, ANN, born 1770, died 2 October 1803. [St Anthony's mi, Montserrat]

URQUHART, ALEXANDER, a time expired servant, from Barbados aboard the Hopewell, a sloop, master William Murphy, from Barbados bound for Antigua on 8 November 1679. [TNA]

URQUHART, GORDON, born 23 February 1786 in Rosskeen, Ross-shire, son of Reverend Thomas Urquhart and his wife Johanna Clunes, died 15 September 1808 in St Croix. [F.7.68]

VALANE, JACOB, on Saba, petitioned the Dutch West India Company in Amsterdam in 1772. [DNA.Inv.1151]

VAN BELL, PETER, possibly on New Tortula alias Ter Holen in 1698, a planter and free denizen of St Kitts in 1699; factor on St Thomas for the African Company of Emden in 1699; in Nevis, a petition re black slaves of his seized in St Kitts 1704; an agent in St Kitts of the Brandenburg Company in 1711; a planter there in 1712-1717. [JCTP:15.5.1704] [SPAWI.1684.1563; 1698.156; 1699.648/685; 1711.391][PCCol.1680-1720:459; 1704;119]

VAN BEVERHOUDT, LUCAS, in the Dutch Leeward Islands in 1704.

VAN DER BURGH, Captain, a planter in St Kitts, dead by 1714. [SPAWI.1714.630]

VAN DER POOL, ANN, in St Kitts, probate 1790, PCC. [TNA]

VAN DER POOL, JAMES PILKINGTON, a Councillor of St Kitts in 1775. [PCCol.1766-1783.573]

VAN DER POOL, JOHN, a Councillor of Nevis by 1773, dead by 1775. [JCTP.80.117; 82.59][PCCol.1766-1783.568]

VAN DER POOL, THOMAS PILKINGTON, a Councillor of Nevis, in 1775. [JCTP.82.78]

VAN ESSEN, GEORGE, a Dutch Reformed Church minister in St Eustatius in 1740.

VAN LO, PETER, in St Kitts, petitioned for denization in 1662. [SPAWI.1662.269]

VAUGHAN, LOGHLANE, in the parish of Sandy Point, St Kitts on 7 February 1678. [TNA.COI.42]

VAUGHAN, THOMAS WILLIAM, on Saba, petitioned the Dutch West India Company in Amsterdam in 1772. [DNA.Inv.1151]

VEM, THOMAS, aged 27, bound aboard the *Mathew of London*, master Richard Goodladd, for St Kitts on 21 May 1635. [TNA.E157.20]

VER BURGT, FORTIUS, a Dutch Reformed Church minister in St Croix in 1746. [RAK.WIC.429]

VER CHILD, JAMES, President of St Kitts, died in Boston in October 1769. [SM.31.615]

VER CHILD, JASPER, a planter in St Kitts in 1712. [JCTP.P.229]

VER CHILD, PHILIP, a planter in St Kitts in 1712. [JCTP.P.243]

VERDEN, HUGH, in the parish of Sandy Point, St Kitts on 7 February 1678. [TNA.COI.42]

THE PEOPLE OF THE LEEWARD ISLANDS, 1620 - 1860

VIGUERS, BALTHAZER, died on Montserrat, probate 1657, PCC. [TNA]

VINACK, JOHN, in the parish of Sandy Point, St Kitts on 7 February 1678. [TNA.COl.42]

VOLLARD, PETRE, in Antigua in 1709. [SPAWI.1709.487ii]

VON BRUNNEN, ARNOLD, a Dutch Reformed Church minister in St Thomas in 1735. [RAK.WIC.431]

VON FISCHER, JOHAN ADOLPH, a merchant in St Croix in 1770, husband of Agnete Fischer. [RDAG]

VON MUHLENFELS, FREDERICH, Governor of St Thomas, 1764.

VON SCHOLTEN, PETER CARL FREDERIK, Governor General of St Croix in 1827. [SSF]

VON WYNGARDE, JOHAN LUDOVICK, a Dutch Reformed Church minister in the Danish West Indies in 1748. [RAK.WIC.429]

WAAD, SAMUEL, junior, husband of Elizabeth Osborne Briskett, a planter in Montserrat, was executed in May 1654.

WADE, ANDREW AFFLECK, probate 27 February 1767, Fredericksted. [RAK]

WADE, GEORGE, aged 16, bound aboard the *Mathew of London*, master Richard Goodladd, for St Kitts on 21 May 1635. [TNA.E157.20]

WADE, GEORGE, probate 30 September 1769, Fredericksted. [RAK]

WADE, RICHARD, died 14 October 1869. [St Anthony's mi, Montserrat]

WADE, ROBERT, aged 35, aboard the Paul of London, master Jo. Acklin, bound from Gravesend to St Kitts on 3 April 1635. [TNA.E157.20]

WADE, THOMAS, probate 31 March 1769, Fredericksted. [RAK]

WADE, WILLIAM, aged 33, from Bodmin, emigrated via Plymouth aboard the Robert Bonaventure bound for St Kitts in February 1633. [TNA.E157.18]

WALE, THOMAS, in Nevis, probate, 1685, PCC. [TNA]

WALKER, GEORGE, in Antigua in 1753. [NRS.CS96.644]

WALKER, JAMES, aged 30, bound aboard the Mathew of London, master Richard Goodladd, for St Kitts on 21 May 1635. [TNA.E157.20]

WALKER, JOHN, probate 31 March 1769, Fredericksted. [RAK]

WALKER, JOHN, born in Aberdeenshire, settled in St Croix, died in Glasgow on 11 July 1809. [SM.71.560]

WALKER, MATHEW, aged 19, bound aboard the Mathew of London, master Richard Goodladd, for St Kitts on 21 May 1635. [TNA.E157.20]

WALKER, ROBERT, died in St Thomas on 10 May 1813. [EA.5173.130][AJ.3422]

WALKER, THOMAS, aged 19, aboard the John of London, master James Waymoth, bound for St Kitts on 2 October 1635. [TNA.E157.20]

WALKER, THOMAS, a planter in Nevis, a petition, 9 February 1737. [PCCol.1737.395]

WALKER, THOMAS, a surgeon from Kinross, married Jean McAra, eldest daughter of James McAra a merchant in Largs, in St Thomas in 1813. [EA.5134.13]

WALKER, WILLIAM, in Antigua and St Vincent, 1778. [NRS.CS16.1.173]

WALLACE, ROBERT, a Jacobite prisoner transported to Montserrat in 1716. [SPAWI.1716.313][CTB.31.206][CTP.CC43]

WALLACE, Dr....., to Montserrat in 1730. [NRS.GD237.12.35.6]

WALLICH, ..., storekeeper, 3 Company Street, in St Croix in 1802. [RDAG.I/2]

WALLROND, CHARLES WILLS, from Antigua, married Elizabeth Day, in Edinburgh on 18 May 1777. [EMR]

WALROND, Mrs SARAH, born 4 September 1731, died in Antigua on 2 January 1764, wife of Main Swete Walrond, [Upper Walronds gravestone, St Philips]

WALSH, JOHN, in St Kitts, probate, 1638, PCC. [TNA]

WALTER, JOHN JACOB, from Antigua, died in London on 21 December 1828. [GM.98.649]

WALWYN, Mrs ANNE, widow of Reverend John Hutchinson Walwyn in St Kitts, second daughter of the late Reverend Henry Hunter in Norfolk, died at Mount Pleasant, St Kitts, on 27 October 1854. [GM.ns43.105]

WALWYN, ANNE FRANCES, born 1763, third daughter of the late William Walwyn in St Kitts, died in London on 17 October 1841. [GM.ns16.661]

WAND, JANET, widow of John N. Beck a planter in Antigua, services of heirs, 1794. [NRS]

WALWYN, JOHN HUNTER, eldest son of the late Reverend J H Walwyn in St Kitts, died at Mount Pleasant, St Kitts, on 19 April 1849. [GM.ns32.110]

WARD, ELISHA, in St Thomas, Middle Island, St Kitts on 7 February 1678. [TNA.COl.42]

WARD, JAMES, born 1701, died 27 July 1757. [St George gravestone, Terre Basse, St Kitts]

WARD, Mrs SARAH LOUISA, widow of Judge Ward in Nevis, married A Miller, youngest son of Reverend William Miller of Hasfield, Gloucester, on 31 January 1818. [GM.88.176]

WARDEN, JAMES, in St Kitts in 1756. [NRS.NRAS.TD132.50]

WARDEN, JAMES, a merchant in St Croix in 1778. [NRS.CS16.1.173/322]

WARDROPE, ALEXANDER, died in Guadaloupe on 19 August 1810. [SM.72.878]

WARDROP, JOHN, from Glasgow, was admitted as a burgher of St Eustatia on 8 August 1781. [TNA.CO318.8.83]

WARDROP, WILLIAM, a merchant in St Kitts, 1774. [NRS.CS16.1.157]

WARERMAN, NICHOLAS, from Marozion, a husbandman aged 15, who emigrated via Plymouth aboard the Margaret bound for St Kitts in 1634. [TNA.E157.18]

WARNER, ASHTON, died in Antigua on 11 February 1762. [St John's Cathedral]

WARNER, EDWARD, a Councillor of Antigua, 26 September, 1721. [PCCol.App.ii.821]

WARNER, JOHN, in St Kitts, probate, 1630, PCC. [TNA]

WARREN, EDWARD, aged 28, bound aboard the Mathew of London, master Richard Goodladd, for St Kitts on 21 May 1635. [TNA.E157.20]

WARREN, JUNE, wife of John Bell, born 19 February 1866, from Mount Sharon, Ireland, died 28 September 1885. [Antigua Archives]

WARREN, THOMAS, born 1716, Attorney General of the Leeward Islands, died in Antigua on 2 June 1779. [GM.49.423][SM.41.455]

WARRINGTON, ROBERT, aged 20, bound aboard the Mathew of London, master Richard Goodladd, for St Kitts on 21 May 1635. [TNA.E157.20]

WASHINGTON, THOMAS, in Nevis, probate, 1719, PCC. [TNA]

WATERALL, JOHN HENRY, born 1847, son of Wilson Waterall in Rotherham, England, died 22 September 1873. [St Anthony's mi, Montserrat]

WATERS, WILLIAM, a merchant from Bristol, died in Nevis, probate, 1692, PCC. [TNA]

WATKINS, GEORGE, in Nevis, probate, 1673, PCC. [TNA]

WATKINS, Reverend WILLIAM, in Antigua, died 1776. [GM.47.47]

WATKINS, Colonel, in Antigua, was admitted as a burgess of Glasgow on 19 February 1717. [GBR]

WATSON, ABRAM, aged 19, aboard the Paul of London, master Jo. Acklin, bound from Gravesend to St Kitts on 3 April 1635. [TNA]

THE PEOPLE OF THE LEEWARD ISLANDS, 1620 - 1860

WATSON, ALEXANDER, at Halfway Tree, St Kitts, in 1667. [TNA.CO1.42.193]

WATSON, ALEXANDER, a merchant burgess to Glasgow, to Jamaica in 1668, died on Nevis. [NRS.Unextracted processes, 1671]

WATSON, CHRISTOPHER, aged 21, bound aboard the Mathew of London, master Richard Goodladd, for St Kitts on 21 May 1635. [TNA.E157.20]

WATSON, JAMES, died in St Martin's on 14 June 1804. [SM.66.644]

WATSON, JOHN, probate 14 March 1781, Christiansted. [RAK.326.168]

WATSON, MARY, a widow in Montserrat, 1754. [JCTP: 21.6.1759]

WATSON, PETER, a Jacobite prisoner transported to Antigua in 1716. [SPAWI.1716.310][CTB.31.204]

WATSON, THOMAS, aged 29, aboard the Paul of London, master Jo. Acklin, bound from Gravesend to St Kitts on 3 April 1635. [TNA.E157.20]

WATSON, WILLIAM, a Jacobite prisoner transported to Antigua in 1716. [SPAWI.1716.310][CTB.31.204]

WATTS, Mrs CATHERINE, widow of Thomas Watts of the Honorable East India Company Service, married Henry R. Cassin, MD, in Antigua on 30 May 1819. [GM.89.271]

WATTS, Jo., aged 21, aboard the Paul of London, master Jo. Acklin, bound from Gravesend to St Kitts on 3 April 1635. [TNA.E157.20]

WATTS, NICOLAS, aged 18, bound aboard the Mathew of London, master Richard Goodladd, for St Kitts on 21 May 1635. [TNA.E157.20]

WATTS, RICHARD, in Nevis, probate, 1686, PCC. [TNA]

WATTS, Colonel WILLIAM, was appointed Governor of St Kitts an Anguilla in 1660. [CSPC]

WEATHERILL, GEORGE, was appointed a councillor of St Kitts. [JCTP: 15.2.1759]

WEBB, ANTHONY, aged 20, from Lanceston, emigrated via Plymouth aboard the Robert Bonaventure bound for St Kitts in February 1633. [TNA.E157.18]

WEBB, GEORGE, a planter in Nevis, 1738. [TNA.CO.186.3]

WEBB, GEORGE, a planter, with his wife, emigrated via London aboard the Clytus bound for Nevis in 1774. [TNA.T47.9/11]

WEBBE, JOSIAH, in Nevis, probate, 1767, PCC. [TNA]

WEBB, NATHANIEL, the Customs Collector of Montserrat, died in Somerset on 29 January 1741. [GM.11.108]

WEBBER, CLEMENT, a labourer from Beckington, an indentured servant bound from Bristol to Nevis in 1660. [BRO]

WEBLEY, THOMAS, born 1704, died 4 August 1741, his wife Ann died 18 November 1842, and their son Thomas died in 1740. [St George gravestone, Basse Terre, St Kitts]

WEBSTER, JOHN, jr., bound from Greenock aboard the Joanna for Antigua on 9 September 1790. [NRS.E504.15.56]

WEEKS, SYMON, born 1618, a worsted weaver from Exeter, bound from Dartmouth to St Kitts in 1634. [TNA]

WEEKS, THOMAS PYNE, son of William Burt Weeks in Nevis, 1772. [NRS.CS16.1.151]

WEEKS, Dr THOMAS PYM, son of William B. Weekes in Nevis, services of heirs, 1766, [NRS]; a physician in Nevis, married Isabella Livingston, youngest daughter of Dr Livingston in Aberdeen, on 21 April 1789. [GM.59.669][SM.51.361]; she died in Nevis on 14 November 1792. [SM.55.50]

WELLS, NATHANIEL, in St Kitts, probate 1792, PCC. [TNA]

WELLS, WILLIAM FENTON, born 1754, son of William and Elizabeth Wells, died on 12 April 1758; daughter Anstance born 1758, died 29 May 1759; Mrs Elizabeth Wells, born 1711, died 28 June 1759. [St George gravestone, Basse Terre, St Kitts]

WELLS, WILLIAM, in St Kitts, probate, 1794, PCC. [TNA]

WELSH, ... daughter of James Welsh, was born on Du Puys Estate, St Kitts, on 29 October 1863. [S.2639]

WELSH, ... daughter of James Welsh, was born on Needsmust Estate, St Kitts, on 22 November 1863. [S.7918]

WEMYSS, DAVID, in St Kitts in 1776. [NLS.Acc.8793]

WENDEVER, ROBERT, aged 25, bound aboard the Mathew of London, master Richard Goodladd, for St Kitts on 21 May 1635. [TNA.E157.20]

WERSFOLDF,........., from Montserrat, died in Winchcomb, Gloucestershire, on 20 August 1811. [GM.81.287]

WEST, CHARLES AUGUSTUS, born 1754, a surgeon in Tortula, died there in January 1793. [GM.63.767]; his widow Mary Ann did in Montserrat in July 1852. [GM.ns39.104]

WEST, HANS, rector and schoolmaster in Christianstad, St Croix, in 1788.

WEST, ROSINA, fourth daughter of the late Dr West in Antigua, married Francis West in Montserrat on 22 October 1844. [GM.ns23.196]

WEST, WILLIAM, MD, died in Antigua on 23 July 1835. [GM.ns4.446]

WETH, HACHBETH, on Nevis in 1708. [TNA.CO152.157]

WETHERED, THOMAS, Deputy Commissary General, father of a daughter born in Antigua in 1813. [EA.5161.13]

WHARTON, LOUISA FRANCES, third daughter of the late William Wharton a Councillor of St Kitts, married Robert Murray Rumsey, in St Kitts on 12 December 1844. [GM.ns23.311]

WHEELER, THOMAS LUCAS, in St Kitts, probate 1792, PCC. [TNA]

WHITE, BERNARD, in Nevis, probate, 1701, PCC. [TNA]

WHITE, JOHN, in St Kitts, probate 1776, PCC. [TNA]

WHITE, LAWRENCE, in the parish of Sandy Point, St Kitts on 7 February 1678. [TNA.COl.42]

WHITE, Mrs MARY, born 1727, widow of Michael White the Governor of Montserrat, died in London in August 1832. [GM.102.187]

WHITE, MICHAEL, was appointed a councillor of Montserrat. [JCTP:20.2.1759]

WHITE, THOMAS in St Thomas, Middle Island, St Kitts on 7 February 1678. [TNA.COl.42]

WHITEHALL, ROBERT, a merchant from London, died in Nevis, probate, 1691, PCC. [TNA]

THE PEOPLE OF THE LEEWARD ISLANDS, 1620 - 1860

WHITEHEAD, WILLIAM, in Antigua in 1761. [DA.Ogilvie ms.56]

WHITEHEAD, Mrs, widow of William Whitehead in Antigua, died in Winchester on 1 September 1800. [GM.70.908]

WHITMOR, ALICE, born 1609, a spinster from Huniton, Devon, bound from Dartmouth to St Kitts in 1634. [TNA]

WHITSON, JOHN, in Nevis, probate, 1699, PCC. [TNA]

WHITTINGTON, STEPHEN, aged 20, from Lincoln, emigrated via Plymouth aboard the Robert Bonaventure bound for St Kitts in February 1633. [TNA.E157.18]

WHITWOOD, ROGER, in Montserrat, probate, 1693, PCC. [TNA]

WHYTE, DANIEL, a millwright in Tortula, second son of Reverend Thomas Whyte in Libberton, Edinburgh, a deed, 1790. [NRS.RD2.252.1038]

WHITE, MARTHA, in St Kitts, probate 1779, PCC. [TNA]

WILBRAHAM, CORBIN, in Antigua, died 11 November 1757. [GM.27.531]

WILCOCKS, NICHOLAS, aged 21, bound aboard the Mathew of London, master Richard Goodladd, for St Kitts on 21 May 1635. [TNA.E157.20]

WILDRIK, RUDOLFUS, a Dutch Reformed Church minister in St Eustatia post 1765.

WILKIE, HELEN, in St Kitts, services of heirs, 1816. [NRS]

WILKINS, JOHN, infant son of John Wilkins in Jarvis Estate, Grenada, died in May 1780, buried in the family plot of Thomas Jarvis. [St George's burial register]

WILKINSON, Reverend J B, of St Paul's, Antigua, died 1851. [GM.ns35.325]

WILKINSON, MICHAEL, in St Kitts, probate, 1645, PCC. [TNA]

WILLE, JOHN, a felt-maker from Barnstaple in Devon, bound from Dartmouth to St Kitts in 1634. [TNA]

WILLETT, RALPH, in St Kitts, probate, 1795, PCC. [TNA]

WILLIAMS, ANTONY, aged 14, bound aboard the Mathew of London, master Richard Goodladd, for St Kitts on 21 May 1635. [TNA.E157.20]

WILLIAMS, JOHN, a merchant in St Kitts, a petition, 9 February 1737. [PCCol.1737.395]

WILLIAMS, Captain JOHN, a mariner and horse-dealer at Malley's stables, St Croix in 1770. [RDAG.I.50]

WILLIAMS, KATHERINE, an indentured servant bound from Bristol to St Kitts in 1660. [BRO]

WILLIAMS, Mrs MARY, born 1766, of Charles Town, St Paul's, Nevis, died 21 September 1829. [St John's, Fig Tree, Nevis, gravestone]

WILLIAMS, MICHAEL, from Nevis, died in Bath on 6 February 1758. [GM.28.94]

WILLIAMS, RICHARD, from St Cullom, a husbandman aged 30, who emigrated via Plymouth aboard the Margaret bound for St Kitts in 1634. [TNA.E157.18]

WILLIAMS, R E, in Antigua, died in Surrey on 28 November 1826. [GM.96.573]

WILLIAMS, Colonel ROWLAND, in Antigua, 1708. [PCCol.1708.190]

THE PEOPLE OF THE LEEWARD ISLANDS, 1620 - 1860

WILLIAMS, Captain ROWLAND EDWARD, born 1784, late of the 10th Royal Hussars, of Wiston Green, Surrey, and Antigua, married Clara Susan Ross, second daughter of Major General Sir Patrick Ross, in Antigua on 22 January 1828. [EA.6717.239]; from Thames Ditton in Surrey, died in Antigua on 30 May 1852. [GM.ns38.321]

WILLIAMS, SAMUEL, in Tortula, died on 14 December 1757. [GM.27.577]

WILLIAMS, TEAGE, an Irish husbandman aged 18, who emigrated via Plymouth aboard the Margaret bound for St Kitts in 1634. [TNA.E157.18]

WILLIAMS, THOMAS, aged 18, bound aboard the Mathew of London, master Richard Goodladd, for St Kitts on 21 May 1635. [TNA.E157.20]

WILLIAMS, THOMAS, aged 18, bound aboard the Mathew of London, master Richard Goodladd, for St Kitts on 21 May 1635. [TNA.E157.20]

WILLIAMS, THOMAS, a carpenter from Shropshire, an indentured servant bound from Bristol to Nevis in 1660. [BRO]

WILLIAMS, THOMAS, in Nevis, probate, 1767, PCC. [TNA]

WILLIAMS, ..., died 1817. [Antigua gravestone]

WILLIAMSON, ALEXANDER, a surgeon from Edinburgh, died in Montserrat on 29 August 1829. [BM.27.134][AJ.4267][S.1020]

WILLIAMSON, Dr JOHN, formerly a physician in Nevis, died in Kirkton of Tynron in 1804. [AJ.2960]

WILLIAMSON, GRIEVE, and MCNEILL, in St Kitts, 1766. [NRS.CS16.1.125]

WILLIS, BENEDICT FREEMAN, born 1750, elder son of Benedict Willis and his wife Mary, also grandson to Robert Freeman of Antigua, was educated at Eton College, Oxford University, and Lincoln's Inn, died on 13 November 1774. [St George's monumental inscription, Antigua]

WILLIS, JO., aged 29, aboard the Paul of London, master Jo. Acklin, bound from Gravesend to St Kitts on 3 April 1635. [TNA.E157.20]

WILLIS, JOSEPH, second son of Benedict Willis, sailed to England in November 1777, died on return voyage to Antigua on 17 May 1778. [St George's mi, Antigua]

WILLOCK, Mr, a merchant in Antigua, married Fanny Atkinson from Lancaster, England, on 16 March 1777. [GM.47.147]

WILLOX, ALEXANDER, in Antigua in 1761. [DA.Ogilvie ms.54]

WILSON, ALEXANDER, of Shielhall, in St Kitts, 1777. [NRS.CS16.1.171]

WILSON, ANNE, youngest daughter of the late R Wilson in St Kitts, married John Baillie, Sherwood Park, Southampton, on 16 July 1806. [GM.76.774]

WILSON, HENRY BROUNCKER, from St Kitts, graduated MD from Edinburgh University in 1784. [EMG.17]

WILSON, JAMES, MD, in St Martin's, married Catherine Thomson daughter of John Thomson in Jamaica, in November 1798, [AJ.2654], he died in St Martin's in 1804. [AJ.2652]

WILSON, JASPER, born 1739, with his wife Mary, born 1749, via London aboard the Woodley bound for St Kitts in 1774. [TNA.T47.9/11]

THE PEOPLE OF THE LEEWARD ISLANDS, 1620 - 1860

WILSON, JOHN, MD, from St Martin's, graduated MD from Edinburgh University in 1795, [EMG.26]; married Catherine Thomson, daughter of John Thomson in Jamaica, in Glasgow on 7 November 1798. [GC.1122][AJ.2654]

WILSON, JOHN FLEMING, eldest son of George Wilson late of Martin and Wilson, died in St Croix on 2 February 1868. [S.7791]

WILSON, PATRICK, in St Martin's in 1753. [NRS.CS96.644]

WILSON, PHILIP, a planter in St Kitts, eldest son of William Wilson of Soonhope, a deed, 1777, [NRS.RD4.775.1.589]; 1780, [NRS.CS16.1.179]; 1781. [NRS.CS16.1.184]; a deed, 1783. [NRS.RD2.234.787]

WILSON, RICHARD, in St Kitts in 1757, [NRS.GD237.12.47]; a judge in Antigua, died in 1759; in St Kitts, probate 1787, PCC. [TNA] [GM.29.497][SM.20.557]

WILSON, ROBERT, youngest son of William Wilson of Soonhope, a writer in Edinburgh, died in St Kitts on 29 August 1771. [SM.33.614]

WILSON, ROBERT, a skipper and merchant in Tortula, dead by 1800. [GA.T-ARD.13/1]

WILSON, SELINA IRWIN, third daughter of the late J W D Wilson the President of St Kitts, niece of Dr Davis in Bath, died in Lymington on 3 September 1833. [GM.103.284]

WILSON, WILLIAM, of Wilson and Company merchants in Antigua, eldest son of Andrew Wilson the Deacon of the Hammermen Incorporation of Kirkcudbright, died in Antigua on 13 October 1823. [S.412.815]

WILSON, Mr, born 1749, a gentleman and planter, bound via Portsmouth aboard the William and Elizabeth bound for Antigua in 1774. [TNA.T47.9/11]

WINDSOR, MARTHA, a pewter refiner, bound from Bristol to Nevis in 1660. [BRO]

WINFIELD, RICHARD, on Saba, petitioned the Dutch West India Company in Amsterdam in 1772. [DNA.Inv.1151]

WISE, JAMES, born 1784, eldest son of J B Wise in Maidenhead, Thicket, St Croix, died on passage from St Bartholemew to Grenada on 16 September 1816. [GM.87.183]

WOLLASTON, FREDERICK HYDE, fourth son of Reverend Francis Wollaston in Chislehurst, Kent, died in St Kitts in 1810. [GM.80.501]

WOOD, EDWARD, in St Kitts, died in 1824, father of Sophia, Eliza, and John, testament, 1825, Comm. Edinburgh. [NRS]

WOOD, JO, aged 22, bound aboard the Mathew of London, master Richard Goodladd, for St Kitts on 21 May 1635. [TNA.E157.20]

WOOD, JO., aged 18, bound aboard the Mathew of London, master Richard Goodladd, for St Kitts on 21 May 1635. [TNA.E157.20]

WOOD, JOHN, a merchant in St Kitts in 1790. [NRS.CS16.1.173/428]

WOOD, RICHARD, on Saba, petitioned the Dutch West India Company in Amsterdam in 1772. [DNA.Inv.1151]

WOOD, ROBERT N., died 26 November 1826. [St Anthony's mi, Montserrat]

WOODCOCK, SELINA AUGUSTA, daughter of the late James Phipps Woodcock in Antigua, married Reverend Alfred Arrow of Wrexham, Buckinghamshire, in Tenby on 17 November 1846. [GM.ns27.195]

WOODGREENE, JO., aged 16, bound aboard the Mathew of London, master Richard Goodladd, for St Kitts on 21 May 1635. [TNA.E157.20]

WOODLEY, CATHERINE, born 1780, wife of John Woodley a Councillor of St Kitts, daughter of Reverend Dr Horne in Chiswick, died in St Kitts on 15 July 1818. [GM.83.374]

WOODLEY, CHARLES, born 1776, youngest son of the late William Woodley the Governor of the Leeward Islands, died in Plymouth on 22 February 1859. [GM.ns2.6.439]

WOODLEY, JOHN, in St Kitts, probate, 1767, PCC. [TNA]

WOODLEY, SAMUEL, born 1730, died 11 November 1795. [St George gravestone, Basse Terre, St Kitts]

WOODLEY, WILLIAM, Governor of the Leeward Islands, died in St Kitts in June 1793. [GM.63.768], probate, 1796, PCC. [TNA]

WOODLEY, Mrs, widow of the late William Woodley the Governor of the Leeward Islands, died in Bloxworth, Dorset, on 29 March 1813. [GM.83.393]

WOODS, JOHN, from Aughton, Lancashire, an indentured servant from Liverpool bound for St Kitts in 1699. [LRO]

WOOD, JOHN, in St Kitts, a deed, 1775. [NRS.RD4.227.789]

WOODROP, ANN, of the parish of St Thomas, Middle Island, St Kitts, died 15 December 1753, probate 12 April 1755, St Kitts.

WOODROPP, WILLIAM, at Halfwaytree, St Kitts in 1667. [TNA.CO1.42/193]

WOODSTOCK, ROBERT, aged 40, bound aboard the Mathew of London, master Richard Goodladd, for St Kitts on 21 May 1635. [TNA.E157.20]

WOODYER, THOMAS, in St Kitts, married Miss Boyfield in 1785. [GM.55.1005]

WOOLFE, WILLIAM, a Jacobite prisoner transported to Antigua in 1716. [SPAWI.1716.310][CTB.31.204]

WOOLFENDEN, JEREMIAH, from Barbados to Nevis in 1670. [TNA.CO.1]

WOOLWARD, WILLIAM, husband of Mary Herbert, died 18 February 1779. [St John's, Fig Tree, Nevis, gravestone]

WRAXALL, WILLIAM, a mariner from Bristol, died in Nevis, probate, 1692, PCC. [TNA]

WRITT, WILLIAM, from Marozion, a husbandman aged 17, a husbandman who emigrated via Plymouth aboard the Margaret bound for St Kitts in 1634. [TNA.E157.18]

WYKE, ANTHONY, born 1738, Governor of Montserrat, died 20 November 1777. [St Anthony's mi, Montserrat]

WYKE, ANTONY, son of Antony Wyke in Antigua, was educated at Marischal College in Aberdeen in 1782. [MCA.II.358]

WYKE, WILLIAM, son of George Wyke, a planter on Montserrat in 1744. [TNA.CO152.26]

YARDE, JAMES, in St Kitts, probate 1779, PCC. [TNA]

YEAMANS, JOHN, a Councillor of Antigua, 26 September, 1721. [PCCol.App.ii.821]

YEAMANS, ..., Governor of Antigua, 1708. [PCCol.1708.190]

YETTS, D A, married Ann King, daughter of David King, in St John's, Antigua, on 28 October 1809. [DPCA.394]

YOUNG, JOHN, born 1750, a merchant in London, via London aboard the Catherine bound for St Kitts in 1774. [TNA.T47.9/11]

YOUNG, JOHN, a physician in Montserrat, services of heirs, 1792. [NRS]

YOUNG, JOHN, in St Kitts, probate, 1797, PCC. [TNA]

YOUNG, THOMAS, of Youngfield, formerly a surgeon in Tortula, later in London, a sasine, 1763. [NRS. RS.Dumfries.xix.451]

YOUNG, WILLIAM, a Jacobite prisoner transported to Antigua in 1716. [SPAWI.1716.310][CTB.31.204]

YOUNG, WILLIAM, probate 1767, Christiansted. [RAK.8.11]

YUILLE, ROBERT, in Antigua in 1754. [NRS.CS96.647]

THE PEOPLE OF THE LEEWARD ISLANDS, 1620 - 1860

SOME OTHER SHIPPING LINKS

ADA, a brig, Captain Isaac Higgins, from Africa, with passengers, to Christianstaed, St Croix, in 1789. [RDAG]

Adonis, a galley, master William Melville, via Madeira bound for Antigua, with 6 passengers, in 1807. [ARM.CMFun.Vol.600]

Cruel Isle, master Samuel Wilkie, from Falmouth via Madeira bound for St Thomas in 1806. [ARM.CMFun.Vol.600]

Eleanor, a snow, Captain Tadsen, from Guinea, with passengers, to Christianstaed, St Croix, in 1770. [RDAG]

Endeavour, a brig, master Isaac Donaldson, from Falmouth via Madeira bound for Antigua, with 7 passengers in 1808. [ARM.CMFun.Vol.600]

Fredensborg, [formerly the Cron Prindz Christian], master Ole Reinholdt, from Copenhagen in 1753 bound for the Gold Coast, from there with passengers to St Thomas, arriving there in 1755. [SSF]

General Huth, Captain Severin Kock, from Africa with passengers to Christianstaed, St Croix, in 1788. [RDAG]

Indefatigable, a brig, master Cornelius Faulkner, from Falmouth via Madeira bound for Montserrat, with 3 passengers, in 1806; also in 1808 with 3 passengers. [ARM.CMFun.Vol.600]

Lucy, a galley, master Charles Mays, from Falmouth via Madeira bound for St Kitts, with 3 passengers, in 1806, also in 1808. [ARM.CMFun.Vol.600]

Martha Magdelina a brig, master Soren Hoyer, from the Gold Coast to St Croix in 1802. [RDAG.I/2]

THE PEOPLE OF THE LEEWARD ISLANDS, 1620 - 1860

Montesville, master John Eve, from Barcelona to St Croix in 1802. [RDAG.I/2]

Providence of Glasgow, master John Anderson, returned to Glasgow from Antigua in 1672. [NRS.E72.10.2]

Rebecca of Dublin, master James Gollier, trading between Ayr and Montserrat in 1642. [NRS.RD1.544.6]

Resolution, master J Freeman, from Falmouth via Madeira bound for Antigua in 1806. [ARM.CMFun.Vol.600]

Richard and John of London, from Kelburn, Ayr, bound for Antigua in 1686. [W L Clements Library, Misc. Bonds, University of Michigan]

Salmon of Chester, master John Glover, trading between Glasgow and Nevis in 1681. [NRS.E72.19.5]

Swan of Ayr, master David Ferguson, returned to Ayr from Montserrat in 1673 and 1678. [NRS.E72.3.3/4]

Two Friends, a brig, master William Brown, from Falmouth via Madeira bound for St Thomas in 1806. [ARM.CMFun.Vol.600]

Unity of Ayr, master John Hodgson, trading between Ayr and Montserrat in 1673. [NRS.E72.3.3]

THE PEOPLE OF THE LEEWARD ISLANDS, 1620 - 1860

REFERENCES

ABR = Ayr Burgess Roll

AJ   = Aberdeen Journal

ANQ = Aberdeen Notes & Queries

ANY = St Andrews Society of New York

APB = Aberdeen Proprinquity Book

ArBR = Arbroath Burgess Roll

ARM = Regional Archives of Madeira

ASS = Archieven van Sint Eustatius

AUL   = Aberdeen University Library

BBR = Banff Burgess Roll

BFR   = Blake Family Records, London, 1905

BL = Bodleian Library, Oxford

BM   = Blackwood's Magazine

BM = British Museum

BRO = Bristol Record Office

CMR = Canongait Marriage Register

CTB   = Calendar of Treasury Books, series

CTP   = Calendar of Treasury Papers, series

DA   = Dundee Archives

DNA = Netherlands National Archives

DP = Darien Papers

THE PEOPLE OF THE LEEWARD ISLANDS, 1620 - 1860

DPCA = Dundee, Perth, & Cupar Advertiser

EA = Edinburgh Advertiser, series

EBR = Edinburgh Burgess Roll

ECA = Edinburgh City Archives

EEC = Edinburgh Evening Courant, series

EMA = Emigrants Ministers to America

EMG = Edinburgh Medical Graduates

EMR = Edinburgh Marriage Register

F = Fasti Ecclesiae Scoticanae, series

FDJ = Freeman's Dublin Journal, series

FH = Fife Herald, series

FLJ = Freeman's Leinster Journal

FPA = Fulham Papers, American

GA = Glasgow Advertiser, series

GAR = Rotterdam Archives

GBR = Glasgow Burgess Roll

GC = Glasgow Courant, series

GJ = Glasgow Journal, series

GM = Gentleman's Magazine

GUL = Glasgow University Library

HMC = Historical Manuscript Commission

HS = History Scotland, series

THE PEOPLE OF THE LEEWARD ISLANDS, 1620 - 1860

JCTP = Journal of the Committee for Trade & Plantations

KCA = King's College, Aberdeen

LRO = London Record Office

MAGU = Matriculation Albums, Glasgow University

MBR = Montrose Burgess Roll

MCA = Marischal College, Aberdeen

MI = Monumental Inscription

NLS = National Library of Scotland

NRS = National Records of Scotland

NWIC = New West India Company

OABR = Old Aberdeen Burgess Roll

P = Prisoners of the '45

PA = Perthshire Advertiser

PA = Passengers to America

PCC = Prerogative Court of Canterbury

PCCol = Privy Council, Colonial

PRONI = Public Record Office, Northern Ireland

PWI = Prerogative Wills of Ireland

RDAG = Royal Danish American Gazette, series

RAK = Royal Archives, Copenhagen

REA = Register of Edinburgh Apprentices

RGG = Register of Glasgow Graduates

THE PEOPLE OF THE LEEWARD ISLANDS, 1620 - 1860

RSM = Ryland Stapleton ms, Manchester University

RGS = Register of the Great Seal of Scotland

S = Scotsman, series

SG = Scottish Guardian, series

SM = Scots Magazine

SPAWI = Calendar State Papers, America & West Indies

SSF = The Slave Ship Fredenborg

SUL = St Andrews University Library

TCD = Trinity College, Dublin

TNA = The National Archives, Kew

UL = University of Leiden

www.ingramcontent.com/pod-product-compliance
Lightning Source LLC
Chambersburg PA
CBHW062124300426
44115CB00012BA/1798